VISUAL QUICKPRO GUIDE

DVD STUDIO PRO 1.5

FOR MACINTOSH

Martin Sitter

Peachpit Press

Visual QuickPro Guide
DVD Studio Pro 1.5 for Macintosh
Martin Sitter

Peachpit Press
1249 Eighth Street
Berkeley, CA 94710
510/524-2178
800/283-9444
510/524-2221 (fax)

Find us on the World Wide Web at: www.peachpit.com
To report errors, please send a note to errata@peachpit.com

Peachpit Press is a division of Pearson Education

Copyright © 2003 by Martin Sitter

Project Editor: Becky Morgan
Editor: Nikki Echler McDonald
Production Coordinator: Connie Jeung-Mills
Copyeditor: Judy Ziajka
Tech Editor: Don Steele
Compositor: Owen Wolfson
Indexer: Emily Glossbrenner
Cover Design: The Visual Group

ISBN 0-321-11547-3

9 8 7 6 5 4 3

Printed and bound in the United States of America

This book is dedicated to my parents,
Valerie and Keith Macauley,
for the love and support they've
given me throughout the years.

Acknowledgements

In life, meaning is sprinkled upon us like dots spread on a sheet of paper. Connect those dots with the proper lines, and surprise—there's a picture. Thank you, **Marjorie Baer**, for enriching my picture with unexpected dots.

Thank you, **Nikki Echler McDonald**, for keeping a sentinel eye on all proceedings, for sage advice, and for being a friend.

Special thanks to **Don Steele**, my technical Yoda, for safeguarding accuracy and for showing me things I'd have missed.

A deep debt of gratitude and sincere thank you to all my excellent friends at Apple, including *Michael Hinkson*, *Jeff Lowe*, *Tony Knight*, and *Frank Klassen*. Especially, a warm thank you goes to **Aimee Mackey** for those lovely afternoon conversations and for answering all of my many questions.

Cheers to you ALL!

TABLE OF CONTENTS

TABLE OF CONTENTS

INTRODUCTION

In 1996, desktop audio experienced a revolution powered by three key events. Computer processors sped past the 100 MHz mark, making real-time multitrack recording possible for the first time. Stock hard disks expanded to hold gigabytes, instead of megabytes, providing room enough to store huge digital audio files. And most important, with the introduction of the CD-R, it finally became possible to economically mix, master, and *deliver* audio recordings produced entirely on the humble desktop computer.

Six years later, the same revolution that swept desktop audio is hitting desktop video. With processors surpassing the 1-GHz mark, real-time video is at long last a reality. Hard disks sporting vastly increased storage capacities can hold hours of high-bandwidth DV footage on a single drive. And like the CD-R, the DVD-R provides a reliable and inexpensive means of delivery. As consumer DV cameras continue to drop in price, the digital video industry is teetering on the brink of change in how it does business forever.

The CD-R let us share music with anyone who had a CD player, and in a similar fashion, the DVD-R now lets us share video with anyone who has a DVD-Video player. But producing a DVD is not quite as easy as creating a song, because unlike DVD-Video, audio recordings aren't interactive. To create DVD-Video, you need a program that takes separate bits of media (menu graphics, video, audio, and subtitle streams) and assembles them into an intuitive, interactive project ready for display on a television. On the Macintosh, the program that does this best, without a doubt, is Apple's DVD Studio Pro.

DVD Studio Pro's history

DVD Studio Pro was born in 1999 as a suite of DVD authoring tools produced by a small software company called Astarte. The tools in the Astarte package included M.Pack, an MPEG-2 encoding application (**Figure i.1**); A.Pack, an AC-3 audio encoder (**Figure i.2**); and DVDirector, the suite's main DVD-Video authoring application (**Figure i.3**).

When DVDirector first hit the market, it wasn't cheap. Wearing a $5,400 price tag, the program was just too expensive for the average consumer. In April 2000, Apple purchased Astarte and began transforming DVDirector into DVD Studio Pro. Over the next year, Apple updated DVDirector's user interface, tweaked the engine under the hood, and then, in March 2001, it released the program with its new name, DVD Studio Pro.

Figure i.1 Astarte's M.Pack—a great MPEG-2 encoding program and one of the few software-only encoders that works on a G3 Macintosh.

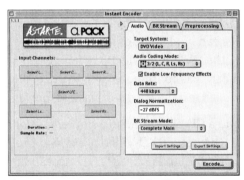

Figure i.2 Astarte's A.Pack. Look familiar?

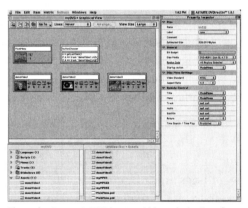

Figure i.3 Astarte's DVDirector. Although the interface has been tweaked and extra features have been added, DVD Studio Pro works much the same as DVDirector did in 1999 (albeit at a fraction of the cost!).

Although Mac OS X was already available when DVD Studio Pro first hit the market, it would take another year and two upgrades before DVD Studio Pro 1.5 for Mac OS X shipped, in April 2002. At that time, Adobe Photoshop 7.0 had just been released, and Apple's Final Cut Pro 3.0 was already taking advantage of the increased performance of Mac OS X to offer real-time video editing. With the inclusion of a killer audio editing application, Bias Peak DV 3.0 (on the DVD Studio Pro installation DVD-ROM), all of the tools needed to make DVD-Video were in place, and all of them worked on Mac OS X.

Today, DVD Studio Pro offers the most comprehensive DVD-Video authoring package available on the Macintosh for a price most desktop video enthusiasts can afford ($999). The program gives you access to almost every aspect of the DVD-Video specification, including scripting! While DVD Studio Pro does have a steep learning curve, once you learn to *think DVD Studio Pro*, you'll be able to create DVDs with sophistication and complexity rivaling those of the best Hollywood production house.

What's new in DVD Studio Pro 1.5?

DVD Studio Pro 1.5 is the first version of the program to work under Mac OS X, and this is undeniably the software's most significant new feature. But there are several other new features that DVD authors will also appreciate. Here are a few of the most important ones:

◆ MPEG-1 Layer 2 Audio is now supported.

◆ DVD Studio Pro 1.5 lets you specify a DVD-ROM folder for inclusion on a hybrid DVD disc. The DVD-ROM folder's file size is accounted for in DVD Studio Pro 1.5's Disc Space indicator.

◆ Using DVD Studio Pro in conjunction with Final Cut Pro 3.0.2, you can now set named chapter markers on the Final Cut Pro timeline and export the markers with your final MPEG-2 video stream. In DVD Studio Pro, these markers show up in the Marker editor, named and ready to go.

INTRODUCTION

Who needs this book?

DVD Studio Pro: Visual QuickPro Guide is designed for busy video professionals and home-based desktop video enthusiasts—in other words, people long on concept, but short on time. A basic understanding of digital video is helpful, but not mandatory; after all, you may be creating the DVD for someone else's video projects. If you're new to digital video and are, for example, learning Final Cut Pro as you work with DVD Studio Pro, you'll still find this book a valuable resource. The first four chapters cover DVD-Video basics and important video issues that beginners will find educational. You'll learn, for example, the differences between computer monitor colors and the broadcast safe colors used on TVs as well as how square computer pixels differ from those used by televisions. Readers with a firm grip on the basics can skip ahead to more advanced chapters.

How to use this book

This is a *task-based reference book*. All aspects of DVD Studio Pro are broken down into simple, easy-to-follow steps packed with pictures so you can see exactly how it all works. If you're new to DVD Studio Pro, you might want to read this book from beginning to end, following all of the steps and figures. If you're using this book as a reference, just hit the index when you have a problem, flip to the page you need, and find your solution.

The book is divided into three parts, each building in theory and complexity on the previous. Part 1 covers DVD-Video basics and explains how to turn video and audio files into assets that DVD Studio Pro understands. Part 2 uses DVD Studio Pro to assemble assets from Part 1 into a fully interactive DVD-Video, complete with menus, tracks, alternate angles, and audio streams. By the end of Part 2, you'll be able to author and burn a complete DVD-Video project onto a DVD-R disc.

Part 3 explores advanced DVD Studio Pro features, such as subtitling, working with alternate languages, and scripting. Parts 1 and 2 will give you a solid foundation in creating DVDs, but it's Part 3 that teaches you how to use DVD Studio Pro's most exciting features, such as scripting, to make your projects come alive. If you're new to scripting, don't worry; DVD Studio Pro makes scripting as simple as speaking English. If you can read this paragraph, you can script like a professional; the last part of this book shows you how.

The companion Web site

Speaking of scripting, all of the example projects in Chapter 17, "Scripting!" are available at this book's companion Web site. The downloads are complete projects, with functioning menus and tracks. In many cases, you can download a project, replace its assets with ones you've prepared on your own, and in minutes have a working project ready to be recorded onto a DVD-R disc.

Visit the *DVD Studio Pro: Visual QuickPro Guide* companion Web site at:
`www.peachpit.com/vqp/dvdsp`.

Getting help

You'll find the Internet to be a valuable source of information on using DVD Studio Pro. There are several Web sites devoted to DVD Studio Pro issues and many forums where you can post questions and get answers. Appendix C, "Online Resources," contains a list of Web sites that you can turn to when the going gets tough.

Keyboard shortcuts

Different people work in different ways. While the mouse is a necessary tool that you'll continuously use to arrange and edit project items, over time you'll find DVD Studio Pro's extensive keyboard shortcuts to be huge time-savers. For a full list of the keyboard shortcuts available in DVD Studio Pro, see Appendix A, "Keyboard Shortcuts."

INTRODUCTION

Part I:
Getting Ready

Part I:
Getting Ready

BEFORE YOU BEGIN

No one hardware setup is ideal for DVD-Video authoring. You can choose among three families of Apple computers, according to your needs: the G4 Power Mac, the G4 iMac, and the G4 PowerBook. Whichever model you choose, you'll likely need to beef it up with a few extra hardware accessories. If you're using an iMac, for example, you'll probably want to add an external hard disk to expand your iMac's storage capacity. If you're building DVD-Videos on an iMac or a PowerBook, you'll need a FireWire DVD recorder to get projects out of DVD Studio Pro and onto a DVD disc. And no matter which computer you settle on, if you intend to distribute your project in large quantities, you'll also need a digital linear tape (DLT) drive to record your DVD-Video in a format that all DVD replicators will accept. The possibilities might seem endless, but the first third of this chapter is designed to help you get past these hardware hurdles by outlining all of the equipment you need to create DVDs.

Your computer is like a thoroughbred racehorse; the better you care for it, the better it performs. DVD Studio Pro uses (and produces) files that may be several gigabytes in size. With all this data racing around your computer, proper hard disk maintenance becomes very important. The second third of this chapter offers tips on keeping your disks optimized and in prime working condition for DVD Studio Pro.

The final third of this chapter shows you how to install DVD Studio Pro and discusses some of the problems you may encounter along the way. If everything goes smoothly with your installation, read on to learn about other software applications that work in tandem with DVD Studio Pro to produce video streams, audio streams, and menu graphics.

Hardware Requirements

DVD Studio Pro requires a Macintosh computer powered by a G4 processor. As of this writing, Apple offers three product lines that are compatible with DVD Studio Pro: The Power Mac G4, the iMac G4, and the PowerBook G4. Each has its own set of advantages.

The Power Mac G4

The most powerful and expandable of all the Apple computers, the Power Mac G4 features three DIMM slots for RAM expansion and three 3.5-inch hard-disk bays. PowerMac G4s also have four PCI slots that can hold third-party sound cards, hardware MPEG-2 encoders, and SCSI cards to connect digital linear tape (DLT) drives to your Mac.

The iMac G4

Apple's new G4 iMac with SuperDrive is a great platform for DVD-Video authoring. Although the iMac comes with a relatively small hard disk, you can safely increase storage capacity by adding external FireWire hard disks to your setup. However, if you intend to replicate your DVD-Video in large quantities, the iMac does suffer from one important limitation: because it has no PCI expansion slots, you cannot add a SCSI card. Without a SCSI card, it is difficult to attach a DLT drive to your iMac, which makes it hard to get your project to a DVD replicator (to learn more about DLT drives, see "Digital Linear Tape (DLT) Drives" later in this chapter).

✔ Tip

■ These days, many replicators accept DVD-R media as a master for replication. Still, if you want copy protection or region coding, you must use a DLT. Before sending anything to a replicator, check to ensure that your format is accepted.

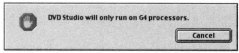

Figure 1.1 If you try to install DVD Studio Pro on a Macintosh G3 computer, this alert dialog box appears.

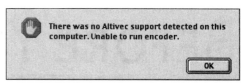

Figure 1.2 If you try to export MPEG-2 video using QuickTime on a G3 Macintosh, you are quickly stopped.

Macintosh G3 Computers

Despite Apple's claims to the contrary, DVD Studio Pro will run under Mac OS 9 on a G3 Macintosh, but the difficulty and limitations of getting it to work are probably not worth your time. If you try to install DVD Studio Pro on a Macintosh G3, for example, the alert box shown in **Figure 1.1** appears, and the installation stops. There are ways to circumvent this, but it's not the only hindrance; to compress MPEG-2 video streams, QuickTime needs the added power of the G4 Velocity Engine (**Figure 1.2**). As a result, G3 users cannot create MPEG-2 video streams. With all these obstacles piling up before you, if all you have is a G3, you should strongly consider upgrading to a G4 Macintosh.

Figure 1.3 Astarte's M.Pack is a discontinued MPEG-encoding application that produces constant- or variable-bit-rate MPEG video streams good enough for DVD-Video use.

The PowerBook G4

If you need portability, then you need the PowerBook G4. The titanium PowerBook is not only the sexiest laptop on the market, but it also lets you author DVD-Video from the comfort of a plane seat or your favorite café patio. Although the PowerBook doesn't come with a DVD recorder, it does have one FireWire port you can use to connect an external DVD recorder.

Additional requirements

If you're using a G4 Macintosh, your system includes all of the base hardware you need to author DVD-Video titles. Nonetheless, take a moment to ensure your system has each of the following Apple recommended components:

◆ At least 128 megabytes of RAM

◆ An Apple-supplied DVD drive

◆ An Apple-supplied AGP graphics card

◆ Display software and hardware capable of displaying 1024 x 768 pixels at thousands or millions of colors.

FYI: Astarte's M.Pack

Several third-party applications can encode MPEG-2 video streams on a G3 Macintosh. Astarte's M.Pack (**Figure 1.3**) encodes MPEG-2 video streams that are comparable in quality to (though not quite as good as) the QuickTime MPEG-2 export option. M.Pack also encodes MPEG-1 streams and offers constant and variable-bit-rate encoding (to learn more about bit rate encoding, see Chapter 3, "Encoding Video Streams").

Unfortunately, Astarte's M.Pack is out of production, and finding a copy is very difficult. From time to time, however, used copies pop up on auction sites like eBay. If you're stuck using a G3 Mac, you might want to start bidding.

FireWire-to-SCSI Converters?

If you want to use a DLT drive but your computer has only FireWire ports, you can buy converters that allow SCSI peripherals to connect to FireWire ports. Orange Micro's Orange Converter, for example, supports data transfer rates of 10 megabytes per second, which is fast enough for use with most DLT drives. For more information, check out the products section of Orange Micro's Web site:

www.orangemicro.com/

Hardware Extras

A few other pieces of hardware will make your life easier as you continue to grow and experiment with DVD Studio Pro. This section describes each of these devices, telling you what they are and why you need them.

Apple SuperDrive

The SuperDrive is the key to getting videos off your computer and onto a television set. In conjunction with DVD Studio Pro, a SuperDrive writes DVD-Videos to DVD-R (general) optical discs that can be read by a set-top DVD-Video player. Depending upon the SuperDrive's age, it uses either the Pioneer DVR-A03 or Pioneer DVR-A04 mechanism (the A04 was launched in April 2002).

The SuperDrive is indeed very versatile. It not only reads most CD and DVD formats (excluding DVD-RAM), but it also records data to DVD-R, CD-R, and CD-RW discs (see **Table 1.1**).

✔ Tips

■ Using the QuickTime MPEG-2 export option and AC-3 audio compression, you can squeeze over two hours of video onto a single DVD-R disc recorded with the SuperDrive. With more aggressive compression settings, the amount of video a DVD disc can store increases, but the trade-off is that you lose video and audio quality.

■ The SuperDrive is capable of writing data to DVD-RW discs, but DVD Studio Pro isn't. To write to a DVD-RW disc, you need to use Roxio's Toast Titanium 5.

Table 1.1

SuperDrive Statistics

Internal Mechanism	Pioneer DVR-A04
DVD Format	DVD-ROM, DVD-Video, DVD-R, DVD-RW
Writes DVD-R at:	2x
Writes DVD-RW at:	1x
Reads DVD-ROM at:	6x
CD Format	CD-ROM, CD-Audio, CD-R, CD-RW, CDI, CD Bridge, CD Extended
Writes CD-R at:	8x
Writes CD-RW at:	4x
Reads CD-ROM at:	24x

External DVD Recorders

An external FireWire DVD recorder is simply a standard Pioneer DVR-A04 placed in an enclosure that connects to your computer via a FireWire cable. If you're planning to purchase a new DVD recorder, consider the high degree of flexibility a FireWire DVD recorder offers. For example, you can move a FireWire DVD recorder between several different computers, lend it to your little brother, and so on (an external FireWire DVD recorder will even work on a FireWire-enabled Windows PC!).

Set-Top DVD-Video player

A set-top DVD-Video player (herein referred to as a DVD-Video player) is a device that connects to your television set to let you view DVD-Videos, including the ones you make with DVD Studio Pro.

DVD-Video players are a bit more finicky than the DVD-ROM drive that came with your Macintosh, and some will not play DVD-R or DVD-RW discs. Should you encounter this problem, it does not necessarily mean that something is wrong with your project. In fact, if your project works correctly in some DVD-Video players but not in others, the problem is very likely an incompatibility between the DVD-Video player and DVD-R or DVD-RW media.

While each new generation of DVD-Video players becomes more tolerant of DVD-R media, a lot of DVD-Video players still prefer professionally replicated DVDs. If you intend to send your project to a replication house, and if your test DVD-R works in several DVD-Video players, rest assured that the final, replicated project will work fine.

✔ Tips

■ Before you purchase a new DVD-Video player, write a DVD Studio Pro project to both a DVD-R and a DVD-RW disc. When you go to the showroom, take these disks with you and try out a few different DVD-Video players. If the player doesn't read your discs, don't buy it!

■ To maximize the readability of your DVD-R discs, write them at only 1x.

■ For a list of Apple-recommended DVD-Video players, check the following Web site: www.apple.com/dvd/compatibility/.

Extra hard disks

At the bare minimum, you need at least twice as much hard disk storage space as the size of your project's encoded source files. If your project uses around 4 gigabytes of source files, you will need an additional 4 gigabytes of free storage space to hold the finished, multiplexed project (for a grand total of 8 gigabytes in storage). The reality, however, is that you need a lot more hard disk space than that. Happily, new Power Mac G4 computers ship with hard disks of at least 40 gigabytes. When properly partitioned and maintained, this disk provides a decent amount of storage space.

Ideally, you should have at least two hard disks for DVD-Video authoring (see "Optimizing Your Hard Disk" later in this chapter). When buying a new hard disk, remember: speed is king! Although 5400 RPM hard disks are inexpensive, they are not fast enough for optimum use with DVD Studio Pro. Stick with hard disks of at least 7200 RPM.

✔ Tip

■ Always purchase a hard disk from a company known for high quality, such as Maxtor or IBM.

Digital Linear Tape (DLT) drives

Currently the SuperDrive can record only to single-layer DVD-R or DVD-RW discs, which have a capacity of 4.7 billion bytes of data (to learn more about single-layer and dual-layer DVD disks, see Chapter 2, "DVD Basics"). Dual-layer DVDs can store more data, but to produce one you must send your project to a qualified DVD replication house.

Some DVD replicators will take an external FireWire hard disk drive, or even copy a DVD-R disc that contains your finished DVD-Video. While increasing numbers of replicators are beginning to offer these services, most still accept *only* DLT tapes. This may seem like a senseless limitation; nonetheless, if you want to produce a dual-layer DVD-Video project, you should purchase a DLT drive. (For detailed information on writing your project to DLT tape, see Chapter 13, "Finishing the DVD.")

The internal mechanisms of all DLT drives are made by Quantum. As of this writing, there are four DLT drives suitable for use with DVD Studio Pro: the DLT 2000 XT, DLT 4000, DLT 7000, and DLT 8000. Of the four, the DLT 4000 is perhaps the most popular choice, with used units cheap and plentiful at online auction sites. To learn more about DLT drives, go to the Quantum Web site: www.quantum.com/.

✔ Tip

■ For DVD-Video authoring, stick to DLT III tapes. DLT IV tapes offer extra storage, but you don't need all that space, so why pay for it? Some DVD replicators won't accept type IV tapes anyway.

Table 1.2

DLT III vs. DLT IV Tapes

	DLT III	DLT IV
Cost (Approximate)	$30	$60
Color (Typically)	Gray	Black
Durability (Uses)	500,000	1,000,000
Native Capacity	10 GB	40 GB
Compressed Capacity	20 GB	80 GB
Native Transfer Rate	1.5 Mbps	3 Mbps
Compressed Transfer Rate	3 Mbps	6 Mbps
DLT 2000 Compatible	Yes	No
DLT 4000 Compatible	Yes	Yes
DLT 7000 Compatible	Yes	Yes
DLT 8000 Compatible	Yes	Yes

DLT Things to Remember

If you plan to purchase a DLT drive, keep two things in mind. First, all DLT drives use SCSI, so you'll need to install a SCSI card in your computer. Second, DLT tapes are not cheap and you need two of them to produce one dual-layer DVD (one DLT tape per layer). Prices range from around $30 (USD) for one DLT III tape to over $60 (USD) for one DLT IV tape. **Table 1.2** outlines the key differences between these two varieties.

The DLT1

If you go to the Quantum Web site, you might be tempted by a DLT drive called a DLT1. Although the Quantum DLT1 writes to Type III and Type IV DLT tapes, some replication houses do not accept tapes recorded on this drive.

Officially, DVD Studio Pro doesn't support the DLT1 either. In reality, however, depending on your computer setup and SCSI card, DVD Studio Pro may recognize the DLT1 as a DLT 7000, enabling you to write to the drive. Still, until DVD Studio Pro fully recognizes the DLT1, you'll probably have more luck trading it in for a real DLT 7000.

The Matrox RTMac

Video looks different on a computer than it does on a television set (see Chapter 3, "Encoding Video Streams"). If you're editing your own video using Apple Final Cut Pro or Adobe After Effects, you'll want to see that difference for yourself by connecting your computer to an NTSC monitor. The problem? To get the signal out of your computer and onto a TV you need third-party video hardware, such as the Matrox RTMac, to perform the translation.

The Matrox RTMac includes a PCI card, cable, and breakout box, which outputs video from your computer to the television. It also lets you capture video from, or record video to, analog sources such as a VHS or non-FireWire DV camera. When it comes to designing motion menus or color correcting your source video files, the Matrox RTMac is indispensable. To learn more, go to: www.matrox.com/.

HARDWARE EXTRAS

Optimizing Your Hard Disk

DVD-Video uses huge files, and moving all of that data around can take a toll on your Mac. To avoid problems later, you'd be wise to get your hard disk in shape now and keep it in shape. This section outlines simple rules and techniques that you can use to keep your hard disk running in top condition.

Defragmenting your hard disk

The number-one enemy of any DVD Studio Pro author is a heavily fragmented hard disk. DVD Studio Pro likes to work with continuous, uninterrupted data streams. Fragmentation divides these streams into many smaller parts, which slows down your system and leads to problems when it comes time to build your completed DVD-Video project.

A fragmented disk is also forced to work much harder than an unfragmented disk. This increased wear and tear may cause a fragmented disk to fail much sooner than a properly maintained disk.

There are two ways to keep your disks in good shape:

◆ Regularly defragment your hard disks with a disk utility such as Symantec's Speed Disk:

www.symantec.com.

◆ After you've finished a project, back up your media files and then erase your media hard disks to completely remove all files. Just make sure to *back up everything!* Erasing a hard disk removes all data on that disk (for safety's sake, it's better to use Speed Disk).

✔ Tip

■ As a rule of thumb, if you can hear your hard disk working (clicking and jigging) your disk is probably fragmented. It's time to run Speed Disk!

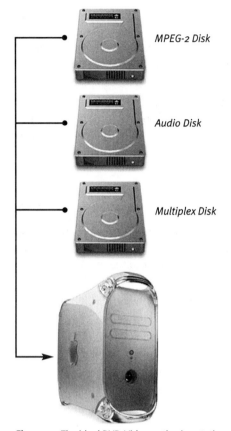

Figure 1.4 The ideal DVD-Video authoring station uses three hard disks: one for MPEG-2 assets, one for audio assets, and one to hold the finished, multiplexed DVD-Video project (these can be a mixture of internal and external FireWire hard disks).

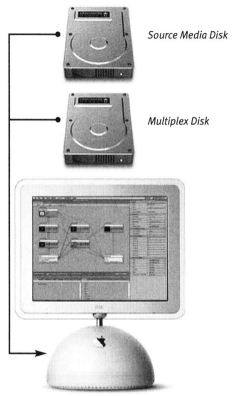

Source Media Disk

Multiplex Disk

Figure 1.5 A common DVD-Video authoring setup has only two hard disks. Use one for the source files and the second for the finished, multiplexed DVD-Video project (a mixture of internal and external FireWire hard disks is acceptable).

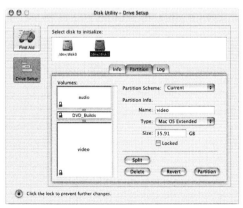

Figure 1.6 To partition a hard disk, use the Disk Utility that comes with Mac OS X.

Using multiple hard disks

Ideally, you should have at least three hard disks to use DVD Studio Pro: one for audio files, one for MPEG-2 files, and one for the final, multiplexed DVD Studio Pro project (**Figure 1.4**). If you have only two hard disks, use one to hold your source files and the second for the multiplexed project (**Figure 1.5**).

iMac G4 users have only one internal hard disk at their disposal. Fortunately, external FireWire hard disks are fast enough for use with DVD Studio Pro. With the iMac's two FireWire ports, you can expand your iMac to include as much hard disk storage space as you need.

If external FireWire hard disks are a bit beyond your budget, then consider partitioning your current hard disk. While a partitioned hard disk is not as good as three separate hard disks, it is easier to maintain and preferable to keeping all of your files lumped together.

✔ Tip

- To partition a hard disk, use the Drive Setup utility (Mac OS 9) or Disk Utility (Mac OS X) that came with your Macintosh (**Figure 1.6**). When you partition a hard disk, you erase *all* of the content currently stored on that disk, including files stored in other partitions on the same disk, *so be careful!*

OPTIMIZING YOUR HARD DISK

About QuickTime Pro

QuickTime adds multimedia abilities to all graphic, video, and audio editing programs that support QuickTime's component technology. DVD Studio Pro authors use QuickTime Pro to compress digital video into MPEG-2 video streams—a very handy feature. However, for QuickTime Pro Player to export MPEG-2 video streams, you must have both DVD Studio Pro and QuickTime Pro installed and registered for use with your computer.

✔ Tip

■ When you install DVD Studio Pro, an MPEG Export option is added to QuickTime (**Figure 1.7**).

Installing QuickTime

If you're using Mac OS X, QuickTime is already installed on your computer. You need simply to unlock QuickTime Pro Player using the QuickTime registration key located on the "Read This Before Installing DVD Studio Pro" leaflet that came with your DVD Studio Pro DVD-ROM.

Mac OS 9 users, however, may need to jump through a few extra hoops, as DVD Studio Pro 1.5 on Mac OS 9 needs QuickTime 5.0.5 or later. This version has been out for awhile, so you may already have it on your computer. If not, you'll need to install it. QuickTime 5.0.5 is included on the DVD Studio Pro DVD-ROM, inside the folder labeled "DVD Studio Pro Mac OS 9."

✔ Tip

■ In Mac OS 9, if you install DVD Studio Pro before QuickTime Pro, there's a small chance that QuickTime will not recognize the MPEG Export component (**Figure 1.8**). Consequently, you should install and register QuickTime before you install DVD Studio Pro.

Figure 1.7 Once you've registered both DVD Studio Pro and QuickTime, a Movie to MPEG-2 Export option is added to QuickTime Pro Player.

QuickTime MPEG Encoder

Figure 1.8 When you install DVD Studio Pro, this MPEG Export component is added to either the QuickTime Extensions folder in Mac OS 9 or the QuickTime folder in Mac OS X.

Figure 1.9 The QuickTime installer is located on your DVD Studio Pro DVD.

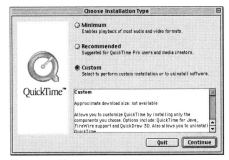

Figure 1.10 From the Choose Installation Type window, click Custom to continue to a new screen where you can specify the exact QuickTime components to be installed on your computer.

Figure 1.11 Click Select All to install all of QuickTime's components on your computer.

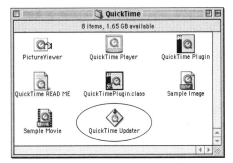

Figure 1.12 The QuickTime Updater application is located inside the QuickTime folder on your hard disk.

To install QuickTime:

1. Insert the DVD Studio Pro DVD-ROM into your CD/DVD-ROM drive.

   A DVD Studio Pro icon appears on your desktop.

2. Double-click the DVD Studio Pro icon.

3. Open the DVD Studio Pro Mac OS 9 folder.

   A window opens that includes the DVD Studio Pro installer icon and a separate QuickTime folder.

4. Double-click the QuickTime Folder.

   A window opens to reveal the QuickTime installer icon (**Figure 1.9**).

5. Double-click the QuickTime installer icon.

   The QuickTime installation application opens. Follow the onscreen instructions until you arrive at the Choose Installation Type window (**Figure 1.10**).

6. In the Choose Installation Type window, select Custom and then click Continue.

   The QuickTime Installer window opens.

7. In the QuickTime Installer window, click Select All (**Figure 1.11**) and then choose Continue.

8. After QuickTime has finished installing, restart your computer.

   After your computer restarts, you are ready to register your copy of QuickTime.

✔ Tip

- To make sure you always have the latest version of QuickTime, it's a good idea to regularly use the QuickTime Updater application (**Figure 1.12**) or check the QuickTime Web site:

  www.apple.com/quicktime

ABOUT QUICKTIME PRO

To register QuickTime Pro Player:

1. Open QuickTime Player.

2. Choose QuickTime > Preferences > Registration (Mac OS X) or Edit > Preferences > Registration (Mac OS 9).

   The QuickTime Registration window opens (**Figure 1.13**).

3. Click the Edit Registration button.

   In Mac OS X, you can type your registration information directly in the Registration window's three text boxes.

   In Mac OS 9, a dialog box opens asking for your QuickTime registration information (**Figure 1.14**).

4. Enter your registration information, making sure that all capital letters, spaces, and numbers are included.

5. Click OK.

   The information in the QuickTime Registration window is updated, and QuickTime Pro Player is unlocked.

✔ Tip

■ To find your QuickTime registration information, locate the documentation that came with your copy of DVD Studio Pro and look on the leaflet titled "Read This Before Installing DVD Studio Pro."

Figure 1.13 The QuickTime Registration window. If your copy of QuickTime is not registered, the Registered To, Organization, and Number text boxes are empty.

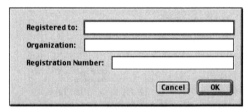

Figure 1.14 The QuickTime Edit Registration dialog box for Mac OS 9.

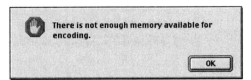

Figure 1.15 In Mac OS 9, if you have less than 25 MB of RAM allocated to QuickTime, attempting to export MPEG-2 video streams results in this alert dialog box.

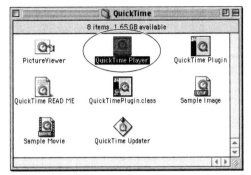

Figure 1.16 To allocate more RAM to QuickTime Player, begin by selecting the QuickTime Player application icon.

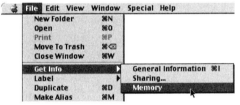

Figure 1.17 Choose File > Get Info > Memory to open the QuickTime Player Info dialog box.

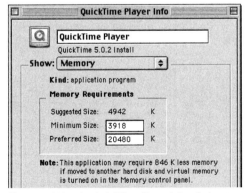

Figure 1.18 Use the QuickTime Player Info window to increase QuickTime's preferred RAM allocation to an amount greater than 25 MB.

Allocating RAM

If you're using Mac OS X, the operating system automatically allocates as much RAM as QuickTime needs to run properly. Under Mac OS 9, however, QuickTime Pro Player is allocated a mere 10 MB of RAM by default. This is not enough memory for QuickTime to export MPEG-2 video streams. If you attempt to export MPEG-2 video streams without increasing QuickTime's RAM allocation, you will be presented with the alert box in **Figure 1.15**. To avoid this alert, give QuickTime Pro Player at least 25 MB of memory (at least 40 MB is recommended).

To increase QuickTime Player's RAM allocation:

1. If QuickTime Player is currently open, choose File > Close.

   QuickTime Pro Player must not be running. If it is running, you will not be able to access the memory text fields in step 4.

2. Locate and select the QuickTime Player application icon on your hard disk (**Figure 1.16**).

   If you're having a hard time finding the QuickTime Player icon, open Apple's Sherlock and search for QuickTime Player.

3. With the QuickTime Player application icon selected, choose File > Get Info > Memory (**Figure 1.17**).

   The QuickTime Player Info dialog box opens (**Figure 1.18**).

4. In the Preferred Size text box, enter a number greater than or equal to 25600 (25 MB).

5. In the top-left corner of the QuickTime Player Info dialog box, click the close box.

   The QuickTime Player Info dialog box closes.

ABOUT QUICKTIME PRO

Installing DVD Studio Pro

Installing DVD Studio Pro is a fast process that provides no surprises. Simply insert the DVD Studio Pro DVD-ROM, launch the DVD Studio Pro installer, and follow the directions that appear on your screen (**Figure 1.19**).

The DVD Studio Pro installer places five important pieces of software on your computer:

◆ DVD Studio Pro

◆ A.Pack

◆ Subtitle Editor

◆ Apple DVD Player

◆ QuickTime MPEG Encoder

Once you've installed DVD Studio Pro, you must register it before it can be used. Registering DVD Studio Pro also enables the QuickTime MPEG Encoder.

Registering DVD Studio Pro

The first time you launch DVD Studio Pro, a dialog box opens asking for your registration information. After you correctly enter this information, DVD Studio Pro opens.

To register DVD Studio Pro:

1. From the Finder, double-click the DVD Studio Pro application icon.

   DVD Studio Pro begins to launch, but is interrupted by the dialog box shown in **Figure 1.20**.

2. Enter your registration information in the dialog box.

   The serial number for your copy of DVD Studio Pro is located on the "Read This Before Installing DVD Studio Pro" leaflet.

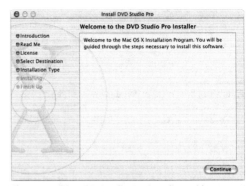

Figure 1.19 The DVD Studio Pro installer guides you through the installation procedure.

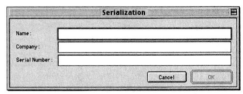

Figure 1.20 To authorize DVD Studio Pro, enter your registration information in the Serialization dialog box.

INSTALLING DVD STUDIO PRO

Figure 1.21 The Extensions Manager lets you specify which extensions will be enabled the next time you start (or restart) your Macintosh.

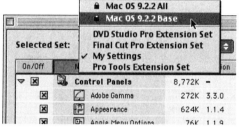

Figure 1.22 The Mac OS 9 Base extension set turns off all extensions that may cause conflicts with the DVD Studio Pro installer.

3. Click OK.

The dialog box closes, and DVD Studio Pro opens. Congratulations! You are ready to start making DVDs. Mac OS 9 users, however, should take a moment to allocate more memory to DVD Studio Pro (see the "DVD Studio Pro RAM Issues" sidebar later in this chapter).

Troubleshooting Mac OS 9 installations

Under some circumstances, Mac OS 9 users have reported errors while trying to install DVD Studio Pro. These errors are often caused by extension conflicts and can sometimes be avoided by restarting your computer using the Mac OS Base extension set before installing DVD Studio Pro.

To enable the Mac OS 9 Base extension set:

1. Choose Apple > Control Panels > Extensions Manager.

The Extensions Manager opens (**Figure 1.21**).

2. From the Selected Set pop-up menu, choose Mac OS 9.x Base (**Figure 1.22**).

To enable the Mac OS Base extension set, you must restart your computer.

continues on next page

3. At the bottom of the Extensions Manager window, click the Restart button.

   Your computer shuts down and restarts using the Mac OS 9 Base extension set.

4. Install DVD Studio Pro (see "Installing DVD Studio Pro" earlier in this chapter).

5. After DVD Studio Pro is successfully installed, follow steps 1 through 3 to reset your extensions to the normal extension set.

Figure 1.23 Ever wonder why DVD Studio Pro starts so fast? This figure shows the RAM usage of Photoshop, DVD Studio Pro, and Final Cut Pro after the programs are launched, but before any files have been opened. To simply run DVD Studio Pro requires less RAM than the other two programs.

Figure 1.24 A relatively complex project consumes a significant portion of DVD Studio Pro's RAM allocation.

DVD Studio Pro RAM Issues

In Mac OS 9, DVD Studio Pro is allocated 62,502 kilobytes of RAM memory by default. The program itself uses a very small amount of this RAM (**Figure 1.23**). However, as you add more and more content to your project, DVD Studio Pro uses up more and more of its RAM allocation (**Figure 1.24**).

To be safe, you should allocate at least 128 megabytes of RAM to DVD Studio Pro. If you don't have that much to spare, then continue using DVD Studio Pro, but be warned: you may have problems previewing projects using DVD Studio Pro's default RAM allocation.

To increase DVD Studio Pro's RAM allocation, select the DVD Studio Pro application icon, and choose File > Get Info > Memory. An Info dialog box opens that lets you assign RAM to DVD Studio Pro.

Figure 1.25 DVD Player for Mac OS X (top), and Mac OS 9 (bottom).

Using DVD Player

Apple's DVD Player is used to preview DVD-Video projects from your hard disk before you build them to a DVD-R or send them to a replication house on DLT. Make sure you have the current version of DVD Player by visiting Apple's software arena:

www.apple.com/software/.

If DVD Player wasn't previously on your computer, it is installed with DVD Studio Pro (**Figure 1.25**).

✔ Tip

- Mac OS 9 users should make sure they have DVD Player 2.7 or later installed. Earlier versions sometimes had trouble keeping DVD video synchronized with its audio, causing extreme panic in DVD-Video authors unaware of this fact. DVD Player 2.7 is included in the Mac OS 9.2.2 update installer, located in the Mac OS 9 Updates folder on the DVD Studio Pro DVD-ROM.

USING DVD PLAYER

Software Extras

DVD Studio Pro is not a content creation program; it's a content assembly program. Before you can produce a DVD-Video project, you must prepare source material, such as edited video, menu graphics, audio, and subtitles. To develop this content, you will use applications including Apple's Final Cut Pro, A.Pack, and Subtitle Editor, as well as Adobe Photoshop.

Adobe Photoshop

You'll use Photoshop to create your projects' interactive parts, including menus, buttons, and highlight overlays. You can also use Photoshop to create still images for DVD-Video slideshows (see Chapter 8, "Photoshop Layer Menus," for more information).

✔ Tip

- If you don't have Photoshop, don't worry, Apple's got you covered. The DVD Studio Pro DVD-ROM contains a copy of Corel PhotoPaint 10, which produces layered Photoshop files that you can use in DVD Studio Pro.

Apple A.Pack

A.Pack compresses digital audio into small, efficient Dolby AC-3 audio streams optimized for DVD-Video playback. A.Pack can compress stereo audio streams as well as multichannel surround streams, allowing you to bring the ambiance of the big screen into the living room. To learn more about using A.Pack, see Chapter 4, "Encoding Audio Streams."

When you install DVD Studio Pro, A.Pack is automatically installed on your hard disk in the same folder as DVD Studio Pro.

Apple Final Cut Pro 3

Final Cut Pro 3 is a Macintosh program used for editing video and compositing motion menus for use with DVD Studio Pro. You don't necessarily need Final Cut Pro 3; in fact, some DVD Studio Pro authors prefer to use Adobe Premiere for editing video and Adobe After Effects for compositing motion menus (in a pinch, even QuickTime Pro Player will suffice!). However, Final Cut Pro 3.0.2 gives DVD Studio Pro authors a great new feature that lets you set DVD Studio Pro chapter markers right on the Final Cut Pro timeline, which is something no other video editing application can do (see Chapter 3, "Encoding Video Streams").

Apple Subtitle Editor

The Subtitle Editor application is used to generate text subtitles that are synchronized to your video streams. To learn more about using the Subtitle Editor, see Chapter 16, "Subtitles."

When you install DVD Studio Pro, the Subtitle Editor is automatically installed on your hard disk in the same folder as DVD Studio Pro.

Bias Peak DV 3.0

Peak DV 3.0 is an audio editing application that works under both Mac OS 9 and Mac OS X. Even better, Apple gives it to you for free (it's included on your DVD Studio Pro DVD-ROM). Peak DV includes several stock digital signal processing (DSP) filters such as a de-esser, audio peak limiter, dynamic range compressor, and equalizer. If its stock audio filters don't provide the effect you're looking for, you can expand Peak DV 3.0's abilities by adding Steinberg Virtual Studio Technology (VST) compatible audio filters.

Roxio Toast Titanium 5

Toast Titanium 5 lets you copy DVD-R discs, record multiple copies of a DVD-R disc from a single DVD-Video image saved on your hard disk, and even write DVD-Video projects onto a CD that your Macintosh reads just like a DVD-Video disc (see Chapter 13, "Finishing the DVD").

✔ Tips

■ Toast is relatively inexpensive, and its cost is quickly recouped by its ability to record DVD-RW discs, which saves you from wasting DVD-Rs as you test your projects.

■ If you're using an external FireWire DVD writer, be sure to upgrade to Toast Titanium 5.0.2 or higher (a free upgrade for registered Toast Titanium 5 users). Version 5.0.2 includes expanded support for external DVD writers as well as a few FireWire bug fixes that will keep you from turning DVD-Rs into expensive coasters.

Extra! Extra!

There are a few other applications that all DVD Studio Pro authors should also consider using:

Digidesign Pro Tools Free. If you're on a budget, check out this free audio editor. It lets you edit and master digital audio files, and it supports Digidesign Pro Tools Real-Time Audio Suite (RTAS) audio effects plug-ins (normalizers, reverbs, delays, and so on); it does not include surround mixing capabilities. Download it from: www.digidesign.com.

Steinberg Nuendo. Nuendo is an audio post-production system that includes support for multichannel surround mixing and Virtual Studio Technology (VST) audio effects plug-ins. Find out more at: www.nuendo.com.

Emagic Logic Audio Platinum 5. Logic Audio offers features similar to Nuendo's (including surround mixing and support for VST audio effects plug-ins), but also contains advanced MIDI editing features. Find out more at: www.emagic.de.

Discreet Cleaner 5. On its own, Cleaner 5 creates MPEG-2 streams of a slightly higher quality than those created by the QuickTime MPEG-2 export option. In conjunction with its companion plug-in, MPEG Charger, Cleaner 5 provides high-quality MPEG-2 compression. Find out more at: www.discreet.com.

SOFTWARE EXTRAS

DVD BASICS

What are the differences between DVDs and CDs? How much data can a DVD store? What's DVD-Video? If you're just getting into DVD, this chapter will answer some basic questions about how DVDs work. But as the chapter unfolds, we'll also discuss increasingly complex (and important) aspects of the DVD-Video specification, culminating in a description of the DVD-Video data structure and how this structure relates to DVD Studio Pro. If you find the final sections of this chapter hard to grasp, don't worry. Later, if you need to use this information, you'll know it's there, waiting.

Before we get into the nitty-gritty of how DVDs work, let me offer this one disclaimer: The DVD-Video specification is large and complex. Although you'll get all the info you need to confidently author DVD-Video with DVD Studio Pro, no one chapter can discuss all aspects of the DVD-Video specification. If you find you want to go deeper into the underpinnings of DVD-Video, visit Jim Taylor's DVD FAQ at:

www.dvddemystified.com/.

DVD vs. CD

If you physically compare a DVD to a CD, you won't see many differences. A DVD's edges may feel slightly smoother, but other than that, a standard DVD is indistinguishable from a standard CD (**Figure 2.1**).

Though they appear identical on the surface, a DVD can store much more data than a CD. You can cram up to 4.37 computer gigabytes of data on a DVD. That's over six times as much data as a standard 700-megabyte CD-ROM disc will hold. So what's the difference? How do DVDs pack so much more information onto that little optical disc?

Pits and tracks

The CDs and DVDs you buy from a store come in two varieties: ROM discs and recordable discs. ROM discs are replicated in huge quantities by specialized facilities that stamp the data directly onto the disc's surface. For a recordable disc, a tightly focused, high-powered laser etches marks into an organic dye recording layer sandwiched between two (or more) layers of molded plastic. Use a microscope to inspect a stamped or recorded disc, and you'll see that the data is represented by very small pits arranged in a tiny track that spirals out from the center of the disc toward its edge.

When you place the disc into a CD or DVD-ROM drive, the laser follows a track in the disc, reading its pits in much the same way that a record needle follows the groove on a vinyl record, reading the bumps in the vinyl. In the case of a CD-ROM drive, the infrared laser's wavelength (about 780 nanometers) is relatively long and not terribly accurate by DVD standards. A DVD-ROM drive, on the other hand, uses a more advanced red laser (that's *red*, not *infrared*) with a shorter wavelength (635 or 650 nanometers) and a narrower focus. As a result, it can precisely follow a DVD's densely spun data tracks, reading the smaller pits.

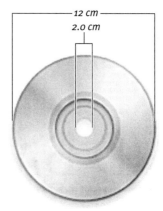

Figure 2.1 Both CDs and DVDs share the same physical dimensions. Both are 12 cm in diameter and 0.12 cm thick, and both have a 2.0-cm hole in the middle.

Out of the Blue

Several companies are working on a new breed of DVD-R recording devices that use a blue (or violet) laser with a wavelength of around 405 nanometers. With this more focused laser, these devices can record over 27 gigabytes of data on a single layer of a DVD-R disc! That's more than six times the storage capacity of today's DVDs.

Like today's DVDs, these next-generation discs will also come in dual-sided and/or dual-layered varieties, which means they may potentially store a staggering 100+ gigabytes of information! Working prototypes of these machines have been unveiled by Sony, Toshiba, and a few other manufacturers. Stay tuned!

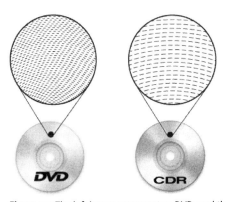

Figure 2.2 The left image represents a DVD, and the right image represents a CD. Data pits on a DVD are smaller and packed much more closely together than data pits on a CD.

Labeling DVDs

Most people label their CD-Rs and DVD-Rs with a black felt-tip Sharpie. Some people prefer to print a label and stick it on the disc. With CD-Rs, this works fine, but attaching a stick-on label to a DVD-R is not recommended. If the label is even remotely off-center, the DVD will wobble as it spins. This makes it hard for the reading laser to lock onto the DVD's smaller track, which in turn makes it hard for the laser to read those tiny pits.

For a truly professional touch, check out the new generation of CD/DVD printers (use Apple's Sherlock to search the Web for CD Printers). These printers print in color directly on the surface of any *inkjet-printable* DVD-R. Inkjet-printable DVD-Rs have a special ink absorption layer that allows the ink to set. If the DVD does not have an inkjet-printable surface, don't print on it! Doing so causes the ink to puddle and slide off the disc, which may damage the disc and your printer.

Storage capacity

Today, the standard CD-ROM disc holds up to 700 megabytes of data in one layer, on one side of the disc only. A similarly configured DVD-ROM disc, with one layer and one side, can hold up to 4.37 gigabytes of data (did you think DVDs held 4.7 gigabytes of data? See the sidebar "Billions of Bytes vs. Gigabytes" later in this chapter).

So why, you may ask, do DVDs have such a vastly increased storage capacity? CDs and DVDs are physically the same size. Both contain pits and tracks. What's the difference? Well, on a DVD the pits are smaller and closer together, and the track is wound much more tightly than the pits and track on a CD (**Figure 2.2**). These two differences together allow DVDs to fit significantly more data on the surface area of the disc.

But DVD-ROM discs do not stop at 4.37 gigabytes of storage space. Unlike CD-ROM discs, DVD-ROM discs can have two data layers, or 7.95 gigabytes of data per side! If that's not enough storage space, there are also double-sided DVD-ROM discs that double the disc's capacity by pressing data onto both the bottom and top surfaces of the disc. **Table 2.1** lists the four most common types of DVD-ROM discs and their corresponding storage capacities.

The following list details the storage capacities and layer configurations of the five most common optical discs available today:

CD-ROM. A CD-ROM disc is a single-sided, single-layer disc that can store up to 700 megabytes of data (0.75 billion bytes).

DVD-5. At the low end of the DVD spectrum sits the DVD-5. DVD-5s are single-layer, single-sided discs that store up to 4.37 gigabytes of data (4.7 billion bytes).

continues on next page

DVD VS. CD

DVD-9. A DVD-9 is a dual-layer, single-sided disc that stores up to 7.95 gigabytes of data (about 8.54 billion bytes).

DVD-10. A DVD-10 has a single data layer on both the top and bottom sides of the disc. Combined, these two layers store up to 8.75 gigabytes of data (about 9.4 billion bytes).

DVD-18. A DVD-18 is a double-sided disc, where each side contains dual data layers. Combined, the four layers of a DVD-18 store up to 15.9 gigabytes of data (about 17.08 billion bytes).

✔ Tip

■ A dual-layer DVD contains a semitransparent data layer that the reading laser must penetrate as it harvests information from the top data layer. This semitransparent layer reduces the entire disc's reflectivity, making it harder for the reading laser to focus. Consequently, data cannot be stamped onto a dual-layer disc as densely as it can be stamped onto a single-layer disc, so dual-layer DVDs store slightly less than double the data of a single-layer disc.

Table 2.1

CD-ROM and DVD-ROM Disc Storage Capacity

Media Type	Capacity (Computer GB)	Capacity (DVD GB)	Data Sides	Data Layers per Side
CD-ROM	0.68 GB	0.75 GB	1	1
DVD-5	4.37 GB	4.7 GB	1	1
DVD-9	7.95 GB	8.54 GB	1	2
DVD-10	8.75 GB	9.4 GB	2	1
DVD-18	15.9 GB	17.08 GB	2	2

DVD vs. CD

Billions of Bytes vs. Gigabytes

You may have read that DVDs hold up to 4.7 gigabytes of data. This number is misleading. In fact, DVDs store up to 4.7 *DVD gigabytes*, which is not the same as *computer gigabytes*. Confused? Here's how it works: A DVD actually holds 4.7 *billion bytes* of information. However, in computer terms, one kilobyte is equal to 1,024 bytes, one megabyte is equal to 1,024 kilobytes, and one gigabyte is equal to 1,024 megabytes. There's a lot of extra "24s" hanging around, and indeed, if you do the math, 4.7 billion bytes actually equals approximately 4.37 computer gigabytes. The difference in perceived data storage is over 300 megabytes!

Because you're using a computer to make your DVDs, this book uses the computer storage numbers (unless otherwise stated). For quick reference, Table 2.1 will help you to convert between computer and DVD storage capacities.

About DVD Formats

DVD formats fall into two categories: physical formats and logical formats.

A DVD's physical format reflects the way the DVD itself is put together. All DVDs conform to one physical format or another. For example, a disc is either a DVD-R or a DVD-RAM, but not both.

Regardless of the disc's physical format, each DVD also contains a logical format reflecting the type of data held on the disc. A blank DVD-R, for example, contains no data and consequently has no logical format. If you record a DVD-Video project onto the disc, you give it a logical format (DVD-Video, of course). If you record computer files onto the disc (HTML, QuickTime movies, and so on), it becomes a DVD-ROM disc with a corresponding logical format. Put both DVD-Video and computer data onto the disc, and you create a hybrid DVD.

DVD physical formats

Physical format determines how the DVD is physically configured, including how the pits are stamped or recorded and other low-level characteristics that you, as a DVD-Video author, seldom need to worry about. Just be sure you use the appropriate disc for your purpose, and everything will work fine. For example, if you want to record a DVD using your SuperDrive, you must use a DVD-R (General) and not a DVD-R (Authoring) or a DVD-RAM disc.

DVD-ROM. DVD-ROM is a read-only format similar to a CD-ROM disc, but it stores much more information. A DVD-ROM disc can hold games, a series of QuickTime movies, MPEG-2 video, text files, or any other type of data.

DVD-R. DVD-R is a write once, read many times format similar to CD-R. Using a SuperDrive and DVD Studio Pro (or a third-party application like Roxio's Toast Titanium 5), you can write data to a DVD-R disc and retrieve that data later.

There are two types of DVD-R media: General and Authoring. If you're using a SuperDrive (Pioneer DVR-A04), you can write only to DVD-R (General) media. The second variety, DVD-R (Authoring), is used with professional DVD-recordable drives, including Pioneer's DVR-S201.

continues on next page

ABOUT DVD FORMATS

DVD-RW. DVD-RW is a write many times, read many times format similar to CD-RW. DVD-RW provides all the benefits of DVD-R, but discs can be erased and rewritten up to 1,000 times.

Most new DVD-Video players can read DVD-RW discs, which dramatically decreases your materials costs. You can build your DVD-Video project on a DVD-RW disc, for example, and then test that project in a DVD-Video player. If there's a problem with the project, simply fix it and rerecord the disc without wasting a DVD-R disc.

DVD-RAM. For archiving data and backing up your DVD Studio Pro projects, nothing beats DVD-RAM. DVD-RAM lets you write to the disc in multiple sessions, similar to the way a floppy or Iomega Zip disk works (DVD-RW, on the other hand, uses "disc at once" recording, which means the whole disc must be recorded in a single session).

DVD-RAM discs will not play in most DVD-Video players and consequently are not recommended for testing DVD-Video projects. A DVD-RAM drive is good to have, but to utilize DVD Studio Pro to its full potential, you must also have a DVD-R recorder like the Apple SuperDrive.

DVD+R and DVD+RW. DVD+R does more or less the same thing as DVD-R: that is, it lets you record up to 4.37 gigabytes of data onto a DVD disc. However, DVD+R uses a different recording process than DVD-R. Consequently, DVD+R discs *cannot* be recorded with a SuperDrive, and they are not supported by DVD Studio Pro.

✔ Tip

■ If you have a SuperDrive (Pioneer DVR-A04) in your computer, you can record only DVD-R (General) or DVD-RW blank discs. DVD-R (Authoring) will not work, nor will DVD+R, DVD+RW, or DVD-RAM.

DVD-R: General vs. Authoring

In the beginning, there were only DVD-R Authoring discs. As DVDs made inroads into the general consumer market, DVD-R General discs were created. There are a couple of differences between DVD-R General and DVD-R Authoring discs:

DVD-R General uses a recording wavelength of 650 nanometers, and DVD-R Authoring uses a recording wavelength of 635 nanometers. Consequently, you cannot record to a DVD-R Authoring disc in a DVD-R General drive.

DVD-R Authoring discs are capable of storing Cutting Master Format (CMF) information on the disc. This allows DVD-R Authoring discs to be used as masters for DVD replication.

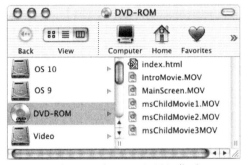

Figure 2.3 When you place a DVD-ROM disc into your DVD drive, the DVD-ROM icon (shown at the top of the figure) appears on your desktop. If you open the DVD and look at its file structure, you'll see that the DVD contains only data files.

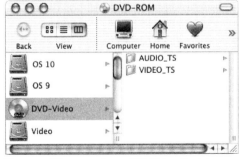

Figure 2.4 When you place a DVD-Video disc into your DVD drive, the DVD-Video icon (shown at the top of the figure) appears on your desktop. If you open the DVD and look at its file structure, you'll see a VIDEO_TS folder (typically, there will also be an AUDIO_TS folder on the disc).

DVD logical formats

Logical format refers to the type of data that a DVD holds. There are three logical DVD formats of interest to DVD Studio Pro authors: DVD-ROM, DVD-Video, and hybrid DVD (in which the disc contains both DVD-ROM and DVD-Video content).

DVD-ROM. A DVD-ROM disc holds any type of file you would normally find on your computer's hard disks (**Figure 2.3**).

DVD-Video. A DVD-Video disc contains DVD-Video that can be read only by DVD-Video players. The video data is stored inside a VIDEO_TS folder at the disc's root level (**Figure 2.4**).

Hybrid DVDs. A hybrid DVD contains a VIDEO_TS folder at the disc's root level, but also has other folders housing data files. These other folders may include HTML pages, QuickTime movies, Word documents, or any type of file you would normally find on your computer's hard disk.

DVD-Audio. DVD-Audio discs are designed to replace the audio CD format. Due to the increased storage space available on a DVD, DVD-Audio discs deliver higher-quality audio than that found on a standard stereo, 16-bit, 44.1 kHz audio CD. In fact, a DVD-Audio disc can hold multichannel, 24-bit surround audio at sample rates of up to 192 kHz. DVD Studio Pro does not create DVD-Audio discs.

✔ Tip

■ DVD logical formats exist independently of DVD physical formats. If you archive your Pro Tools sessions by recording them onto a DVD-R disc, for example, you have effectively created a DVD-ROM disc. If you record a DVD-Video project onto a DVD-R disc, you've created a DVD-Video disc.

Editing in DVD Studio Pro

Until DVD-Video came along, VHS video was the only full-motion video format that we could play on our television sets. VHS video is a linear format with many limitations, including a lack of interactivity, no random-access capabilities, and audio and video streams of an often questionable quality. For a generation raised on video games and the Internet, a Fast Forward button is just not good enough. Let's face it; VHS video is boring.

DVD-Video significantly enhances the video experience by adding interactivity, support for multiple video streams, high-quality surround audio, dynamic alternate language streams, and scripting capabilities that allow DVD-Video authors to create immersive video environments and games. Unlike VHS video, DVD-Video is loaded with possibilities, and DVD Studio Pro is designed to help you make the most of them. Here's a quick look at what you can do:

Tracks. In DVD Studio Pro, a track is a container that holds video, audio, and subtitles. Each track holds at least one video stream, and you can use a maximum of 99 tracks in any DVD Studio Pro project.

Multiple angles. Each track can have up to eight alternate camera angles on top of the main video stream (for a total of nine different camera angles). These camera angles may supply anything from an alternate view of a sports event to a wireframe composite that lets you get under the skin of a 3D animation. If viewers want to switch angles, they can press the Angle button on their remote controls, and the DVD player will cycle through each alternate angle in succession.

Menus. A menu provides a visual backdrop for buttons. A menu can be a still Photoshop or PICT file (still menu) or an MPEG-2 video (motion menu).

Buttons. Buttons allow viewers to interact with the DVD-Video project. Each menu can have up to 36 buttons.

Slideshows. A slideshow is a series of still images and/or MPEG video segments that plays sequentially from beginning to end. Each slide may advance automatically after a certain interval or may be programmed to advance when the viewer presses the Next Track button on the DVD player's remote control.

Audio streams. Uncompressed PCM (AIFF, WAV, SDII), MPEG-1 Layer 2, and digitally compressed AC3 audio streams are accepted by DVD Studio Pro 1.5 (DVD Studio Pro 1.2 and below do not support MPEG-1 Layer 2 audio). These audio streams can be mono, stereo, or multichannel surround. Each track (or slide in a slideshow) may have up to eight different audio streams.

Subtitles. Subtitles are used for closed captions or to supply text translations of your movie in alternate languages. DVD Studio Pro supports up to 32 subtitle streams per track. Each subtitle is synchronized with the track's video and audio streams, and each can use a maximum of four colors (2 bits per pixel).

To create subtitles, you use the Subtitle Editor application that comes with DVD Studio Pro.

Table 2.2

DVD Region Coding Compatibility	
REGION	GEOGRAPHIC AREA
Region 1	Canada, USA
Region 2	Europe, Japan, the Near East, Egypt, and South Africa
Region 3	East Asia, Hong Kong, and South Asia
Region 4	Australia, the Caribbean, Central and South America, New Zealand
Region 5	Africa, India, Mongolia, Pakistan, North Korea, the states of the former USSR
Region 6	China
Region 7	Reserved
Region 8	Special purpose (for in-flight DVD-Video players installed in airplanes)

Scripting. Scripting programs your DVD-Video to make its own decisions. Through scripting, you can tell a menu to highlight the button corresponding to the last track played, program a track to loop a set number of times, create a Random button that randomly plays all of the tracks in the project, passcode protect certain tracks and/or menus, and more.

Region coding. Region coding lets you, as a DVD-Video author, decide where in the world your DVD-Video disc will play (see **Table 2.2**). All DVD-Video players are hardwired with a certain region code at the time they are manufactured. When you place a DVD-Video disc into a DVD-Video player, the player checks the DVD's region code against its own. If the codes match, the DVD player allows you to view the disc. If the codes are different, the disc won't work.

EDITING IN DVD STUDIO PRO

Copy Protection

Copy protection prevents viewers from dragging your DVD-Video's media files onto their computers (**Figure 2.5**) or copying them to an analog recording device such as a VHS tape recorder. Two forms of copy protection are available to DVD Studio Pro:

CSS. CSS stands for Content Scrambling System. CSS uses an encryption system to scramble each sector of the DVD-Video disc. DVD Studio Pro provides an option that lets you copy protect your DVD-Video disc using CSS. You can do this, however, only if you build your DVD-Video disc on a DLT tape and send it to a qualified replication house, where the appropriate encryption keys are inserted.

Macrovision. Macrovision copy protection (also known as the Analog Protection System, or APS) is used to prevent consumer DVD users from recording a DVD-Video disc to a VHS tape. If a Macrovision-protected DVD is recorded to VHS, the signal appears to be inverted or posterized (rather like those channels above the ones you've paid for). In other words, Macrovision degrades the signal to a point where most consumers will not enjoy watching it.

✔ Tip

■ DVD-R (General) discs do not allow you to protect your content using CSS.

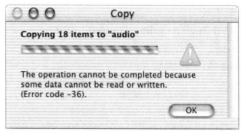

Figure 2.5 If you try to drag the contents of a copy-protected DVD-Video onto your hard disk, this alert dialog box appears.

Using Macrovision

To use Macrovision copy protection, you must enter into a usage agreement with Macrovision Corporation. For more information, contact Macrovision:

◆ Telephone: (408) 743-8600

◆ Fax: (408) 743-8610

◆ Email: acp-info@macrovision.com

◆ Web site: www.macrovision.com

COPY PROTECTION

DVD Studio Pro Workflow

Although there's no set way to produce a DVD-Video project, in general you'll find yourself following a similar routine almost every time.

1. Use programs such as Apple Final Cut Pro, Adobe Photoshop, and Peak DV 3 to create source files (audio and video streams, menu and slideshow graphics).

2. Encode video and audio, respectively, to MPEG-2 and AC-3 streams.

3. Import assets into DVD Studio Pro.

4. Create one or more tracks, including alternate angles, subtitles, markers, and stories.

5. Create menus and buttons to allow the viewer to interact with and navigate your DVD-Video.

6. Enhance the DVD-Video by adding scripts, slideshows, and Web links.

7. Build the project on your hard disk.

8. Record the project to a DVD-R, DVD-RW, or DVD-RAM disc (or a DLT if you intend to send the project to a replication house).

✔ Tip

- At each applicable step of the process, you should also use DVD Studio Pro's Preview mode to preview your project, ensuring that everything works correctly.

DVD STUDIO PRO WORKFLOW

About DVD-Video Data Structure

This section provides an overview of the DVD-Video data structure and how it relates to DVD Studio Pro (**Figure 2.6**). This is not meant to be an all-encompassing description of the DVD-Video data structure.

Groups of pictures

The MPEG group of pictures (GOP) is the smallest unit of random access available to DVD Studio Pro. For example, all markers lock onto the first frame of a GOP (markers are discussed in Chapter 10, "Creating Markers and Stories"). A single GOP represents 15 frames of NTSC video, or 12 frames of PAL video. To learn more about GOPs, see Chapter 3, "Encoding Video Streams."

Video object units

A video object unit (VOBU) contains one or more MPEG GOPs. A VOBU can be between 0.4 and 1.2 seconds long, which means that a VOBU typically holds two full GOPs. You may experience build errors when one or more VOBUs in your MPEG streams are less than 0.4 second long. To learn more, see Chapter 13, "Finishing the DVD."

Cells

A cell is a collection of VOBUs and their corresponding audio packets. DVD Studio Pro does not give you access to cells.

Programs

A program is analogous to a single chapter in a track. A chapter represents the segment of an MPEG video, as defined by markers set in the Marker window (see Chapter 10, "Creating Markers and Stories"). By default, every track has one chapter, and consequently one program. As you supply the track with more markers, you create more chapters, and thus more programs in the program chain.

DVD Studio Pro allows you to create up to 99 individual programs, or chapters, per track.

Program chains

A program chain is a sequential group of programs. In DVD Studio Pro, a story is equivalent to a program chain (for more information on stories, see Chapter 10, "Creating Markers and Stories").

The title area

The title area collects program chains, or in the case of DVD Studio Pro, stories. Each title area can hold up to one story.

The video title set

The DVD-Video format allows each DVD-Video disc up to 99 video title sets (VTSs). In DVD Studio Pro, each track and slideshow is assigned to one of the 99 VTSs. If your project has 66 tracks, for example, there is room left for only 33 slideshows.

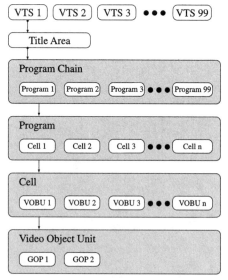

Figure 2.6 The DVD-Video data structure.

ENCODING
VIDEO STREAMS

Trying to cram uncompressed digital video onto a DVD disc is a lot like attempting to squeeze an elephant into a shoebox—size definitely matters. Digital video, when uncompressed, is very large. Without some method of squeezing it down to a manageable size, you're not going to fit much of it on a DVD. Uncompressed digital video also suffers from a high data rate, and DVD-ROM drives simply can't read uncompressed digital video fast enough to display it at its full frame rate and resolution. Fortunately, you can solve both size and speed issues at the same time using MPEG compression.

There's an old saying in the world of video compression: Garbage in, garbage out! The quality of your MPEG video streams is directly dependent upon the quality of the source video you put through the encoder. The first part of this chapter shows you how to prepare source video for compression and provides other tips that will make your video streams look as clear and sharp as possible.

Video compression is an involved process, and you probably have a lot of questions about how MPEG compression works. What exactly *is* MPEG compression? What's the difference between MPEG-1 and MPEG-2 Video? What happens under the hood of MPEG compression utilities such as the QuickTime MPEG Encoder? The second half of this chapter provides background theory that answers these questions, and many others. After the theory lesson is over, this chapter finishes by exploring the QuickTime MPEG Encoder and all of its various settings. If you read this chapter from start to end the QuickTime MPEG Encoder will seem self-explanatory—it's extremely easy to use.

Preparing Source Video

DVD Studio Pro's basic appeal lies in its ability to transfer edited video from your computer to an optical disc that plays on a TV. There are, however, some important differences between the way computers and televisions display video. This section discusses those differences and shows you how to work around them.

NTSC vs. PAL

Broadcast video has two major competing standards: NTSC (National Television Standards Committee) and PAL (Phase Alternation Line). DVD Studio Pro lets you work with either standard, but each project must be either NTSC or PAL, not both.

NTSC. NTSC video uses a screen resolution of 720 x 480 pixels per frame and a frame rate of 29.97 frames per second. If you live in North America, this is your standard.

PAL. PAL video uses a screen resolution of 720 x 576 pixels per frame and a frame rate of 25 frames per second. If you live in Europe (including the United Kingdom), this is your standard.

Tables 3.1 and **3.2** categorize many (but not all) countries by their broadcast standard. Take a moment to look at these tables. As you develop the project, keep your target market in mind and be sure to use the correct standard for your source video streams.

✔ Tips

- NTSC is by far the dominant video standard, and consequently most PAL DVD-video players will actually play NTSC DVDs (provided the DVD's region coding allows it). On the flip side, almost no NTSC DVD-video players play PAL DVDs.

- Playing an NTSC DVD-Video on a PAL player can lead to problems, including poorly reproduced color and stuttering playback. If your DVD is to be distributed in both Europe and North America, you should consider making two completely separate discs: one PAL and one NTSC.

Table 3.1

NTSC Countries		
Antigua	Ecuador	Panama
Bahamas	El Salvador	Peru
Barbados	Greenland	Philippines
Belize	Guam	Puerto Rico
Bermuda	Guatemala	Saint Kitts
Bolivia	Guyana	Samoa
Burma	Honduras	Taiwan
Canada	Jamaica	Tobago
Chile	Japan	Trinidad
Colombia	South Korea	USA
Costa Rica	Mexico	Venezuela
Cuba	Nicaragua	Virgin Islands

Table 3.2

PAL Countries		
Africa	Cyprus	Pakistan
Afghanistan	Europe	Paraguay
Argentina	Hong Kong	Qatar
Australia	India	Saudi Arabia
Bahrain	Indonesia	Singapore
Bangladesh	Israel	Sri Lanka
Brunei	Jordan	Thailand
Cameroon	Kuwait	Turkey
Canary Islands	New Zealand	Uruguay
China	Oman	Yemen

PREPARING SOURCE VIDEO

About safe zones

Televisions blast electron beams at the picture tube's surface, causing phosphors on the face of the tube to emit red, green, and blue light. As you move towards the edges of the screen, the electron beams become less accurate, and visual distortion occurs. Televisions hide this distortion "in the wings," or past the visible edges of the screen, using a process called *overscanning*.

Overscanning causes your video's displayed resolution to be less than that defined by the NTSC and PAL standards. For example, you may have created your NTSC video streams at a resolution of 720 x 480 pixels per frame, but some televisions may display only 640 x 430 (or less) of those pixels. The video is not resized to fit within these shrunken dimensions; in fact, all those extra pixels are hidden past the visible boundary of the screen. On televisions, the edges of your video are always cut off.

To compensate for this, there are two *safe zones* you can use to ensure your viewers see everything they are supposed to see. These safe zones are called the *action safe* and *title safe* zones:

Action safe zone. The action safe zone is represented by a rectangular border set five percent in from the edges of your video (**Figure 3.1**). For NTSC video, that's 36 pixels from the left and right edges, and 24 pixels from the top and bottom edges. You should always assume that everything outside the action safe zone will *not* be seen by viewers watching your DVD-Video on a television set.

Title safe zone. The title safe zone is represented by a rectangular border set 10 percent in from the edges of your video (refer to Figure 3.1). For NTSC video, that's 72 pixels from the left and right edges, and 48 pixels from the top and bottom edges. Older televisions overscan more than newer ones, so you must be sure to set all text (including closed captions and subtitles) and key images inside the title safe zone.

✔ Tips

■ For motion menus, make sure all buttons are placed inside the title safe zone, or they may get sliced from view, cut in half, or otherwise truncated.

■ Computers display video at its full dimensions, so nothing gets cut off. If your DVD-Video is destined only for computer playback, you do not need to design with the safe zones in mind.

To enable the title safe overlay in Adobe After Effects, click this button.

Figure 3.1 The action safe and title safe zones as shown in Adobe After Effects.

Using safe zones

All video-editing programs provide overlays that define the action and title safe zones. As you prepare your source video, you should occasionally turn these overlays on and check that important visual content falls within the safe zones.

As DVD Studio Pro is designed to work in concert with Apple Final Cut Pro, the following numbered step shows you how to turn on the title safe overlay in Final Cut Pro. Adobe Premiere and After Effects, however, also contain these overlays.

To enable the title safe overlay in Final Cut Pro:

1. Click either the Final Cut Pro Viewer or Canvas window to select it.

   The Viewer and Canvas windows usually fill the top two-thirds of your screen (they're the windows you look at as you edit your video in Final Cut Pro).

2. Choose View > Title Safe (**Figure 3.2**).

   The action and title safe zones are drawn on top of the video (**Figure 3.3**). As you edit your video, make sure that no important action falls outside of these safe zones.

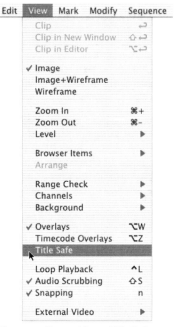

Figure 3.2 Choose View > Title Safe to enable the Final Cut Pro title safe overlay.

Figure 3.3 The video and title safe overlays. Make sure that all important video events fall within the inner rectangle.

Table 3.3

Broadcast Safe Colors

Color	Standard RGB Value	Broadcast Safe RGB Value
Red	255, 0, 0	204, 0, 0
Green	0, 255, 0	0, 204, 0
Yellow	255, 255, 0	153, 153, 0
Black	0, 0, 0	15, 15, 15
White	255, 255, 255	235, 235, 235

About color depth

Televisions cannot display as many colors as computer screens. In particular, televisions have a very hard time displaying bright red, green, yellow, white, and even deep black (**Table 3.3**). If you don't filter these colors out of your video, they will appear to *bleed* into surrounding areas, making the overall image look mushy. To avoid this problem, use the Broadcast Safe color filter that comes with your video editing application (this filter is sometimes called Broadcast Colors or NTSC Colors). On the computer screen, your bright yellows turn a bit brown, reds deepen, and pure white (also known as *super white*) becomes noticeably gray, but on a television set, everything will look perfect.

About MPEG Video

Although the 4.37 gigabyte storage capacity of a typical DVD-R disc might seem like a lot, in digital video terms, it's a drop in the bucket. A digital video compressed using the DV codec uses 216 megabytes of storage per minute of footage. That's over one gigabyte per five minutes, which means that without some more efficient form of compression, you could store only 20 minutes of DV on a single layer DVD-R disc.

Happily, the good people of the Moving Picture Experts Group invented MPEG video compression, which dramatically reduces digital video file size while maintaining the full motion, resolution, and visual quality of the source video file. MPEG video comes in two flavors: MPEG-1 and MPEG-2.

MPEG-1 video

MPEG-1 is the preferred format for video compact discs (VCDs). However, due to its relatively low bit rate (typically 1.4 Mbps, with a maximum of 1.8 Mbps), MPEG-1 is restricted to a resolution of 352 x 240 pixels (NTSC) or 352 x 288 (PAL)—less than half the resolution of broadcast-quality video. In North America, MPEG-1 is more commonly seen on the Internet than on video store shelves. Nonetheless, MPEG-1 is a legal format for a DVD-Video title, and DVD Studio Pro lets you use MPEG-1 video streams in your projects.

MPEG-2 video

MPEG-2 video is the preferred format for DVD-Video titles, and it is the format you will typically use while authoring in DVD Studio Pro. MPEG-2 video provides a resolution of 720 x 480 at 30 frames per second (NTSC) or 720 x 576 at 25 frames per second (PAL), with a maximum bit rate of 9.8 Mbps. In other words, MPEG-2 video provides full-motion, full-resolution, broadcast-quality video at a data rate that most new computers and all DVD-ROM drives can handle.

About MPEG-2 Compression

Video is a progression of still images that flick by in rapid succession. If you stop a video, you see a single image, called a *frame*. The frame itself is made of a grid of colored dots, called pixels. As video frames progress, these dots change color, creating the effect of motion.

To efficiently encode digital video, it must be compressed both spatially (within the video frame) and temporally (over time, or across several video frames). MPEG encoders start by breaking the video into several small segments called Groups of Pictures (GOPs). The first frame in a GOP (technically, the *I-frame*, but more on that in a moment) is spatially compressed using a process similar to JPEG compression for still images. With the first frame completely compressed, the encoder moves on to the next frame and checks to see if blocks of color have shifted or changed. Where blocks of color have shifted, the encoder creates a *motion vector* to represent this change.

Motion vectors

MPEG encoders divide the video frame into blocks (called *macroblocks*) and then search through surrounding frames, looking for similar blocks. If the encoder finds a similar block, it creates a motion vector to describe how far the block has moved. This is a major boon to compression because instead of re-encoding each color block, the MPEG encoder need only record a small number representing how far that color block has moved within the frame.

Take, for example, a video of a zeppelin floating through the sky. The macroblocks composing the zeppelin don't change in color as the zeppelin floats along, and there is no need to spatially re-encode those blocks. Instead, a motion vector is used to describe the movement of the zeppelin (or rather, the movement of the macroblocks composing the zeppelin).

✔ Tip

- Motion vectors work well wherever large blocks of color move together. Panning shots (where the whole frame moves sideways) compress well, while zooms (where the camera focuses in on a particular object, causing it to grow larger in relation to other objects in the frame) do not.

ABOUT MPEG-2 COMPRESSION

GOPs

MPEG encoding utilities begin the compression process by breaking the source video into small segments called groups of pictures (GOPs), as shown in **Figure 3.4**. According to the DVD-Video format, a GOP must be no larger than 18 pictures, or frames of sequential video. It's more common, however, to use a GOP size of 15 for NTSC video and 12 for PAL video (roughly equivalent to two GOPs per second of video).

A GOP is composed of one intra frame (I-frame), followed by several predicted frames (P-frames) and bidirectional predicted frames (B-frames), as shown in **Figure 3.5**.

I-frames. Each GOP begins with an I-frame (sometimes called a reference frame). An I-frame contains all of the data needed to fully re-create the source video frame, and is spatially compressed in a process similar to JPEG still-image compression. I-frames are equivalent to keyframes in other forms of digital video compression.

P-frames. Using motion vectors, a P-frame calculates the difference between itself and the frame before it. Areas not accounted for by motion vectors are instead encoded with the same process used to compress an I-frame. Consequently, P-frames contain only data that has changed.

B-frames. B-frames are encoded similarly to P-frames, except all motion vectors are bidirectional, or mathematically derived from both the previous and following frames.

MPEG-2 Video Stream

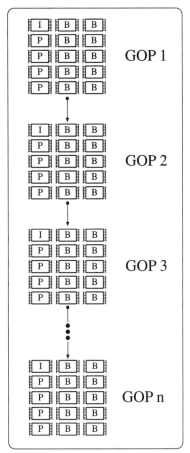

Figure 3.4 An MPEG-2 video stream is divided into many groups of pictures (GOPs).

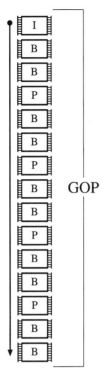

GOP

Figure 3.5 A standard MPEG-2 GOP contains 15 frames, each of which is an I-, P-, or B-frame. This figure shows a typical distribution of I-, P-, and B-frames within a GOP.

✔ Tips

■ The QuickTime MPEG Encoder is fixed at a GOP of 15 pictures. Some compression utilities allow you to set your own GOP size (Cleaner 5 with MPEG Charger, for example). But unless you know exactly what you're doing, stick with a GOP size of 15 pictures.

■ Because only I-frames contain all of the data needed to completely re-create the source frame, the thumbnails that appear on Track tiles and the images you see as you scrub through the Marker window are all I-frames (to learn more, see Chapter 10, "Creating Markers and Stories").

ABOUT MPEG-2 COMPRESSION

Shooting Video for Optimum Compression

MPEG encoders compress video temporally, over time. This feature produces very small, high-quality MPEG files, but only if blocks of color (macroblocks) within the video remain constant from frame to frame. While shooting the source video for your DVD project, you can do a few things to make sure your video compresses at the best possible quality:

Use a tripod. No matter how steady your hand, if you "shoot from the hip," or hold the camera, there will inevitably be some twitches and shakes in your footage. However slight, these twitches cause pixels to jiggle around the frame, and jiggling pixels increase the bit rate needed for high-quality compression. Use a tripod to eliminate these unwanted and hard-to-compress twitches.

Shoot against a solid background. Solid blocks of color compress better than noisy backgrounds. If at all possible, set up your shot against a backdrop of uniform color.

Choosing Bit Rates

Using the QuickTime MPEG Encoder, you can compress your MPEG-2 streams at bit rates ranging from 1 to 9.8 Mbps. As a rule of thumb, the higher the bit rate, the better the quality of the resulting MPEG-2 video stream. Scenes that include a high degree of motion (transitions, cuts, zooms, and so on) need a higher bit rate to achieve the same quality as scenes with a lower degree of motion (a newscaster seated in front of a backdrop).

There are a couple of limitations that you must respect when encoding video streams:

Obey the upper limit. MPEG-2 video allows a maximum bit rate of 9.8 Mbps, which falls just within the current maximum DVD-Video data rate of 10.08 Mbps. While it may be tempting to set the MPEG Encoder to the maximum, don't do it. In fact, you should never use a bit rate higher than 8 Mbps; go beyond that and you leave very little headroom for audio and subtitle streams. Plus, some DVD-Video players will not smoothly play MPEG-2 video encoded at bit rates higher than 8 Mbps.

Know your audience. DVD-Video players contain dedicated hardware for decoding MPEG video streams. In general, DVD-Video players have no problem handling MPEG-2 streams encoded at 8 Mbps.

This is not the case with some computers, which typically use software MPEG-2 decoders that rely on the computer's CPU for their processing power. While newer computers are fast enough to decode MPEG-2 video streams at any bit rate, slower computers (especially laptops) have a hard time keeping up with data rates higher than 6 or 7 Mbps.

✔ Tips

- If your DVD uses a lot of video, be sure to create a bit budget. In many cases, the bit budget will tell you exactly what bit rate is needed to squeeze all of the video onto the DVD disc. To learn more about bit budgets, see Appendix B, "Making a Bit Budget."

- For most applications, 8 Mbps is a much higher bit rate than you need to preserve the quality of your source content. Unless a scene has a lot of motion, a bit rate of between 5.4 and 6 Mbps is often enough to maintain quality.

- If your DVD-Video disc is intended for computer playback, make sure you compress your video streams accordingly and test your finished project on as many computers as possible before you replicate it.

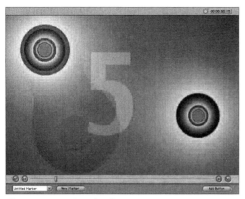

Figure 3.6 An example of extreme compression artifacts. This MPEG stream was compressed at 1 Mbps. Note the presence of blocks and the jagged edges around the number. If you could see this screenshot in color, you would also notice that the colors are not as vibrant as in the original.

Testing Bit Rates

The trick to video compression is selecting a bit rate that's low enough to provide the smallest possible file size, but high enough to maintain your source content's visual quality. Low bit rates produce files that take up less space on the DVD, and they also make it easier for the DVD-Video player to play the disc. However, if you use too low a bit rate, compression artifacts will creep into your video (Figure 3.6).

If you're not sure what bit rate to use, run a few tests before compressing the entire source video file. Open the file in QuickTime Pro Player and slice out a couple of 10-second chunks. Choose sections that have quite a bit of motion, such as panning shots or transitions. Then compress these sections at several different bit rates and see which setting gives you the best quality at the lowest bit rate. Once you've determined the appropriate bit rate, go back and compress the entire source video using that setting.

Bit-rate encoding

MPEG-2 video streams can be compressed using constant-bit-rate (CBR) or variable-bit-rate (VBR) encoding.

CBR encoding. In constant-bit-rate encoding, picture quality fluctuates while the data rate remains constant. As its name implies, CBR encoding compresses your video at a data rate that never changes. If you compress your digital video at 5.4 Mbps, then each second of video uses exactly 5.4 megabits of data.

You generally don't want to use CBR encoding for MPEG-2 compression. CBR encoding allocates low-motion scenes more bits than are needed, while high-motion scenes often do not get enough bits (leading to digital artifacts such as blocking, color distortion, and motion degradation, as seen in **Figure 3.6**).

VBR encoding. In variable-bit-rate encoding, the picture quality stays constant, but the data rate fluctuates. VBR encoding allocates only as many bits as needed to low-motion scenes, while high-motion scenes are given more bits to avoid digital artifacts. This allows simple scenes to use less storage space, while more complex scenes are given extra bits to account for all that extra motion. The result is higher quality MPEG-2 video.

The QuickTime MPEG Encoder uses VBR encoding.

Compressing MPEG-2 Video

If you've diligently read this chapter, you're armed with all the theory you need to compress great-looking MPEG-2 video streams. Now it's time to put that theory into action.

To compress MPEG-2 video streams:

1. Open a digital video in QuickTime.

2. Choose File > Export (**Figure 3.7**); or press Command-E.

    The Export dialog box opens (**Figure 3.8**).

3. Navigate to the directory where you want to save your exported MPEG file and enter a name for it in the Save As text box (in Mac OS 9, this is the Save Exported File As text box).

4. From the Export pop-up menu, select Movie to MPEG 2 (**Figure 3.9**).

    In the Save As text box, a .m2v file extension is added to your movie's name. This is the QuickTime MPEG-2 file extension.

Figure 3.7 From QuickTime Player, begin the MPEG-2 encoding process by selecting File > Export.

Figure 3.8 The Export dialog box.

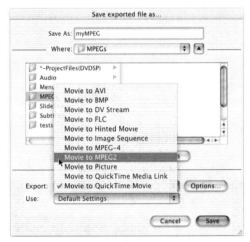

Figure 3.9 From the Export pop-up menu, choose Movie to MPEG2.

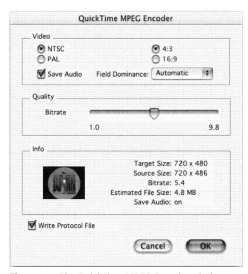

Figure 3.10 The QuickTime MPEG Encoder window.

Figure 3.11 Select the video standard (NTSC or PAL) that matches your source video.

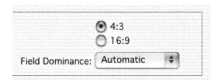

Figure 3.12 Choose 4:3 for normal DVD-Video projects, or 16:9 for widescreen projects.

5. Click the Options button.

The QuickTime MPEG Encoder window opens (**Figure 3.10**).

6. Select either the NTSC or PAL radio button (**Figure 3.11**).

For video destined for playback in North America, select the NTSC radio button. For video destined for playback in Europe, select the PAL radio button.

7. Select either the 4:3 or 16:9 radio button (**Figure 3.12**).

For most purposes, you should select the 4:3 radio button. Select the 16:9 radio button only if you're sure that this is the correct aspect ratio for your video. To learn more about 16:9 (widescreen) video, see Chapter 14, "Widescreen: 16:9."

continues on next page

Saving Audio

If your source video has one or more audio tracks, the QuickTime MPEG Encoder strips those audio tracks out and encodes them separately once it has finished encoding the MPEG-2 video stream. The audio from your source video may be in any format that QuickTime understands and at any bit depth and sample rate. QuickTime takes this source audio and converts it to a single 48 kHz, 16-bit stereo AIFF file ready for import into DVD Studio Pro or A.Pack. The AIFF file itself is saved in the same folder as the newly created MPEG-2 video stream, with the same name but a different file extension (.aif). To learn more about encoding audio for DVD Studio Pro, see Chapter 4, "Encoding Audio Streams."

COMPRESSING MPEG-2 VIDEO

47

8. If your source video has audio, select the Save Audio checkbox (**Figure 3.13**).

To learn more, see the sidebar "Saving Audio" earlier in this chapter.

9. Set the Field Dominance pop-up menu to match the field dominance of your source video (**Figure 3.14**).

For source video in the DV format, Automatic works well. If your source video is not compressed using the DV format, or if you know the field dominance (also called field order) of your video, choose the appropriate setting. To learn more, see the sidebar "What Are Fields?" at the bottom of this page.

10. Using the Quality slider, choose an appropriate bit rate (**Figure 3.15**).

A bit rate of between 5 and 8 is generally sufficient to maintain the source content's quality. To learn more about using the Quality slider, refer to the section "Choosing Bit Rates" earlier in this chapter.

11. Check the QuickTime MPEG Encoder's Info section to make sure that all of your settings are correct and click OK.

The QuickTime MPEG Encoder window closes.

Figure 3.13 Check Save Audio and the QuickTime MPEG Encoder saves a 16-bit, 48kHz stereo AIFF file of the movie's audio along with the MPEG-2 video stream.

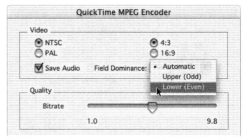

Figure 3.14 It is important to select the correct field dominance. If you don't know which setting is correct, choose Automatic.

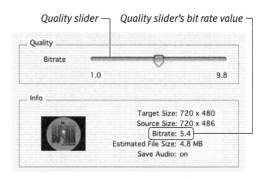

Figure 3.15 The Quality slider sets your MPEG-2 stream's bit rate with a numerical value that's displayed in the Info section below the slider.

What Are Fields?

Televisions display video as an ever-changing series of odd and even lines called fields. Fields create smoother motion on televisions by breaking each frame into two sets of alternating lines that flick by at double the perceived frame rate. When you edit video on a computer, these two sets of alternating lines are *interlaced* together to create one frame, making the editing process easier, but causing frames from high-motion scenes to exhibit a comb-like effect on a computer monitor. If you notice this as you edit with DVD Studio Pro, don't worry; everything will look fine when you play the completed project.

COMPRESSING MPEG-2 VIDEO

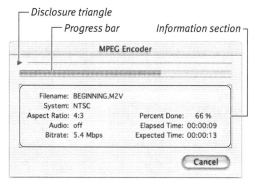

Figure 3.16 The QuickTime MPEG Encoder's progress window.

Figure 3.17 A protocol file sums up the MPEG-2 settings used to encode a video stream.

12. In the Export dialog, click Save.

The QuickTime MPEG Encoder's progress window opens (**Figure 3.16**). To learn more, see the section "The Progress Window" later in this chapter.

And that's all there is to it! When the encoder's progress bar hits the right edge of its display area, your MPEG-2 video stream is encoded and ready for import into DVD Studio Pro.

✔ Tips

■ The QuickTime MPEG Encoder is tuned to compress source video streams that use the DV codec. If you're using source video of a different codec, such as Animation or Sorenson, the stream will take longer to encode.

■ If your source video's resolution is different from the standard resolution for NTSC video (or PAL video, if you're compressing a PAL MPEG stream), the QuickTime MPEG Encoder automatically adjusts the encoded stream to the correct dimensions.

Using Protocol Files

A protocol file stores information about an encoded MPEG-2 video stream, including its file name, bit rate, aspect ratio, and field order (**Figure 3.17**).

If you select the QuickTime MPEG Encoder's Write Protocol File check box, QuickTime creates a text file with a .pro file extension and saves that file in the same destination folder as the MPEG-2 video stream. Over the course of a day, you may continue to encode MPEG streams to the same folder, and QuickTime will update the original protocol file (QuickTime writes one protocol file per folder per day; as soon as the clock switches over at midnight, QuickTime creates a new protocol file).

The Progress Window

When the QuickTime MPEG Encoder's progress window first opens, you see a progress bar that advances as your video compresses and an information section that provides you with encoding details (refer to Figure 3.16). The left side of the information section displays the compression parameters you set in the QuickTime MPEG Encoder window. The right side provides detailed information about encoding progress, including the percentage compressed, the elapsed time in compression, and the estimated time needed to fully encode the video stream.

Watching while encoding

To watch your video as it encodes, click the disclosure triangle at the top left of the progress bar and your video will appear (**Figure 3.18**). While it's entertaining to watch the video as it compresses, you should be warned that previewing during encoding slows down the process by approximately 20 percent. If time is at a premium, collapse the preview area and take the opportunity to make yourself a cup of tea.

✔ Tip

■ While previewing the video, you may notice that the picture lurches, or jumps. Don't worry; this is normal behavior (in fact, if you look at the progress bar, you will see that it jumps in unison with the picture). If you've read the earlier section on GOPs, you know that only I-frames contain all the information needed to completely reconstruct the source video frame. The lurches you see reflect the preview picture jumping from I-frame to I-frame.

Figure 3.18 The progress window with the preview area expanded. Previewing slows down encoding by about 20 percent.

THE PROGRESS WINDOW

Audio and the progress window

If you selected the Save Audio option, the progress bar will be divided in half, with the first half representing the time needed to encode the MPEG stream, and the second half representing the time needed to encode the audio stream. The progress bar may seem to crawl along the first half at an unusually slow pace, but once it hits the audio section in the second half, it dramatically speeds up, racing toward the finish line. If you haven't selected the Save Audio check box, the progress bar is not divided and reflects only the time needed to encode the MPEG stream.

Quality, Speed, Price—Pick Two!

While searching for high quality MPEG-2 compression utilities, many DVD-Video authors turn to Discreet's Cleaner 5 with MPEG Charger. This combo offers a software-only encoding option that provides MPEG-2 video encoding at both constant and variable bit rates. But depending on the speed of your computer, compressing a feature-length video (one-and-a-half hours) could take up to an entire week or more! That's 1/52 of a year.

Whether or not Cleaner 5 with MPEG Charger offers better quality than the QuickTime MPEG Encoder is a topic of some debate. However one thing's clear; it's much more expensive. For more information, visit Discreet at //www.discreet.com/.

THE PROGRESS WINDOW

Using Final Cut Pro

The similarities between the look and feel of Final Cut Pro and DVD Studio Pro should be enough to convince you that Apple designed the two applications to work together. In fact, Final Cut Pro includes features that not only integrate with DVD Studio Pro, but also speed the process of creating a DVD-Video.

One dramatic time-saving feature is Final Cut Pro's QuickTime export option, which encodes MPEG-2 video streams directly from Final Cut Pro. This lets you avoid rendering out a finished DV file, which not only saves you time, but also saves hard disk storage space.

But that's not all. You can also set DVD Studio Pro markers right in Final Cut Pro's timeline. When you export your MPEG-2 streams from Final Cut Pro, these markers are encoded into the MPEG-2 stream and appear inside DVD Studio Pro, named and ready to go.

To export MPEG streams from Final Cut Pro:

1. From within Final Cut Pro, choose File > Export > QuickTime (**Figure 3.19**). A Save dialog box opens (**Figure 3.20**).

2. Name your MPEG stream and navigate to the folder you want to save it in.

3. From the Format pop-up menu, choose MPEG2.

4. Click Options. The QuickTime MPEG Encoder opens.

5. Follow the same steps as outlined earlier in the section "To compress MPEG-2 video streams."

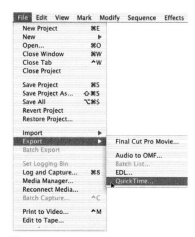

Figure 3.19 You can access the QuickTime MPEG Encoder from Final Cut Pro by choosing File > Export > QuickTime.

Figure 3.20 Look familiar? Choosing to export to QuickTime opens a standard QuickTime export dialog box.

✔ Tip

- DV uses approximately one gigabyte of storage space for every five minutes of video. For a one-and-a-half-hour video, you need over 18 gigabytes of free storage space! Avoid rendering out this huge DV file by encoding your MPEG-2 video streams directly from Final Cut Pro.

Timeline — — *Markers* — *Playhead*

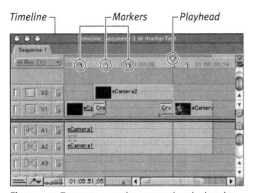

Figure 3.21 To create a marker, move the playhead to the frame where you wish to place the marker and press the M key on your keyboard.

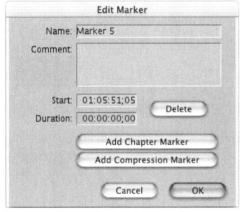

Figure 3.22 The Edit Marker window.

Encoding markers

Final Cut Pro 3.0.2 introduced the ability to set DVD Studio Pro compression and chapter markers right in Final Cut Pro's timeline. When you encode your Final Cut Pro project into MPEG-2 video, these markers are included in the stream.

Compression markers force an MPEG I-frame on an exact frame of your video stream. For example, your video clips may contain areas of abrupt visual change such as zooms and fast pans. To help avoid compression artifacts, you may insert compression markers before, and/or after these sections.

Chapter markers are similar to compression markers, except that they also store chapter names. Later, when you import the stream into DVD Studio Pro and create a track from it, these chapter names appear in the track's Marker editor (see Chapter 10, "Creating Markers and Stories").

To set markers in Final Cut Pro:

1. In the Final Cut Pro timeline, make sure no clips are selected.

2. Position the playhead on the frame where you wish to place a marker.

3. Press the M key.

   A new marker is created in the timeline (**Figure 3.21**).

4. Without moving the playhead, press the M key a second time.

   The Edit Marker window opens (**Figure 3.22**).

5. In the Name text box, enter a name for the marker.

continues on next page

USING FINAL CUT PRO

6. Do one (or both) of the following:

To create a compression marker, click the Add Compression Marker button.

To create a chapter marker, click the Add Chapter Marker button.

The Comment text box updates to display the type of marker(s) you've created (**Figure 3.23**).

7. Export an MPEG-2 video stream as described earlier in the section titled "To export MPEG streams from Final Cut Pro."

✔ Tips

■ There must be at least one second between chapter and compression markers or they will be ignored. Markers may not be set within one second of the beginning or end of a video clip.

■ All video streams in multi-angle tracks must have I-frames in exactly the same places (see Chapter 7, "Using Tracks"). Setting chapter or compression markers in Final Cut Pro greatly increases the chance that your video streams will not have corresponding I-frames. Consequently, you should not set markers in video streams that you plan to use in multi-angle tracks.

■ If you accidentally create the wrong type of marker, highlight it in the Comment text box and press the Delete key.

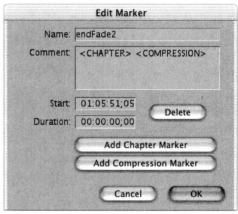

Figure 3.23 The Comment text box lists the markers that you've added to this frame.

Figure 3.24 To create a Final Cut Pro reference movie, choose File > Export > Final Cut Pro Movie.

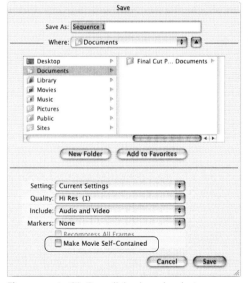

Figure 3.25 In this Save dialog box, deselect Make Movie Self-Contained. The final file will be a reference movie.

Creating reference movies

A reference movie is a small file that contains all the Final Cut Pro edit information (including markers), but no media. Instead, a reference movie points to, or references, the original video clips used by Final Cut Pro. Reference movies take up very little space on your hard disk (when compared to a fully-rendered DV file) and thus provide a perfect solution when hard disk storage space is at a premium, but you're not quite ready to encode the final MPEG-2 stream.

To create a Final Cut Pro reference movie:

1. From within Final Cut Pro, choose File > Export > Final Cut Pro Movie (**Figure 3.24**).

   A Save dialog box opens (**Figure 3.25**).

2. Name your MPEG stream and navigate to the folder that you want to save it in.

   continues on next page

3. If you've used Final Cut Pro to specify compression or chapter markers for use in DVD Studio Pro, choose DVD Studio Pro Markers from the Markers pop-up menu (**Figure 3.26**).

4. Deselect the Make Movie Self-Contained check box.

If you don't deselect this check box, Final Cut Pro renders a self-contained movie, which is a complete, full-file-size version of the edited video.

5. Click Save.

Final Cut Pro creates a reference movie.

✔ Tips

■ To compress the reference movie as MPEG-2 video, open it in QuickTime Pro Player and follow the steps outlined earlier in the section "To compress MPEG-2 video streams."

■ Don't delete the source files for your Final Cut Pro project. If you delete those source files, the reference movie has nothing to reference (after all, the reference movie contains no media files of its own).

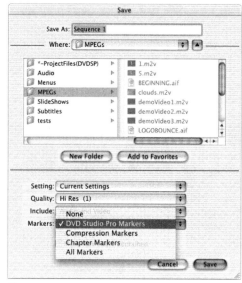

Figure 3.26 To encode your markers directly into the reference movie, choose All Markers from the Markers menu.

ENCODING AUDIO STREAMS

If you're like most DVD-Video authors, you're coming to DVD Studio Pro from a video background, which might make creating and encoding audio seem difficult at first. And, it isn't easy. In fact, preparing good-quality audio is just about the toughest part of creating a DVD-Video.

Tough, but not impossible. Apple kindly includes a copy of Bias Peak DV 3 with DVD Studio Pro to help ease the process. Peak DV 3 works on both Mac OS 9 and Mac OS X and makes optimizing your audio streams easier by allowing you to remove background noise, widen stereo images, and normalize audio levels so that they consistently hit your viewers at a constant volume.

After you've cleaned up your audio, you can either import it directly into DVD Studio Pro or use A.Pack, Apple's AC-3 encoder, to compress the files. Audio sucks up bandwidth, leaving little room for actual *video* if left uncompressed; A.Pack helps solve this problem by compressing mammoth audio files into much smaller AC-3 streams that sound almost as good as the originals.

AC-3 compression, however, takes a while to master. Although seasoned sound designers will appreciate the control that the encoder offers, audio newcomers face a daunting array of choices. AC-3 encoding poses a lot of questions for the audio novice, so if you're ready to face the music, let's dive right in.

About Digital Audio

When you record a sound into your computer, the sound must be *digitized*, or changed from an analog wave into a series of digital numbers that the computer can understand. Computers sample sound by capturing the voltage level of an analog sound wave a certain number of times per second. When played back in rapid succession, this series of voltage numbers creates a pulsing electrical signal that drives a speaker—in other words, these fluctuating voltage levels are turned back into sound that we can hear.

The file's *sampling rate* reflects the number of times per second its voltage is sampled, or recorded (**Figure 4.1**). A file sampled 48 thousand times per second, for example, has a sampling rate of 48 kHz. When creating DVD-Videos with DVD Studio Pro, you'll most often sample your files at 48 kHz. Although the program accepts 96 kHz files, these audio streams are so large in file size that they barely leave any room on the disc for other project items, like video. Sure, they sound great, but nobody likes a bandwidth hog.

✔ Tips

■ A 16-bit, stereo PCM audio file at 48 kHz has a bit rate of 1.5 Mbps—about 15 percent of the data rate available to your DVD-Video (16-bit, 96 kHz PCM files double that bit rate to 3 Mbps). This doesn't leave much room for alternate audio streams, subtitles, or even a high-data-rate MPEG-2 video stream. To conserve bits, convert your PCM audio to Dolby Digital AC-3 files.

■ CD audio uses a sampling rate of 44.1 kHz, while audio in DVD-Video uses a sampling rate of 48 or 96 kHz. Consequently, your DVD-Videos will usually sound better than an audio CD! To learn how to convert CD audio to a format DVD Studio Pro understands, see "Converting Audio Formats" later in this chapter.

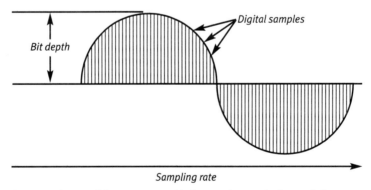

Figure 4.1 Where each line intersects with the waveform, a single sample is recorded. For 48-kHz audio, the waveform is sampled 48,000 times per second.

Understanding bit depth

Bit depth is the amplitude portion of the sampling process; in other words, bit depth represents a sample's *sound*. Often called quantization (see the sidebar "Rounding Down Your Sound" on the next page), bit depth defines the number of discreet voltage steps used in the sampling process. For example, a 16-bit audio file uses 65,536 discreet voltage steps to represent the sound at each particular sample. A 24-bit audio file uses 16,777,216 discreet voltage steps. With all those millions of extra voltage steps, a 24-bit file usually represents the source audio much more realistically than does a 16-bit file. Think of a staircase: a staircase with lots of steps looks smoother than one with few steps. In a similar fashion, an audio wave with a higher bit depth sounds smoother, or more natural, than one with a lower bit depth.

DVD Studio Pro understands both 16- and 24-bit audio files. Earlier versions of DVD Studio Pro (1.2 and below) had problems dealing with 24-bit AIFF files, as did the original version of DVD Studio Pro 1.5. In both the Preview mode and on the written disc, 24-bit AIFF files hiss noticeably. Fortunately, 24-bit SoundDesigner 2 files do not suffer from this problem in DVD Studio Pro version 1.5, and the DVD Studio Pro 1.5.1 update fixes the 24-bit AIFF problem.

✔ Tip

- A.Pack has no problem encoding 24-bit AIFF, WAV, or SoundDesigner 2 files. If your source audio is 24-bit, use A.Pack to turn it into an AC-3 stream. To learn more, see "About AC-3 audio" later in this chapter.

Rounding Down Your Sound

No matter how accurate your recording, a digital audio file will never exactly represent the analog wave. In **Figure 4.2**, the audio wave crosses the y axis somewhere between 80 and 90 Hz. If we zoom in, we see that the intersection occurs near 87.5 Hz. We could zoom in closer and get a more exact value, but no matter how powerful the measuring equipment, we can never zoom in close enough to get the exact value of where the wave crosses the y axis. That said, you must have an exact number in order to digitize sound. The only way to get that number is to *quantize* the audio to a set bit depth.

Quantization reduces large blocks of information to more manageable chunks by rounding numbers to a preset scale. For example, when you round numbers to the nearest 10, you are quantizing them. The number 84 would be rounded down to 80, and 87 would be rounded up to 90. In a similar way, a sampled sound's voltage is quantized to the nearest voltage step, as defined by the file's bit depth. 16-bit audio has 65,536 discrete voltage steps available, and 24-bit audio has 16,777,216 discreet voltage steps. Because 24-bit audio has millions of voltage steps, it provides a much more accurate representation of the original sound wave.

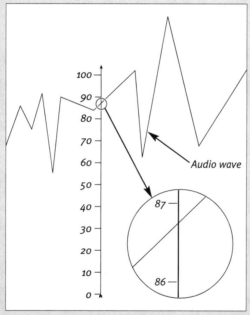

Figure 4.2 No matter how small the number, you will never be able to exactly measure a sample's voltage. Consequently, computers quantize the sample's voltage to the nearest value, as defined by the audio file's bit depth.

Figure 4.3 To convert your audio files to a format that DVD Studio Pro understands, open them in QuickTime and choose File > Export.

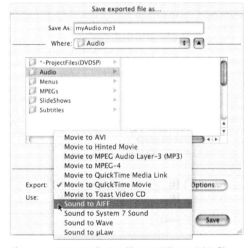

Figure 4.4 DVD Studio Pro likes AIFF linear PCM files, so choose Sound to AIFF from the Export pop-up menu.

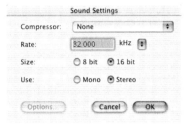

Figure 4.5 Use the Sound Settings dialog box to convert your audio file to stereo and set its bit rate to 16-bit.

Converting audio formats

If your files are in an audio format other than 16-or 24-bit, 48 or 96 kHz AIFF (for example, MP3, Q-design, or CD-Audio), use QuickTime Pro Player to convert these files to 16-bit, 48 kHz AIFF files that DVD Studio Pro understands.

To convert audio to 48 kHz:

1. Open the digital audio file in QuickTime Pro Player.

2. Choose File > Export (**Figure 4.3**). The File Export dialog box opens.

3. Name your file and choose a folder to save it in.

4. From the Export pop-up menu, choose Sound to AIFF (**Figure 4.4**).

5. Click the Options button. The Sound Settings dialog box opens (**Figure 4.5**).

6. From the Rate pop-up menu, choose 48.000 (**Figure 4.6**).

continues on next page

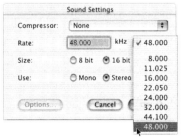

Figure 4.6 Choose 48 kHz from the Rate pop-up menu.

ABOUT DIGITAL AUDIO

7. In the center of the Sound Settings dialog box, choose 16-bit for the Size setting and Stereo for the Use setting.

8. In the lower right corner of the Sound Settings dialog box, click OK.

The Sound Settings dialog box closes, leaving the File Export dialog box open on your screen.

9. In the File Export dialog box, click Save.

QuickTime converts the audio file into a 48-kHz AIFF file that may be directly imported into DVD Studio Pro or encoded to AC-3 using A.Pack.

✔ Tip

■ If your project includes songs ripped from audio CDs, keep in mind that audio CDs use a sampling rate of 44.1 kHz at a depth of 16 bits. This is not a legal sampling rate for DVD. You will need to convert all songs from audio CDs to 48 kHz digital audio files before you import them into DVD Studio Pro.

To check sample rate and bit depth:

1. Open the digital audio file in QuickTime Pro Player.

2. Choose Movie > Get Movie Properties or press Command-J (**Figure 4.7**).

The Properties window opens.

3. From the left pop-up menu, choose Sound Track, and from the right pop-up menu, choose Format (**Figure 4.8**).

The Properties window displays the audio file's format, including its sample rate, number of channels, sample size (bit depth), and method of compression. If the sampling rate does not say 48 kHz, you must convert the audio file as demonstrated earlier in the task "To convert audio to 48 kHz."

Figure 4.7 To check an audio file's sample rate, use QuickTime Pro Player. Open the file in QuickTime and choose Movie > Get Movie Properties.

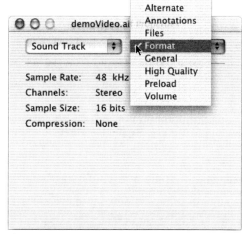

Figure 4.8 The Movie Properties window, displaying the sound track's format information.

Understanding Audio Formats

DVD-Video players the world over are *required* to decode linear pulse code modulated (linear PCM) and Dolby AC-3 audio streams. Most PAL DVD-Video players will also decode MPEG 1 Layer 2 audio streams, and new to DVD Studio Pro 1.5, you can include MPEG 1 Layer 2 audio in your projects. This format, however, is not widely supported on NTSC DVD-Video players, so if you want anyone outside of Europe to hear your DVD-Video, you should use only linear PCM or AC-3 audio streams in your DVD-Video projects.

✔ Tip

■ DVD Studio Pro creates DVD-Videos that comply to either version 1.0 or version 1.1 of the DVD-Video Specification. Version 1.0 uses PCM and/or AC-3 audio only, while version 1.1 uses PCM, AC-3, and/or MPEG 1 Layer 2 audio streams.

About PCM audio

There's no mystery to the PCM format; it's simply uncompressed digital audio in AIFF, WAV, or SoundDesigner II (SDII) format. Audio editing tools such as Propellerheads Reason or Peak DV 3 produce PCM audio. When you render your Final Cut Pro movies, the audio is recorded in PCM format (AIFF). In other words, all digital audio begins as a linear PCM file.

DVD Studio Pro requires all PCM audio files to meet the following specifications:

◆ AIFF, WAV, or SDII format

◆ Mono or stereo channels

◆ 16/24-bit resolution

◆ 48/96 kHz sampling rate

About AC-3 audio

AC-3 is a perceptual audio coding system that analyzes an audio signal and throws away the parts we can't hear. As it turns out, we don't hear a lot, which allows AC-3 encoders to produce audio streams with compression ratios of up to 12:1 over PCM audio.

AC-3 encoders use a process called *masking* to determine which sounds are audible. Masking occurs when high-volume frequencies drown out their low-volume neighbors, making the low-volume frequency bands less noticeable or even completely inaudible (see the sidebar "Real-Life Masking"). Before encoding an audio file, an AC-3 encoder divides it into many narrow frequency bands. It next searches through those frequency bands to determine which ones are the loudest, and then looks at neighboring frequency bands to see if they contain enough sound to be heard. Frequency bands that are too low in volume are *masked* by the louder ones. AC-3 encoders largely ignore masked frequencies, assigning fewer bits to masked frequencies than to their more audible counterparts.

✔ Tip

■ AC-3 encoding is a *lossy* compression system. Because some of the original data gets thrown away, the AC-3 stream is only a close approximation, and not an exact recreation of the original digital audio file.

Real-Life Masking

Here's how masking works: Imagine that you and a friend are sitting in your car at a stoplight, with the windows rolled up, listening to some AM radio. A low-rider pulls up beside you with R&B pumping loud enough that your car shakes in rhythm with the subpulses. You can no longer hear the subfrequencies coming from your AM radio, because the bass from the other car overpowers, or *masks*, them. You can, however, still hear the complaints from your friend in the passenger seat. Why? Well, your friend's voice is loud and in a frequency range far enough from the bass range that it is not masked (try opening the window).

About AC-3 Encoding

AC-3 is *the* audio standard for DVD-Video. In fact, all DVD-Video players are required to contain an AC-3 decoder. DVD-Video players also support linear PCM and a few other audio formats, but if you want to be sure that your sound reaches the viewer, use AC-3 encoding.

An AC-3 file can have up to six channels, allowing for fully supported 5.1 surround sound. AC-3 files are also encoded with hints that allow the decoder to dynamically alter the file's volume. These hints, called control parameters, ensure that your DVD-Video's audio maintains a consistent volume level across all programs.

5.1 surround sound

5.1 surround sound uses six discreet channels to feed speakers arranged in a matrix around a central point (**Figure 4.9**). A 5.1 surround field has three full-spectrum speakers in the front, two in the back, and one subwoofer for reproducing low-frequency effects (the subwoofer may be placed anywhere in the room).

continues on next page

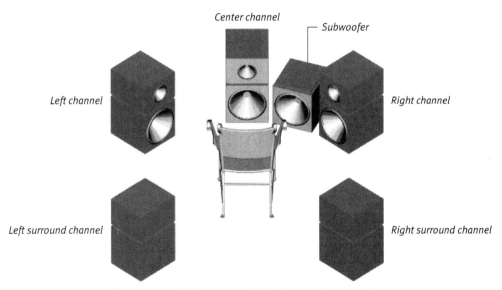

Center channel

Subwoofer

Left channel

Right channel

Left surround channel

Right surround channel

Figure 4.9 A typical 5.1 surround mix includes a stereo signal fed to both the left and right speakers, a dialog track in the center channel, surround effects in the left surround and right surround channels, and low frequency effects in the subwoofer channel. The result is a three-dimensional sound field surrounding the listener.

ABOUT AC-3 ENCODING

AC-3 decoders deal with 5.1 surround streams in a very clever way. When faced with a surround signal, the decoder directs each channel in the AC-3 file to the appropriate speaker. If there are fewer than 5.1 channels available to the decoder, it downmixes the surround stream into a configuration that works with the available speakers. Consequently, if the viewer has a two-speaker stereo system, the center, left surround, and right surround channels are *downmixed*, or blended into the left and right speakers. The viewer still hears everything, just not exactly as the audio engineer intended.

✔ Tip

- Subwoofers reproduce frequencies of only up to 120 Hz, while all other speakers are full range (up to 20 kHz). The limited frequency range of the subwoofer is said to represent only 10 percent, or 0.1, of a full channel: hence, 5.1 surround sound.

Control parameters

Control parameters are hints sent with the encoded AC-3 file that tell the decoder how to play the AC-3 stream. Control parameters include the dialog normalization setting, dynamic range profile, and downmix options, all of which are explained later in this chapter.

Control parameters do not alter the AC-3 stream itself. You set control parameters when you encode the AC-3 file, but it's up to the playback device to interpret and apply them. Currently, most (if not all) DVD-Video players are capable of decoding control parameters.

✔ Tip

- Some AC-3 decoders allow the viewer to determine how control parameters are applied. Most viewers don't mess with these settings, so rest assured that all control parameters should be correctly interpreted by the majority of AC-3 decoders out there.

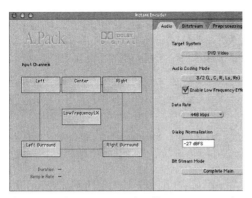

Figure 4.10 The Instant Encoder allows you to encode AC-3 files one at a time.

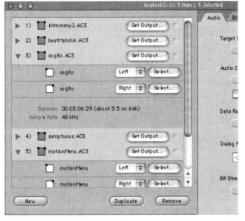

Figure 4.11 The Batch Encoder lets you set up several AC-3 encoding jobs at the same time. The Batch Encoder looks similar to the Instant Encoder, but instead of an Input Channel matrix occupying the left side, there's a batch list that holds multiple audio files.

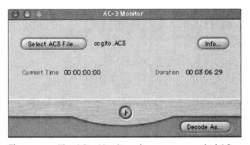

Figure 4.12 The AC-3 Monitor plays your encoded AC-3 streams. You'll use the AC-3 Monitor to make sure that dialog normalization and dynamic range compression are correctly applied, and that all surround streams sound good when downmixed into stereo.

About A.Pack

Apple's A.Pack is an AC-3 encoder that converts 48 kHz PCM audio files into Dolby Digital AC-3 audio streams (A.Pack currently does not support 96 kHz PCM files). A.Pack has three main parts: the Instant Encoder (**Figure 4.10**), the Batch Encoder (**Figure 4.11**), and the AC-3 Monitor (**Figure 4.12**).

The Instant Encoder is the main encoding window, which you use when you want to encode audio files one at a time in a single *encode job*. The left side of this window contains an Input Channel matrix used to assign audio files to the AC-3 stream's left, right, and surround channels; the right side contains tabs that define encoding settings such as the file's encoded bit rate and dialog normalization value. The Batch Encoder offers the same functions as the Instant Encoder, but as an added bonus, the Batch Encoder groups multiple encode jobs together so you can compress them all at once. The AC-3 Monitor is a playback utility you can use to preview your encoded AC-3 files and ensure they were encoded correctly (it also lets you decode AC-3 files back into PCM audio streams, which can be a lifesaver if you need to alter the AC-3 stream's sound).

continues on next page

✔ Tip

■ If you can't see the Instant Encoder's encoding settings, click the green button at the top left of the Input Channels section (**Figure 4.13**). This button expands or hides the encoding settings section.

Launching A.Pack

The DVD Studio Pro installation utility places A.Pack in the same folder as DVD Studio Pro. To launch A.Pack, find its application icon in the DVD Studio Pro folder on your hard disk.

To launch A.Pack:

1. Double-click the A.Pack application icon (**Figure 4.14**).

   The A.Pack splash screen appears (**Figure 4.15**).

2. Click the splash screen.

   A.Pack launches, and the Instant Encoder window opens (refer to Figure 4.10).

Figure 4.13 If the encoding settings section is missing, click the window's expansion button to reveal it.

Figure 4.14 The A.Pack application icon is located in the same folder as DVD Studio Pro.

Figure 4.15 Click the A.Pack splash screen to dismiss it instantly.

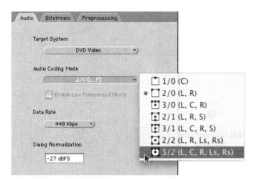

Figure 4.16 The Audio Coding Mode menu defines the channel configuration for your AC-3 file.

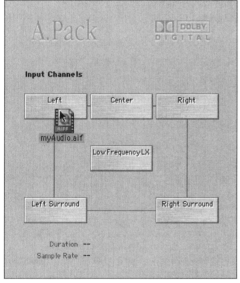

Figure 4.17 The Input Channels matrix reflects the selected audio coding mode. Assign PCM files to A.Pack input channels by dragging them from the Finder onto the channel buttons.

Encoding AC-3 Audio

Converting PCM audio into an AC-3 file is called an *encoding job*. And it *is* a job. There are no shortcuts or set formulas to help you bluff your way through it—you need to know how all of A.Pack's settings work to encode an audio stream.

Although the number of settings you'll have to configure varies for every project, you'll always have to determine an audio stream's volume and bit rate and the number and configuration of its channels to set A.Pack correctly. Once these settings are made, all the rest falls into place. In general, you'll perform the following steps when encoding an AC-3 stream in A.Pack:

Choose an audio coding mode. The audio coding mode determines how many channels your final AC-3 audio stream will contain and sets their configuration within the surround sound field (**Figure 4.16**).

Assign audio files to input channels. Assign audio streams to channels by dragging and dropping PCM files onto channel buttons in the Input Channels matrix (**Figure 4.17**).

continues on next page

ENCODING AC-3 AUDIO

Set the bit rate. The bit rate (measured in kilobits per second, or kbps) sets the combined data rate of all channels within the AC-3 file (**Figure 4.18**). Higher bit rates increase the AC-3 file's fidelity, but also create large file sizes.

Set dynamic range controls. You control your AC-3 stream's volume level using several settings, including dialog normalization, dynamic range-compression profile, and RF overmodulation (**Figure 4.19**). This is perhaps the most confusing aspect of AC-3 encoding, so to help you through it, all of the necessary settings are described in separate sections in this chapter.

Downmix surround sound. Surround AC-3 files contain hints that tell the decoder in a DVD-Video player how to turn multichannel sound into a stereo signal (**Figure 4.20**). Setting the downmix settings incorrectly can cause parts of the downmixed audio to play back at the wrong volume, creating unpleasant spikes in your sound.

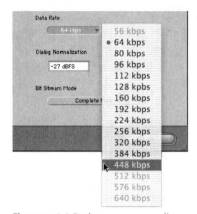

Figure 4.18 A.Pack compresses audio files at bit rates ranging from 64 kbps for a mono stream to 448 kbps for a 5.1 surround stream.

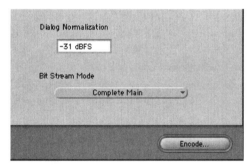

Figure 4.19 The dialog normalization setting is critical to the proper playback of your AC-3 file. This number also controls all other dynamic range settings (compression profile, RF overmodulation, and so on), so make sure you set it right!

Figure 4.20 Downmix settings determine how the AC-3 file will sound when decoded by DVD-Video players with fewer channels than the AC-3 audio stream.

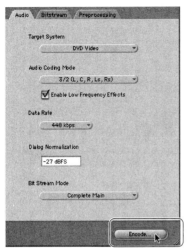

Figure 4.21 After you've defined your encoding settings, click the Encode button to begin compressing an AC-3 file.

Encode your audio. The Encode button sits in the lower-right corner of the Instant Encoder (**Figure 4.21**). Clicking this button launches the Instant Encoder status window. Use the status window to monitor A.Pack's progress while encoding (**Figure 4.22**).

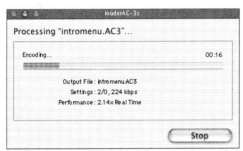

Figure 4.22 The Instant Encoder's status window follows the encoder's progress.

A.Pack Quick Settings

For rush jobs, start with the default A.Pack settings, enter an audio coding mode to give the file the correct number of channels, and then use these encoding settings (leave all the rest at their default values):

◆ **Bit rate:** Stereo: 196 kbps. 5.1: 448 kbps

◆ **Dialog Normalization:** –31

◆ **Compression preset:** None

Using Audio Coding Modes

The audio coding mode determines the speaker configuration for your AC-3 file. Each audio coding mode is defined by two numbers separated by a forward slash (**Figure 4.23**). The first number represents the number of speakers across the front of the audio field; the second defines the number of speakers across the back. For example, 1/0 is a single mono signal with sound coming only from the center channel, 2/0 represents stereo audio, and any other combination yields some form of multichannel or surround sound.

To select an audio coding mode:

1. In the Instant Encoder's Audio tab, click the Audio Coding Mode drop-down menu (refer to Figure 4.23).

   The menu lists several audio coding modes, from mono up to 5.1 surround sound.

2. Choose an audio coding mode.

   The Input Channels matrix updates to show the configuration that you've chosen (**Figure 4.24**).

3. If your audio has a low-frequency effects channel (a subwoofer channel), select the Enable Low Frequency Effects check box (found directly under the Audio tab's Audio Coding Mode menu).

   In the Input Channels matrix, the low-frequency effects channel is enabled.

✔ Tip

- If you've assigned a full-spectrum audio file to the low-frequency effects channel, on the Instant Encoder's Preprocessing tab select LFE Channel section > Apply Low-Pass Filter. This filter removes all sound above 120 Hz from the LFE channel.

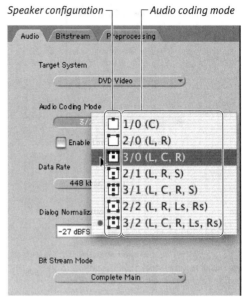

Figure 4.23 To help you visualize the target speaker configuration, the left side of the Audio Coding Mode menu provides small icons that show how channels will be arranged within the audio field.

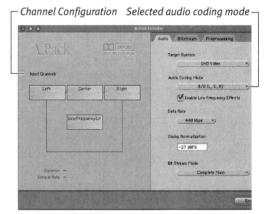

Figure 4.24 The buttons on the left side of A.Pack's Instant Encoder show the selected audio coding mode's channel configuration.

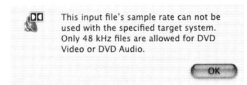

Figure 4.25 For DVD-Video purposes, A.Pack accepts only PCM files with a sampling rate of 48 kHz.

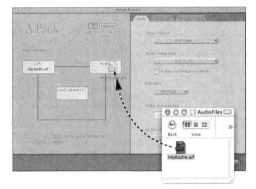

Figure 4.26 To assign audio files to A.Pack input channels, drag the audio files from the Finder directly onto the correct Input Channel buttons.

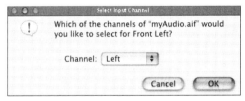

Figure 4.27 If the source file has more than one channel, the Select Input Channel dialog box lets you pick which one to assign to the A.Pack Input Channel button.

Assigning Input Channels

In A.Pack, you assign PCM audio files to input channels by dragging the files onto the appropriate Input Channel buttons. Unlike DVD Studio Pro, which accepts 48- and 96-kHz audio files, A.Pack accepts only files sampled at a rate of 48 kHz (**Figure 4.25**). If your audio uses any other sampling rate, you'll need to convert it before assigning the audio to an input channel (to learn how to convert your audio files to 48 kHz, see "Converting Audio Formats" earlier in this chapter).

To assign an audio file to a channel:

1. In the Finder, select an audio file.

2. In A.Pack's Instant Encoder window, drag the audio file onto an Input Channel button (**Figure 4.26**), or click the Input Channel button and select an audio file from the Select File dialog box.

   If the audio file has more than one channel, the Select Input Channel dialog box opens (**Figure 4.27**).

continues on next page

3. From the Channel menu, select the correct audio track for the input channel.

If your source audio file is stereo, the Channel menu lists both the left and right audio tracks (**Figure 4.28**).

4. Repeat steps 1 to 3 until all input channels have been assigned a source audio track.

✔ Tips

- In Mac OS 9, if your source audio file has more than two tracks, the Channel menu lists the name of each track (**Figure 4.29**).

- If you have a QuickTime movie that contains video as well as audio, you can still drop it into A.Pack. A.Pack ignores everything but the audio tracks. (You can even drop a Final Cut Pro reference movie directly into A.Pack!)

Figure 4.28 When you add a stereo PCM file to an A.Pack Input Channel button, A.Pack lets you choose either the left or right channel.

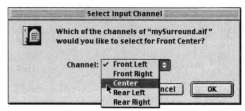

Figure 4.29 When you add a multichannel PCM file to an A.Pack Input Channel button in Mac OS 9, A.Pack lets you choose the proper channel by name.

Faking Surround Sound

A.Pack allows you to combine audio tracks from different files together in one encoding job. You can use this technique to fake a surround audio mix by, for example, assigning a stereo song to the front left and right speakers, a narration track to the center channel, and stereo ambient sound (crowd noise, blowing wind, and so on) to the rear left and right speakers. When combining audio from different files into one encoding job, the files used should be the same length. If your source files vary in length, A.Pack equalizes them by adding silence to the end of the shorter audio streams.

At present, most DVD-Video players are hooked up to stereo playback devices. If you're faking a surround mix, make sure you test the AC-3 file to ensure that it sounds good when the surround channels are downmixed into stereo.

Assigning Multiple Channels

Assign multiple audio files to multiple A.Pack input channels at once by simply attaching these extensions to the end of any AIFF, WAV, or SDII file:

- L. Left. *myAudio.L*
- R. Right. *myAudio.R*
- C. Center. *myAudio.C*

- Sub. Low-frequency effect. *myAudio.Sub*
- Ls. Left surround. *myAudio.Ls*
- Rs. Right surround. *myAudio.Rs*

In the Finder, select all of the audio files and then drag the selection directly onto the Instant Encoder's Input Channel matrix (**Figure 4.30**). Each file automatically jumps to the correct Input Channel button.

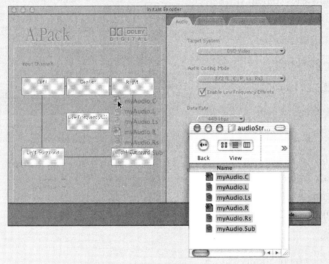

Figure 4.30 By adding special extensions to audio file names, you can drag multiple files into A.Pack at one time. These files automatically assign themselves to the correct input channels.

Choosing a Bit Rate

The bit rate you choose (**Figure 4.31**) depends on how many channels your AC-3 file needs and how much storage space you have available on your DVD disc. The ear is more critical than the eye, and viewers are more likely to enjoy a DVD-Video with poor visual and high audio quality than vice-versa. Consequently, you should give audio streams the highest possible setting given your DVD disc's storage capacity.

Here are some guidelines to help you select the correct bit rate:

◆ **Mono:** 64 to 128 kbps

◆ **Stereo:** 192 to 224 kbps

◆ **5.1 surround:** 224 to 448 kbps

To choose a bit rate:

1. In A.Pack, select the Audio tab.

2. From the Audio tab's Data Rate menu, choose a bit rate (refer to Figure 4.31).

   The AC-3 stream is set to be encoded at the selected bit rate.

✔ Tips

■ 192 kbps provides high-quality stereo streams.

■ 448 kbps is recommended for 5.1 streams.

■ Still not sure if there's enough space on your DVD disc to encode that 5.1 track at a full 448 kbps? Check out Appendix B, "Making a Bit Budget."

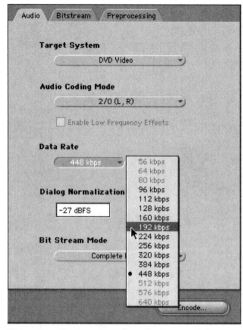

Figure 4.31 The Data Rate drop-down menu lists possible bit rates for your AC-3 file. If you've selected DVD Video from the Target System drop-down menu, only DVD-Video compatible data rates are selectable.

Table 4.1

Dialog Normalization Values	
SOURCE AUDIO	DIALOG NORMALIZATION
DV camera	−31
Dance music	−8
Television broadcast	−14
Orchestra	−25
Movie sound track	−31

Setting Volume Levels

In audio terms, *normalization* is a process in which the volume level of one (or several) audio programs is altered to a set (normalized) level. Using the same principle, *dialog normalization* raises or lowers the volume of an audio program to ensure that all *dialog* reaches the listener at the same average volume level.

For all dialog to play back at consistent levels, you must determine the dialog normalization value (DNV) for your audio stream and key that value into A.Pack. When the decoder processes the AC-3 stream, it reads the file's DNV and alters the stream's volume accordingly. **Table 4.1** shows typical DNVs needed to match several different source audio streams to the standard volume level of a DVD-Video.

✔ Tips

- In DVD Studio Pro 1.2 and below, the Preview mode does not decode dialog normalization information. If your track volume levels jump all over the place in Preview mode, don't worry; everything should work fine once the project is built to disc (for more on building a DVD-Video, see Chapter 13, "Finishing the DVD").

- Dialog normalization is not available for PCM audio streams.

Matching TV Volumes

You may not have noticed, but people on TV talk much louder than their silver screen counterparts. On television, the average dialog level is mixed in at about −14 dB, while for movies the level is more like −31 dB. You can hear it for yourself by opening Peak DV 3 and recording the audio from both a TV show and a movie distributed on DVD. The TV show is always louder.

If you want your DVD-Video's volume to match the TV standard, figure out the audio streams' DNV as described in the task "To determine the DNV" on the next page; then subtract 15. This lower DNV should get your audio close to the levels on a television. (To avoid *gain pumping* and other unwanted volume fluctuations, you may also need to set the file's compression profile to None, as described in the section "About Dynamic Range Control" later in this chapter).

To determine the DNV:

1. Open the audio file in Peak DV 3.

2. Find a section of the audio file that's dialog only (**Figure 4.32**).

3. Play the file and look at the volume meter in Peak DV 3's Transport window (**Figure 4.33**).

   Watch the audio levels as the dialog plays. You'll notice that they bounce between a low and a high level.

4. Determine the average volume level of the file's dialog (**Figure 4.34**).

   This is your audio file's DNV. It takes a bit of practice to determine your audio file's average volume level. As you watch the

level meter bounce between its high and low values, at first you'll be tempted to choose a number right in the middle. In fact, the average volume level of dialog is often much closer to the lowest volume level. For more information, see the sidebar "Volume vs. Average Volume" later in this chapter.

✔ Tip

■ Don't forget to register Peak DV 3. Registering makes you eligible to receive bonus material that includes a free set of 29 VST plug-ins, which work in Mac OS X (or at least, that was the deal as this book was written; regardless, membership always has its advantages...).

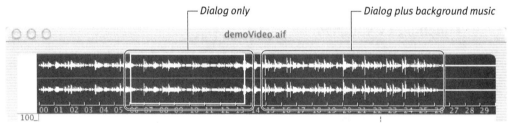

Figure 4.32 An audio program in Peak DV 3. To find the file's dialog normalization number, you don't want any background music interfering with your readings, so locate a section of the audio program that contains nothing but dialog.

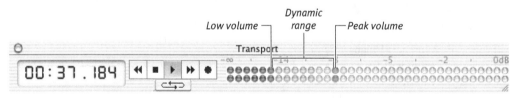

Figure 4.33 Peak DV 3's Transport window has a volume meter that visually shows you how loud your audio file is, in dB.

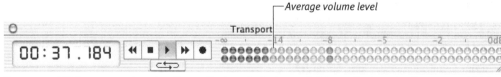

Figure 4.34 A file's average volume level is usually closer to the low end of the audio stream's volume range. This is your audio file's dialog normalization value.

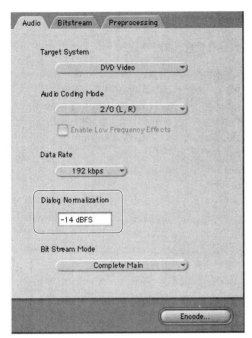

Figure 4.35 Type your audio stream's dialog normalization value into A.Pack's Dialog Normalization text box.

To enter the DNV:

1. In A.Pack, choose the Instant Encoder's Audio tab.

2. In the Dialog Normalization text box, enter the DNV for your audio stream (**Figure 4.35**).

✔ Tips

■ If your source audio came off a DV camera and has passed through the production chain relatively unaltered, you can set dialog normalization to –31. No signal attenuation will be applied, and the DV camera's audio will retain a volume level equivalent to the one at which it was recorded.

■ How do you determine the DNV of an instrumental source audio track that doesn't have any dialog? Here's a trick. Open the file in a multitrack audio editor such as Digidesign Pro Tools Free; then import a dialog track and run it on top of the instrumental (go on—fire up that microphone). Adjust the dialog track so that it fits well into the mix and then play the dialog track by itself (solo the dialog track). Use this dialog track's average volume level as the DNV for your instrumental AC-3 file.

■ When you're trying to determine a file's DNV, it often helps to set up a batch and encode multiple versions of the same AC-3 file, each with a different DNV (see "About Batch Lists" later in this chapter). You can then audition these files with A.Pack's AC-3 monitor to see which one sounds the best (see "Auditioning AC-3 Files" later in this chapter).

SETTING VOLUME LEVELS

Understanding dialog normalization

In audio terms, when you *attenuate* a track, you lower its volume. Dialog normalization heals discrepancies in volume levels by attenuating *every* AC-3 audio stream by (31 + DNV) dB. If the AC-3 file is a movie sound track, you assign it a DNV of −31. Consequently, the track is attenuated (31 + (−31)) dB. That's 0 dB, which means that the track's volume doesn't change at all. A dance track has a DNV of around −8; at playback, the track is attenuated (31 + (−8)) dB, or 23 dB. This may seem like a lot of volume to cut off, but now the dance track doesn't overpower the love scene, and everyone is happy.

Volume vs. Average Volume

Dialog normalization is generally measured in dBFS LAeq, which is a slightly different volume scale than that found in Peak DV 3. LAeq measures an audio stream's long-term average sound-pressure level and typically yields readings slightly lower than the dB reading of Peak DV 3's volume-level meter.

About Dynamic Range Control

Dynamic range compression works by shaving off an audio track's loudest peaks while boosting its lower volume sections, resulting in quieter loud sections, louder quiet sections, and a more unified volume level for the entire AC-3 file—that is, if you don't foul it up. Miscalculating dynamic range compression can result in *gain pumping*, which causes the track's audio to sound like it's pumping rapidly up and down in volume. In truth, the sound track plays at a fairly constant volume, but because the volume peaks are being noticeably lowered, while the lows are noticeably accentuated, the overall impression is that the volume is jumping back and forth erratically.

With AC-3 files encoded using A.Pack, this problem most often occurs when *the dialog normalization number is set incorrectly.* If your DVD-Video uses loud techno background music, for example, but you've left A.Pack's DNV at the factory default position of −27 with the compression profile set to Film Standard, the sound will appear to increase in volume any time the beat stops pounding. When the beat returns, the sound quiets down. This is called *gain pumping.* To fix the problem, either raise the dialog normalization number to around −8, or turn compression off on the Preprocessing tab's Compression menu.

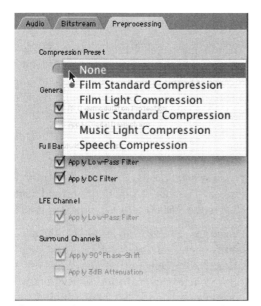

Figure 4.36 The Compression Preset menu lists five preset compression profiles you can use to tame errant volume spikes in your audio programs.

Using compression profiles

AC-3 dynamic range compression (DRC) is divided into three distinct bands. Inside the middle band, called the null band, audio is neither boosted nor attenuated. When audio levels drift outside the null band, they are boosted (increased in volume) or attenuated (lowered in volume) according to a *compression profile*.

Compression profiles come preset by Dolby; you can't change their characteristics. A.Pack lets you choose from a selection of five DRC profiles, all found in the Preprocessing tab's Compression Preset menu (**Figure 4.36**). The characteristics of each profile are listed in **Table 4.2**.

To choose a compression profile:

1. In A.Pack's Instant Encoder, choose the Preprocessing tab.

2. From the Compression Preset menu, choose a DRC profile (refer to Figure 4.36). This DRC profile will be applied to your AC-3 stream as it's decoded.

Table 4.2

Comparing Dynamic Range-Compression Profiles					
PROFILE QUALITY	FILM STANDARD	FILM LIGHT	MUSIC STANDARD	MUSIC LIGHT	SPEECH
Null Band Width	10 dB	20 dB	10 dB	20 dB	10 dB
Null Band Range (dB)	(–31 to –21)	(–41 to –21)	(–31 to 21)	(–41 to –21)	(–31 to –21)
Max Boost	6 dB	6 dB	12 dB	12 dB	15 dB
Boost Ratio	2:1	2:1	2:1	2:1	5:1
Max Cut	24 dB	24 dB	24 dB	15 dB	24 dB
Cut Ratio	20:1	20:1	20:1	2:1	20:1

When in Doubt, Don't!

If you don't have time to test your AC-3 streams to make sure that the compression profile is correct, choose None from the Preprocessing tab's Compression menu. No compression always sounds better than poorly applied compression, which can lead to gain pumping or *transient distortion* (when low-volume sounds, such as a chair being moved offscreen or the camera man's breathing, are increased in volume).

About Downmixing

When a 5.1 audio program is played on a 5.1 surround system, the result is nothing short of spectacular. Crowds thunder behind you and bombs explode in the back right corner of the room as all of the video's sounds conspire to make you feel like you're smack in the center of a larger-than-life movie moment.

When that same surround signal plays back on a stereo with just two front speakers—well, what happens to the crowd noise? Without the two back speakers, there's nothing to reproduce the sound. *Surround downmixing* solves this problem by adding audio from the surround speakers into the stereo channels.

The missing center channel poses a similar problem. Many 5.1 mixes include dialog only in the center channel, with music and effects (dialog reverb, chorusing, and so on) in the left and right channels. This gives a voice tremendous presence, but only if there's a center channel: if you remove the center channel from the mix, the dialog disappears. On a stereo system, the AC-3 decoder downmixes the center channel into both the left and right channels so that all the dialog can still be heard.

Downmixing leads to an increase in the program's overall volume (see the sidebar "Why Attenuate the Downmix?"). You counter this volume increase by reducing the level of the downmixed channels using DVD Studio Pro's Center Downmix and Surround Downmix menus, found on the Bitstream tab in the Instant Encoder.

Why Attenuate the Downmix?

When you combine audio signals, certain parts of the new signal sound much louder than either of the source signals do when they're played separately. Here's a simple test that demonstrates this fact:

Open a mono audio file in a multitrack audio editor. Give it a quick listen. Then duplicate the mono file so two versions of it are playing at the same time. Create a stereo signal by panning one version hard left and the other hard right. If you listen closely, you'll notice that this new stereo signal is louder than the original mono signal (typically by about 3 dB).

Downmix attenuation counters this volume increase, allowing stereo decoders to play the signal at the correct volume.

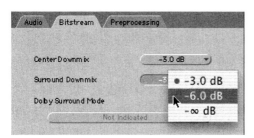

Figure 4.37 To ensure that your multichannel AC-3 files downmix properly, choose a downmix attenuation value from both the Center and Surround downmix options (typically the default value of –3.0 works just fine).

To attenuate the downmix:

1. In A.Pack's Instant Encoder, choose the Bitstream tab.

2. *Do one of the following:*

   To attenuate a center channel downmix, select a value from the Center Downmix menu.

   or

   To attenuate a surround downmix, select a value from the Surround Downmix menu (**Figure 4.37**).

✔ Tips

■ The low frequency effects (LFE) channel is not downmixed into other channels. If the viewer's AC-3 decoder lacks an LFE channel, no LFE content is heard. To guard against this, mix a bit of the LFE channel into the audio stream's left and right channels when producing the source audio.

■ If you don't want the surround channels to be downmixed into the main stereo stream, set the Surround Downmix menu to ∞ dB (refer to Figure 4.37).

■ After creating a 5.1 stream, open it in the AC-3 monitor and check out your downmix settings. If you hear any unwanted volume spikes, re-encode the stream using a lower downmix setting.

ABOUT DOWNMIXING

Other AC-3 Settings

There are still a few AC-3 encoding settings that we haven't covered. All of the remaining settings can be left at their default values, and your AC-3 file will turn out just fine. If you're curious about what they do, read on.

The Target System

The Target System drop-down menu on the Instant Encoder's Audio tab has three settings: DVD-Video, DVD-Audio, and Generic AC-3 (**Figure 4.38**). You're authoring DVD-Video, so select DVD-Video. The other options make extra settings available, but these settings may make your AC-3 stream incompatible with the DVD-Video specification (**Figure 4.39**).

Bit Stream Mode

The Bit Stream Mode menu assigns each AC-3 stream information that a select number of DVD-Video players can use to mix multiple AC-3 files together while the DVD-Video plays. For example, you could provide one AC-3 file of just audio and effects, with up to seven other AC-3 files of dialog in different languages. At run time, the DVD-Video player would check the bit stream mode of each AC-3 file and then mix the correct language into the music and effects file, playing them both simultaneously.

Because very few DVD-Video players understand bit stream modes, you will probably never have to deal with this setting and can leave it at its default of Complete Main (**Figure 4.40**).

✔ Tip

- If you want to learn more about bit stream modes, go straight to the source. Download the *Dolby Digital Professional Encoding Manual* and click to page 107: http://www.dolby.com/tvaudio/.

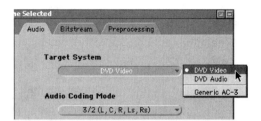

Figure 4.38 For AC-3 files that you intend to bring into DVD Studio Pro, choose DVD-Video as the target system.

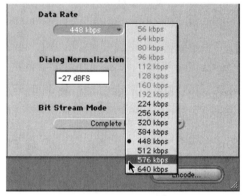

Figure 4.39 If you choose another setting from the Target System menu, your AC-3 files may not be compatible with DVD-Video specifications. Choosing Generic AC-3, for example, lets you encode your files at bit rates higher than 448 kbps. These settings are too high for DVD-Video.

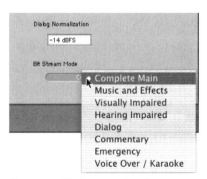

Figure 4.40 Bit stream modes allow some DVD-Video players to mix multiple AC-3 files together as the DVD-Video plays back. You will normally leave the Bit Stream Mode option set to Complete Main.

Figure 4.41 If you're using audio created by someone else (other than you or your client), deselect the Copyright Exists and Content Is Original check boxes.

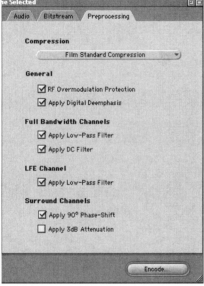

Figure 4.42 The Preprocessing tab hosts a lot of check boxes. Unless you know that you *don't* need one or more selected, leave every box checked, excluding the Apply 3dB Attenuation box.

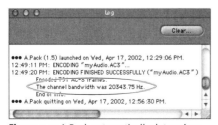

Figure 4.43 A.Pack automatically determines the audio stream's frequency range and applies its full-bandwidth low-pass filter accordingly.

Copyright and content

If you (or your client) produced the audio and own the copyright to your material, leave the Copyright Exists and Content Is Original check boxes on the Bitstream tab selected (**Figure 4.41**). If you're using someone else's audio (with permission, of course), deselect these check boxes.

RF Overmodulation Protection

On the Instant Encoder's Preprocessing tab, leave RF Overmodulation Protection *selected* (**Figure 4.42**).

Some DVD-Video players downmix multi-channel AC-3 files into a signal that's transmitted to the RF, or antenna input, of a television set. Signals sent to the television's RF input are boosted in volume by 11 dB. This can cause the RF signal to *overmodulate*, or distort. To avoid this, select the RF Overmodulation Protection check box.

The Apply Low-Pass Filter

Leave the Preprocessing tab's Apply Low-Pass Filter check box *selected*.

A low-pass filter removes all frequencies above a certain *cutoff* frequency, allowing all sounds below the cutoff frequency to pass through unhindered. Selecting Apply Low-Pass Filter removes all audio frequencies above the range allowed for AC-3 encoding. A normal 48-kHz digital audio file is already safely within this range, but leaving this check box selected acts as a safeguard (A.Pack automatically determines the correct cutoff frequency, as shown in **Figure 4.43**).

The Apply DC Filter

Leave the Preprocessing tab's Apply DC Filter check box *selected*.

Poorly calibrated analog-to-digital converters can introduce DC offset into your recordings (**Figure 4.44**). DC offset can't be heard, but it takes up space in the audio file and consequently consumes encoding bits (particularly in quiet sections of your audio program). For files of the highest fidelity, you don't want to waste bits on something the viewer won't hear, so leave the Apply DC Filter check box *selected*.

Figure 4.44 A digital audio file exhibiting DC offset.

Apply 90° Phase-Shift

The Preprocessing tab's Apply 90° Phase-Shift option produces multichannel bit streams that certain decoders can translate into two-channel Dolby Surround audio streams. Selecting this check box doesn't hurt anything, so leave it checked. This option is available only to files that contain surround channels.

Apply 3dB Attenuation

When big studios create a blockbuster sound track for playback in a movie theater, surround channels are mixed at +3 dB relative to the front channels. If your AC-3 file didn't originate as a Hollywood blockbuster soundtrack, you should *not* select the Preprocessing tab's Apply 3dB Attenuation check box. This option is available only to files that contain surround channels.

OTHER AC-3 SETTINGS

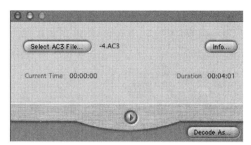

Figure 4.45 The AC-3 Monitor plays AC-3 files. Use it to audition your encoded files to verify dialog normalization and dynamic range compression settings.

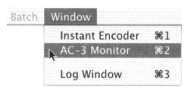

Figure 4.46 To open the AC-3 Monitor, choose Window > AC-3 Monitor.

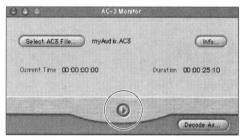

Figure 4.47 After loading an AC-3 file into the AC-3 Monitor, click the Play button to hear how it sounds.

Auditioning AC-3 Files

In audio terms, when you're *auditioning* an audio file, you're listening to it with a critical ear. You might audition an audio file if, for example, you want to check the results of a dialog normalization setting or perhaps to verify that the file's compression profile sounds OK. To audition encoded AC-3 audio streams in A.Pack, you'll use the program's built-in AC-3 Monitor (**Figure 4.45**).

To audition an AC-3 file:

1. From within A.Pack, choose Window > AC-3 Monitor (**Figure 4.46**), or press Command-2.

   The AC-3 Monitor opens (see Figure 4.45).

2. Click the Select AC-3 File button.

   The Select AC-3 File dialog box appears.

3. Use the Select AC-3 File dialog box to select the file that you want to audition.

4. Click the AC-3 Monitor's Play button (**Figure 4.47**).

   The AC-3 Monitor plays the AC-3 file.

   continues on next page

✔ Tips

- The secret to good sound is systematically auditioning all of your AC-3 streams. Open every newly encoded file in the AC-3 Monitor and compare it to your DVD-Video's other AC-3 files. For safety's sake, play a DVD-Video from a major studio and compare its volume level to that of your AC-3 files. If everything sounds about the same volume, you know you've encoded your files correctly.

- To peek at an AC-3 file's encoding settings, open it in the AC-3 Monitor and click the Info button. The AC-3 Stream Information window opens, displaying the file's duration, data rate, dialog normalization number, and several other settings (**Figure 4.48**).

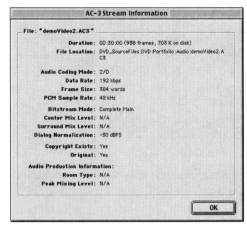

Figure 4.48 Clicking the AC-3 Monitor's Info button launches this AC-3 Stream Information window and reveals the file's encoding settings.

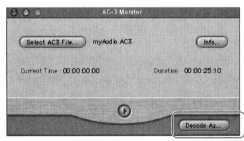

Figure 4.49 To decode an AC-3 file into linear PCM files that you can edit in Peak DV 3 (or any other digital audio editor), open the AC-3 file in A.Pack's AC-3 Monitor and click the Decode As button.

Decoding an AC-3 File

The AC-3 Monitor has a button labeled Decode As (**Figure 4.49**). If you load an AC-3 file into the AC-3 Monitor and click the Decode As button, the AC-3 file is transformed into PCM files that you can open and manipulate in an audio editing program such as Peak DV 3.

Figure 4.50 To create a new batch list, choose File > New Batch List.

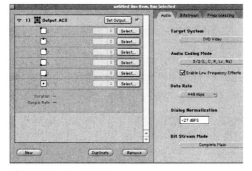

Figure 4.51 A batch list.

Figure 4.52 To add a new encode job to a batch, click the batch list's New button.

About Batch Lists

Batch lists are used to set up multiple encode jobs that you can *batch render* (automatically encode in sequential order). If you've ever batch rendered video files using a program such as Discreet Cleaner 5 or Adobe After Effects, the A.Pack batch list should feel familiar. If you're new to batch rendering, prepare to meet a great labor-saving tool.

To create a new batch list:

◆ Choose File > New Batch List (**Figure 4.50**), or press Command-N.

A new batch list opens (**Figure 4.51**).

To create a new encode job:

◆ At the bottom of the batch list, click the New button (**Figure 4.52**), or press Command-K.

A new encode job appears at the bottom of the batch list (**Figure 4.53**).

Figure 4.53 New encode jobs are added to the bottom of the batch list.

To delete an encode job:

1. In the batch list, select the encode job that you want to delete.

The encode job is highlighted.

2. At the bottom of the batch list, click the Remove button (**Figure 4.54**), or press the Delete key.

A dialog box appears asking if you are sure that you want to remove the encoding job (**Figure 4.55**).

3. Click OK.

The encode job is removed from the batch list.

To encode the batch list:

◆ Click the Encode button in the lower-right corner of the batch list (**Figure 4.56**).

A.Pack encodes the batch, working progressively through files from the top of the batch list to the bottom.

Figure 4.54 Clicking the batch list's Remove button deletes the selected encode job.

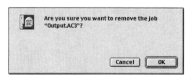

Figure 4.55 A.Pack gives you a second chance to make sure that you want to remove the encode job. If you do, click OK.

Figure 4.56 When your batch is all set up and ready to go, click the Encode button in A.Pack's lower right corner. A.Pack encodes all of the files in the batch list, starting at the top and working its way down to the bottom.

Testing AC-3 Encoding Settings

Batch lists are particularly useful if you're not sure which dialog normalization, compression profile, and/or downmix settings to use with an AC-3 file. Instead of encoding your files one at a time, you can use a batch list to set up several encode jobs, each with different settings. After A.Pack finishes encoding the batch, open the finished AC-3 files in the AC-3 Monitor and check to see which one sounds best.

ABOUT BATCH LISTS

Part II:
DVD Studio Pro

Part II:
DVD Studio Pro

THE DVD STUDIO PRO WORKSPACE

When DVD Studio Pro launches, it defaults to a fresh *workspace*, which consists of the Graphical View, the Property Inspector, the Assets container, and the Project View (**Figure 5.1**). You won't be able to miss the Graphical View—it's the large window in the top left corner of the workspace. This window serves as the foundation for all of your authoring, as it's here that you organize project *assets* (MPEG video, audio streams, subtitles, menus, scripts, and so on) into tiles representing your project's flow.

Directly below the Graphical View sits the Project View and the Assets container. The Project View functions like a filing cabinet, grouping all of the project's items into a hierarchy of nested folders. Located to the right of the Project View, the Assets container works as your project's library. When you import a source file into DVD Studio Pro, it goes directly into the Assets container. From the Assets container, you add assets to the project by dragging them into the Graphical or Project Views.

The right edge of the workspace holds the Property Inspector. The Property Inspector is *context sensitive* and changes to display the unique properties of whichever project item is currently selected.

This chapter unlocks DVD Studio Pro's workspace, taking you on a visual tour of the windows and tools you'll use to make your DVD-Videos. Along the way, you'll explore essential editors and even peek at a few power tools, including the List window (used to manipulate multivalue properties) and Matrix Views (used to connect project elements or quickly locate errors in your authoring).

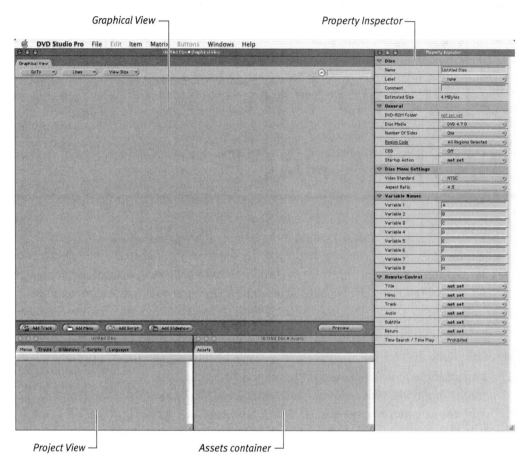

Figure 5.1 The DVD Studio Pro workspace includes all of the windows you see on the screen when DVD Studio Pro first launches.

About the Graphical View

Everything in a DVD-Video fits into one of four categories: Tracks, Menus, Slideshows, and Scripts. In DVD Studio Pro, these categories are represented as *tiles* in the Graphical View (**Figure 5.2**). The Graphical View is basically a large, interactive flow chart that acts like a storyboard, showing you how the parts of your project link together.

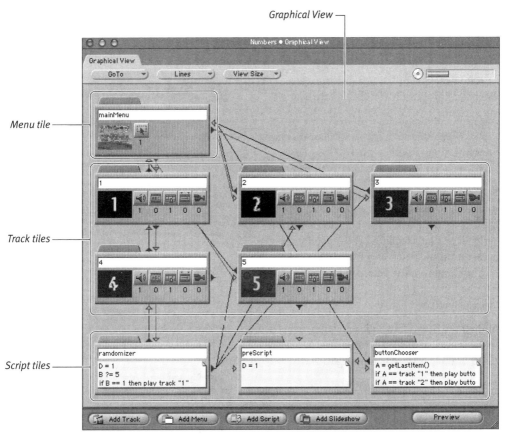

Figure 5.2 The Graphical View looks and acts like a flow chart with tiles that reflect your project's organization. Use the Graphical View to see which tiles are linked together and to clump similar menus, tracks, or scripts into easy-to-find groups.

To open or close the Graphical View:

◆ Choose Windows > Graphical View (**Figure 5.3**), or press Command-1.

Understanding tiles

Each tile has one large thumbnail area and up to five container icons. The thumbnail area provides a visual clue to the tile's contents and hides an editor that's specific to the tile's function. The container icons act as short-cuts to various Project View containers that hold and organize the tile's contents (see "About the Project View" later in this chapter). DVD Studio Pro has four types of tiles, which are differentiated by color (**Figure 5.4**):

Track tiles. Green. Track tiles combine video, audio, and subtitle assets into a single data stream for a DVD-Video.

Menu tiles. Blue. A menu is a still or moving background over which buttons are placed. Menu tiles hold one menu and its buttons.

Script tiles. Orange. Script tiles contain a script editor you use to give your DVD-Video the power to make its own decisions. The script editor also facilitates advanced inter-active scripting (such as a Play All Tracks button) or automatic actions (programming a menu to return to the button of the last track played).

Slideshow tiles. Gray. Slideshow tiles create a linear sequence of still pictures and/or MPEG video that plays from beginning to end.

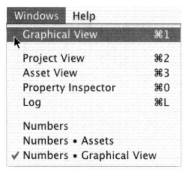

Figure 5.3 If you can't see the Graphical View, choose Windows > Graphical View.

Track tile

Menu tile

Script tile

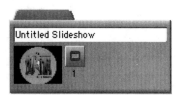

Slideshow tile

Figure 5.4 What can you do with just four tiles? Quite a lot. These four tiles contain every element of your project. From MPEG video straight through to scripts, it's all in the tiles.

Figure 5.5 Create tiles by clicking one of these buttons along the bottom of the Graphical View.

Figure 5.6 To change a tile's name, type a new name in the Name text box.

To create a tile:

◆ At the bottom of the Graphical View, click one of the four Add Tile buttons (**Figure 5.5**).

A new, empty tile is created in the Graphical View.

✔ Tips

■ To move a tile, select it and drag it across the Graphical View.

■ To delete a tile, select it and press the Delete key on your keyboard.

To rename a tile:

1. Select a tile.

2. In the white text box at the top of the tile, drag the pointer across the tile's name.

   The tile's name is highlighted.

3. Type a new name for the tile (**Figure 5.6**).

✔ Tip

■ With a tile selected, you can also use the Property Inspector's Name text box to change the tile's name.

ABOUT THE GRAPHICAL VIEW

Tiles and Track Numbers

DVD-Video players display track numbers based on the order in which Track tiles are created. To keep the player's display synchronized with your track order, you may have to do some planning. Think about how your final DVD-Video will play. Create the Track tiles in the correct order and assign them the proper assets. When you play the disc, the DVD-Video player will display track numbers that reflect the project's track order.

DVD Studio Pro also builds items to disc in the same order as they are listed in the Project View. If you've created your tracks in the wrong order, rearrange the tracks in the Project View and the problem will go away. See "About the Project View" later in this chapter.

Navigating tiles

Tile navigation is the process by which you find and select tiles for editing. Projects with less than a dozen tiles fit neatly in the Graphical View, making tile navigation as simple as clicking the tile you need. Unfortunately, the Graphical View doesn't hold many tiles, and your projects will often outgrow this window's constraints (**Figure 5.7**).

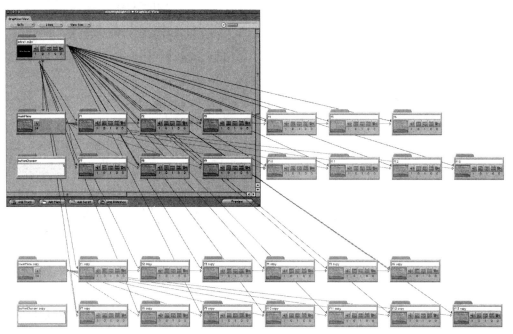

Figure 5.7 Imagine the Graphical View to be a flash light beam: Where the Graphical View shines, you can see your project. Outside its beam, the project still exists, but is hidden from view. To see other parts, you must illuminate them by moving the beam (the Graphical View) over them.

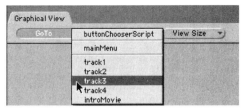

Figure 5.8 The Graphical View's GoTo drop-down menu lists all of the tiles in your project by name. To find a tile quickly, select it from the GoTo menu.

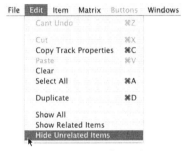

Figure 5.9 The bottom of the Edit menu contains three options that show or hide tiles in the Graphical View. Hide Unrelated Items is particularly useful for checking tile connections in crowded projects.

To find tiles outside of the Graphical View, use the scroll bars along the window's bottom and right edges, or select tiles by name from the GoTo drop-down menu at the top of the Graphical View.

To select a tile:

◆ In the Graphical View, click a tile.

or

◆ From the GoTo drop-down menu, choose a tile by name (**Figure 5.8**).

The tile is selected. If the tile was previously hidden, the Graphical View moves to display it.

✔ Tips

■ The GoTo menu lists tiles by type, starting with Script tiles, and then moving progressively through Menu, Track, and Slideshow tiles.

■ The bottom of the Edit menu contains three options used to display only tiles related to the currently selected tile (**Figure 5.9**). When your screen starts getting cluttered, use these options to hide tiles you're not currently working on.

ABOUT THE GRAPHICAL VIEW

Changing tile size

Using small tiles is the best way to squeeze as many tiles as possible into the Graphical View (**Figure 5.10**). But the added real estate comes at a price: small tiles display only the first 12 characters of the tile name and they lack thumbnail areas and container icons, which makes it difficult to access the tile's elements (you'll have to use the Project View instead).

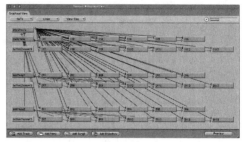

Figure 5.10 The Graphical View, showing small tiles. Small tiles let you squeeze more of your project into the Graphical View.

To change tile size:

◆ From the View Size drop-down menu (at the top of the Graphical View), select a tile size (**Figure 5.11**).

▲ To make all tiles small, choose Small (Shift-Command-S).

▲ To make all tiles large, choose Large (Shift-Command-L).

Figure 5.11 To change tile size, choose an option from the View Size drop-down menu.

✔ Tip

■ To open a Menu, Script, or Slideshow editor from a small tile, double-click the tile or select it and choose Item > Edit (Command-E).

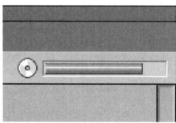

Figure 5.12 The Disc Space indicator shows you how much space is left on the DVD disc. If it turns red, you've put more content into your project than the target DVD disc can handle.

The Disc Space Indicator

The Disc Space indicator in the top right corner of the Graphical View displays your project's approximate file size (**Figure 5.12**). As you add assets to tiles in the Graphical View, the Disc Space indicator increases in size. If you've used up more space than is available on the disc, the Disc Space indictor turns red.

DVD Studio Pro 1.5 lets you pick a ROM folder to include on a hybrid DVD (**Figure 5.13**). DVD Studio Pro calculates the size of the files inside the ROM folder and adds it to the Disc Space indicator. As a result, the Disc Space indicator always represents all the data that will be included on the final DVD disc. To learn more about specifying a DVD-ROM folder for a hybrid DVD disc, see Chapter 13, "Finishing the DVD."

Figure 5.13 For hybrid DVD discs, the DVD-ROM Folder property lets you specify a folder to be written onto the DVD disc along with your DVD-Video project.

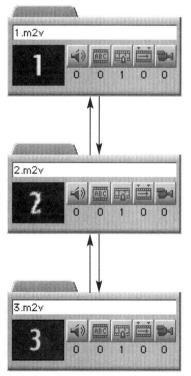

Figure 5.14 Links show you how tiles are connected. The solid triangle indicates the link's source tile and the hollow triangle shows the link's destination tile.

Understanding tile links

Links show tile connections. A link is composed of a line and two arrows that help you determine which tile is connected to which (**Figure 5.14**). The beginning of a link is represented by a solid triangle and the link's destination is represented by a hollow triangle.

You'll typically leave tile links enabled. If your Graphical View is cluttered by link lines, however, you can either turn off link lines or enable them for only the currently selected tiles.

ABOUT THE GRAPHICAL VIEW

To display or hide link lines:

◆ From the Lines drop-down menu (located at the top of the Graphical View), choose an option (**Figure 5.15**).

Depending upon your choice, link lines are all displayed (Always), displayed only for the currently selected tiles (Selected Items), or all hidden (Never).

✔ Tip

■ The Configure option on the Lines menu lets you choose exactly which links the Graphical View displays (**Figure 5.16**). If Always is too much, but Never is not enough, configure your own link style.

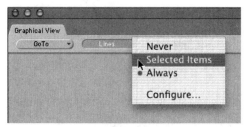

Figure 5.15 The Lines drop-down menu's options hide all links (Never), show only links originating from the currently selected tile (Selected Items), or show all tile links (Always). Select Configure to customize the link display.

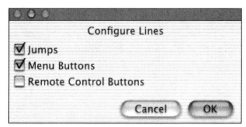

Figure 5.16 Choose Configure from the Lines drop-down menu, and this Configure Lines menu appears. Use the menu to select the type of tile links for the Graphical View to display.

Figure 5.17 The Preview mode plays your DVD-Video just as if the project had been built to a disc and placed in a normal DVD player. The buttons at the bottom of the Preview mode mimic the buttons found on a DVD remote control. Use these buttons to interact with the preview.

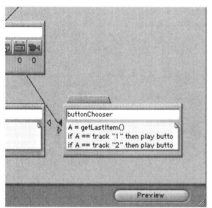

Figure 5.18 To engage the Preview mode, click the Preview button in the Graphical View's lower right corner.

Using the Preview button

From time to time, you'll need to check that everything is snapping together and working the way you need it to. At these moments, you'll turn to DVD Studio Pro's real-time multiplexer: the *Preview mode* (**Figure 5.17**).

The process of converting your project's assets into a format that can be written to a DVD disc is called *multiplexing*. Multiplexing is kind of like taking a bunch of ingredients (your project's assets), mixing them together in a bowl (DVD Studio Pro), and then baking everything into a cake that you can eat (the final DVD-Video). Simply stated, multiplexing takes all of a project's elementary streams (such as a Track tile's MPEG video, subtitles, and audio) and combines them together into a single stream that a DVD-Video player can read.

To engage the Preview mode:

◆ In the lower right corner of the Graphical View, click the Preview button (**Figure 5.18**), or choose Item > Preview.

✔ Tips

■ The Preview mode relies on the Apple DVD Player to work. To ensure the best possible preview playback, make sure that you have the latest version of DVD Player.

■ The Preview mode does not work if DVD Player is currently open.

Previewing in DVD Studio Pro 1.2

With DVD Studio Pro 1.2 and earlier, the Preview mode often doesn't work exactly as expected. Slideshows, for example, sometimes advance before they should, and AC-3 control parameters, including dialog normalization and compression profiles, are ignored (see Chapter 4, "Encoding Audio Streams"). Even worse, in some cases audio falls out of sync with the video, which can be quite disconcerting. Once you build the project and play it in a DVD player, however, everything should work fine. Additionally, some of these problems (particularly audio synchronization issues) are solved by upgrading the Apple DVD Player to version 2.7 or later.

About the Property Inspector

On the right side of the DVD Studio Pro workspace, you will find the Property Inspector (**Figure 5.19**). The Property Inspector is context sensitive and follows just one rule: it always updates to display the currently selected project item's properties.

The Property Inspector arranges similar properties into named *areas*, or sections. By default, the Property Inspector displays all areas. To the left of the area name is a disclosure triangle that you can click to hide (or expand) the area's properties.

To open or close the Property Inspector:

◆ Choose Windows > Property Inspector (**Figure 5.20**), or press Command-0.

If the Property Inspector was not open, it appears on the screen. If it was open, it closes.

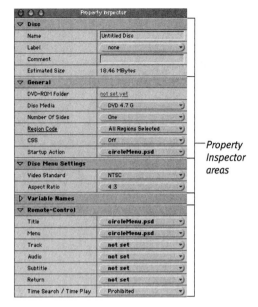

Figure 5.19 The Property Inspector. Similar properties are grouped into areas.

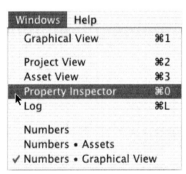

Figure 5.20 If you closed the Property Inspector, open it by choosing Windows > Property Inspector.

What Are Properties?

Depending on the item selected, the Property Inspector shows different *properties*. Properties are your project items' attributes. An MPEG asset, for example, has several properties including its dimensions, bit rate, and format (MPEG-1 or MPEG-2). A Track tile has an entirely different set of properties, including its assigned MPEG asset, the action taken once the track finishes playing, and the way the track responds to the buttons on the remote control.

MPEGs

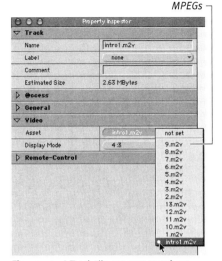

Figure 5.21 A Track tile can accept only an MPEG video as an asset, so only MPEG videos are listed on that Property Inspector's Asset menu.

Collapse Window button
Resize Window button
Close Window button

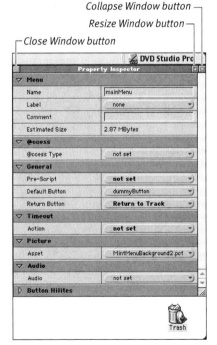

Figure 5.22 In OS 9, click the resize button to trim unused space off the bottom of the Property Inspector, revealing the Trash and the desktop below.

✔ Tips

■ Property menus display only values that make sense for the selected property. The asset property of a Track tile, for example, can be only an MPEG video. As expected, the Asset menu lists MPEG video, but no other project assets (**Figure 5.21**).

■ The Property Inspector usually takes up the whole right edge of the DVD Studio Pro workspace. But in Mac OS 9, the bottom right corner of the screen contains the Trash. To keep the Property Inspector from covering the Trash, click the resize button at the upper right corner of the window (**Figure 5.22**). The Property Inspector shrinks to display only currently available properties, leaving space at the bottom for the Trash.

ABOUT THE PROPERTY INSPECTOR

To expand or collapse an area:

◆ In the Property Inspector, click the disclosure arrow beside the area's name (**Figure 5.23**).

If the area is currently expanded, it collapses, and you can no longer see its properties. If the area is collapsed, clicking the expansion arrow expands it.

✔ Tip

■ You can quickly expand all areas in the Property Inspector by choosing Item > Expand All Properties (**Figure 5.24**), or by pressing Command-9.

Expansion arrows

Figure 5.23 Click the disclosure arrow to show or hide Property Inspector areas.

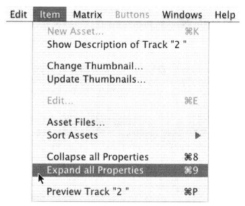

Figure 5.24 Choose Item > Expand All Properties to reveal all Property Inspector areas.

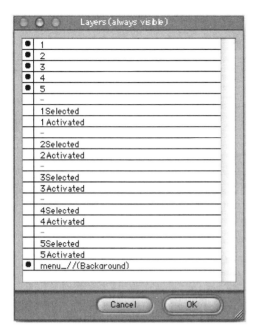

Figure 5.25 A List window. Bullets indicate selected values.

Using the List window

In the Property Inspector, certain properties are underlined. Clicking any underlined property opens a DVD Studio Pro power tool called the List window (**Figure 5.25**).

The List window exists only for properties that can be assigned more than one value. A DVD-Video, for example, can currently have up to seven different region codes. If you look at the disc's Property Inspector, you'll see that Region Code is underlined (**Figure 5.26**). Clicking Region Code opens a Region Code List window used to select one or more compatible regions for your DVD-Video (**Figure 5.27**).

Figure 5.26 Region Code is underlined, indicating that it hides a List window. To launch the List window, click the underlined words.

Figure 5.27 The Region Code List window. Every region is selected, which means that this disc will play in all regions of the world.

The List window contains a list of all the selected property's potential values. To the left of each value sits a selection box in which selected values are bulleted. To the right of the list is a scroll bar. If the list contains more values than will fit in the window, drag this scroll bar to bring hidden values into view.

To open the List window:

1. In the Property Inspector, click an underlined property name.

   The List window opens.

2. *Do one of the following:*

   To select a single value. Click the selection box to the left of the value's name (**Figure 5.28**). If any other value was selected, DVD Studio Pro deselects the old value and selects the new one.

   To select a range of values. Click the selection box for the value highest in the list. This box is the upper limit of the selection range. Next, hold down Shift while clicking the selection box for the value lowest in the list. This is the lower limit of the selection range. All values between the upper and lower limits are selected, including the upper and lower selection limits themselves.

   To select noncontiguous values. Click the selection box of the first value, hold down the Command key on your keyboard, and click the selection box of a second value. Values between the chosen ones remain unselected (**Figure 5.29**).

   To deselect a value. Hold down the Command key on your keyboard and click the selection box. This is the only way to actively deselect a value (remember this when all the values in a List window are selected).

Selection box

Figure 5.28 To select a value from the List window, click its selection box.

First value

Second value

Figure 5.29 To select noncontiguous values from the List window, click the first value, hold down the Command key, and click a second value.

✔ Tip

- In Mac OS X, do not close the List window by clicking the little yellow button in the upper left corner. This compelling little button actually sends the List window to your computer's dock. But DVD Studio Pro's workspace remains locked as long as the List window is open, so until you actually close the List window you will be unable to use DVD Studio Pro.

Disclosure arrows   *Container tabs*

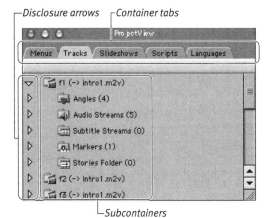

Subcontainers

Figure 5.30 The Project View collects all project items in one window. As projects become larger, you'll find that using the Project View makes it easier to find and edit the various items in your project.

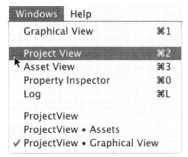

Figure 5.31 If you can't see the Project View, choose Windows > Project View.

Figure 5.32 The number in parentheses indicates the number of items assigned to each container.

Figure 5.33 Links between items are displayed in parentheses.

About the Project View

Most of the time, you'll use the Graphical View to arrange and edit your project. But as your projects grow more complex, the increased number of tiles makes the Graphical View difficult to navigate. At these times, the Project View awaits (**Figure 5.30**).

The Project View contains a series of five tabs listing all of your project's elements. These tabs (also called *containers*) are the Menus, Tracks, Slideshows, Scripts, and Languages containers. Each container has a series of sub-containers that hold assets or other project elements. To gain access to a subcontainer's contents, you click the disclosure arrow on its left side or double-click the subcontainer to open it in a separate window.

To open or close the Project View:

◆ Choose Windows > Project View
(**Figure 5.31**), or press Command-2.
If the Project View was not visible, it opens. If it was open, it closes.

✔ Tips

■ If items are assigned to a subcontainer, the number of assigned items is printed in parentheses to the right of the subcontainer (**Figure 5.32**).

■ If an item is linked to another item, parentheses to its right display an arrow followed by the linked item's name (**Figure 5.33**).

■ If an item's name is printed in italics, that item is incomplete (some of its properties have not been set). Track tiles, for example, must have at least one MPEG video, so if that crucial asset remains unassigned, the Track tile's name will appear in italics. DVD Studio Pro will not multiplex or preview your project if any item names are in italics. When you see italics, make sure you track down and fix the problem.

Working in the Project View

Think of the Project View as a file cabinet holding your DVD-Video project. Open the Project View, and you see five tabs. Clicking a tab reveals its contents, which in most cases consists of a series of subcontainers that look like folders. Subcontainers can hold other subcontainers and/or project assets, such as MPEG video, subtitle streams, scripts, and so on (**Figure 5.34**). Collectively, Project View subcontainers and assets are called *items*.

To add an item to a container:

1. From the tabs across the top of the Project View, select a container tab. In this example, the Tracks tab is selected (**Figure 5.35**).

2. Choose Item > New Track (**Figure 5.36**), or press Command-K.

   A new, untitled item is added at the bottom of the container (**Figure 5.37**).

✔ Tip

■ The Item menu is context sensitive. Depending on which type of tab you've selected from the top of the Project View, the Item > New option will display a different "new item" value.

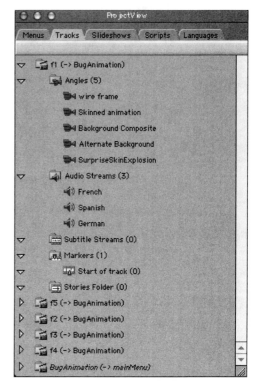

Figure 5.34 Click the resize box to make all of the tab's items visible.

Figure 5.35 To add an item to a Project View container, first select the container.

Figure 5.36 Next, choose Item > New (the New Item option is context sensitive and creates only items that belong in the selected container).

Figure 5.37 The new, untitled item is added at the bottom of the container.

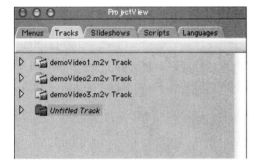

Figure 5.38 From the Project View, to change an item's name, you first need to select it.

Name text box

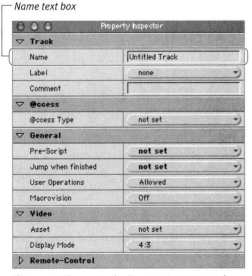

Figure 5.39 Then go to the Property Inspector and change the name in the Name text box.

To rename an item:

1. In the Project View, select an item (**Figure 5.38**).

   The Property Inspector updates to show the item's properties.

2. At the top of the Property Inspector, type a new name in the Name text box (**Figure 5.39**).

   Back in the Project View, the item's name changes.

To reorder an item:

◆ Select an item in the Project View and drag it above or below other list items.

To expand all items:

◆ Hold down the Option key while clicking a subcontainer's disclosure arrow.

   The subcontainer expands. If the subcontainer holds nested subcontainers, each nested subcontainer also expands.

Creating container windows

If you need to see the contents of several containers at the same time, drag container tabs out of the Project View. This creates separate container windows that you can position anywhere inside the DVD Studio Pro workspace. (The Assets container, located directly to the right of the Project View in DVD Studio Pro's default workspace, is actually a tab that's been removed from the Project View.)

To open a new container window:

1. In the Project View, select the container's tab.

   The container opens in the Project View.

2. Click the tab and drag it out of the Project View (**Figure 5.40**).

3. Drop the tab anywhere inside the DVD Studio Pro workspace.

   A new container window is created (**Figure 5.41**).

✔ Tip

- If you drag a tab out of the Project View and then close its container, the tab does not reappear in the Project View. To access this tab, you must close the Project View, then reopen it by choosing Windows > Project View (Command-2).

To return a container to the Project View:

◆ Select the container's tab and drag it back into the Project View.

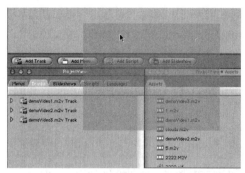

Figure 5.40 To open a container in its own window, drag it out of the Project View.

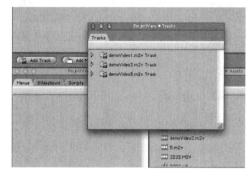

Figure 5.41 The Tracks container has been removed from the Project View.

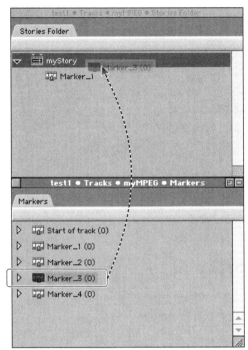

Figure 5.42 By opening subcontainers in their own windows, you can drag items from one container to another.

Figure 5.43 To open a subcontainer in its own window, find it in the Project View and double-click it.

Opening multiple containers

Some situations call for having two or more subcontainers open at the same time, such as when you're adding markers to a story (see Chapter 10, "Creating Markers and Stories"). While there are several ways to do this, the easiest method is to open both subcontainers and drag markers directly into stories (**Figure 5.42**).

To open a subcontainer in its own window:

◆ In the Project View, double-click a subcontainer (**Figure 5.43**).

A new window appears displaying the subcontainer's contents.

About the Assets Container

The Assets container (also called the Assets View) serves as your project's library (**Figure 5.44**). Before you can use a source file in DVD Studio Pro, you must import it into the program where it appears as an asset in the Assets container (importing source files is also covered in Chapter 6, "Setting Up Your Project").

To add an asset:

1. Select the Assets container.

2. Choose Item > New Asset (**Figure 5.45**), or press Command-K.

   The Open dialog box appears.

3. Use the Open dialog box to locate a media file and click Open.

   An asset representing the media file appears at the bottom of the Assets container.

✔ Tip

■ The Assets container is actually part of the Project View. You can drag it back into the Project View (**Figure 5.46**), but you'll probably find this placement inconvenient.

Figure 5.44 The Assets container groups all of your project's assets in one place, similar to the library in Macromedia Flash or Totally Hip LiveStage Professional.

Figure 5.45 To add an asset to the Assets container, choose Item > New Asset.

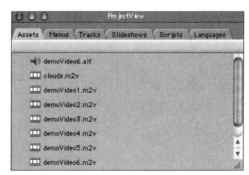

Figure 5.46 The Assets container, happily snuggled back inside the Project View. You'll use the Assets container so much, however, that you'll likely want to leave it in its own window at the bottom of the workspace.

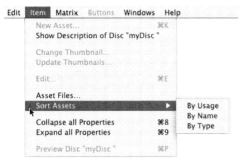

Figure 5.47 Sorting cleans up your Assets container and makes it easier to quickly locate assets.

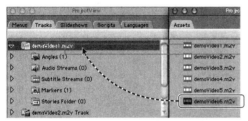

Figure 5.48 To assign a new asset to an item in the Project View, select it in the Assets container and drag it onto a Project View item.

Sorting assets

When the Assets container gets crowded, you must arrange items so that you can quickly find them when needed. DVD Studio Pro lets you organize items by use, name, or type.

To sort assets:

◆ Choose Item > Sort Assets and select a sort option (**Figure 5.47**).

All items in the Assets container are sorted accordingly.

To assign assets to a Project View item:

1. In the Project View, locate the item to which you want to assign an asset.

2. From the Assets container, select an asset.

3. Drag the asset onto an item in the Project View (**Figure 5.48**).

The item is highlighted in black, indicating that you can drop this type of asset onto it. If the item is not highlighted, it isn't compatible with the currently selected asset, and you cannot perform the next step.

4. Drop the asset onto the item.

The asset is assigned to the item.

What's an Asset?

An asset is an alias to a source file on your hard disk (like a pointer that shows DVD Studio Pro where to look to find a media file). When DVD Studio Pro needs the source file, it follows the path defined by the asset, goes out to your hard disk, and grabs the file. You'll learn all about assets in Chapter 6, "Setting Up Your Project."

ABOUT THE ASSETS CONTAINER

About Editors

Click a tile's thumbnail area as shown in **Figure 5.49** to open task-specific windows that are used to edit buttons (**Figure 5.50**), markers (**Figure 5.51**), slideshows (**Figure 5.52**), and scripts (**Figure 5.53**).

Thumbnail area

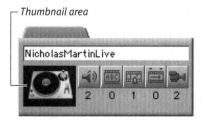

Figure 5.49 To open an editor, click the large thumbnail area on the tile's surface.

Figure 5.50 The Menu editor is used to create up to 36 buttons for each menu. For more information on menus, see Chapter 8, "Photoshop Layer Menus," and Chapter 9, "Highlight Menus."

Marker editor

Figure 5.51 The Marker editor creates markers that define chapters in a track. To learn more about markers, see Chapter 10, "Creating Markers and Stories."

Figure 5.52 The Slideshow editor lets you link images and MPEG video together into a linear presentation. Slideshows are discussed in Chapter 11, "Assembling Slideshows."

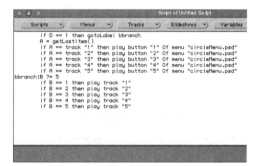

Figure 5.53 The Script editor is used to create complex interactivity for your projects. To learn more about scripting, see Chapter 17, "Scripting!"

Thumbnail area

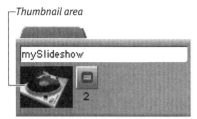

Figure 5.54 Click a tile's thumbnail area to open the editor.

Figure 5.55 You can open tile editors directly from the Project View only if you select a marker, menu, slideshow, or script item.

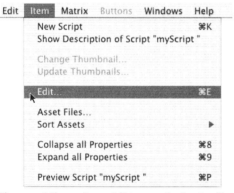

Figure 5.56 Choose Item > Edit to open the item's editor.

To open an editor in the Graphical View:

◆ Click the tile's thumbnail area (**Figure 5.54**).

The editor opens.

To open an editor in the Project View:

1. In the Project View, select a marker, menu, slideshow, or script item.

The item is highlighted (**Figure 5.55**)

2. Choose Item > Edit (**Figure 5.56**), or press Command-E.

The editor that's specific to the selected item opens.

✔ Tip

■ The Item > Edit option is available only when a marker, menu, slideshow, or script item is selected in the Project or Graphical View.

ABOUT EDITORS

117

About Matrix Views

Matrix Views show item connections and relationships as dots on a grid. You use the Matrix Views when you need to quickly relink project elements. Say, for example, that after previewing your project, you decide that tracks 1 and 5 should use a different asset. Using the Asset matrix, you can switch both tracks' assets at one time (**Figure 5.57**). Now, say the next time you preview the project, you notice that several buttons link to the wrong tracks. To figure out where the problem lies, open the Jump matrix for a visual display of the project's links (**Figure 5.58**).

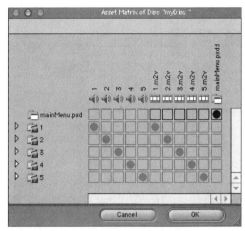

Figure 5.57 Use the Asset matrix to assign assets (top) to tracks and menus (left).

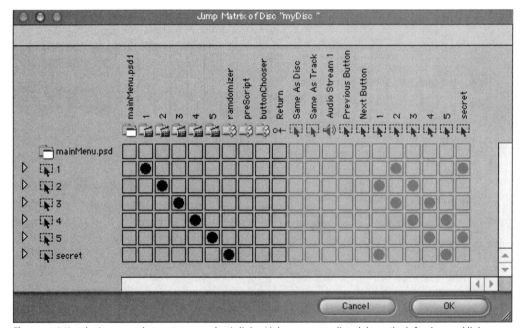

Figure 5.58 Use the Jump matrix to set your project's links. Link sources are listed down the left edge, and link destinations are printed across the top.

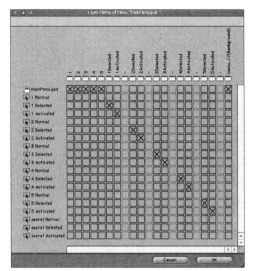

Figure 5.59 Use the Layer matrix to assign Photoshop layers (top) to menu buttons (left).

Item	Matrix	Buttons	Windows	Help
	Assets of Disc "myDisc "			⌘4
	Jumps of Menu "MainMenu.psd "			⌘5
	Layers of Menu "MainMenu.psd "			⌘6

Figure 5.60 To open a Matrix View, choose Matrix and select a Matrix View.

The final Matrix View, called the Layer matrix, links menu buttons to layers in Photoshop files (**Figure 5.59**).

To open a Matrix View:

◆ Choose Matrix and select a Matrix View (**Figure 5.60**).

The selected Matrix View opens.

✔ Tips

■ After a little practice, you'll come to see patterns in the Matrix Views. If you have a problem with your project, you'll often be able to root it out simply by looking at a Matrix View.

■ The Matrix Views display items in the order in which they appear in the Project View. Sometimes this order makes it hard to spot patterns. If need be, close the Matrix View, reorder the items in the Project View, and then reopen the Matrix View.

ABOUT MATRIX VIEWS

SETTING UP
YOUR PROJECT

Chapter 5 introduced you to the DVD Studio Pro workspace. Now that you're feeling at home with this powerful DVD-Video authoring environment, it's time to start a project!

Before you import source files into DVD Studio Pro, you need to set a few basic disc properties. Your project needs a name, for example, and you also need to tell DVD Studio Pro which video standard you'll be working with—NTSC or PAL. Once the standard disc properties are set, you can import source media files to create assets.

Assets are *not* the actual source media files, but rather aliases that point DVD Studio Pro to the original source files on your hard disks. This is an important distinction to keep in mind, especially when you need to update an asset. While designing your project's layout, for example, you might use a short video clip as a placeholder. Once the project is working correctly, you can swap the placeholder for the video file you really want to use. The asset doesn't change; it merely directs DVD Studio Pro to the newly assigned source file on your hard disk. If this seems confusing, don't worry. The second part of this chapter covers assets and their relationship to source files in detail.

Setting Disc Properties

When you first open DVD Studio Pro or create a new project, an empty workspace appears on your screen. Right away, before you create any tiles or even import assets, you should set a few disc properties (**Figure 6.1**).

First and foremost, name your disc. This is an easy step to forget, and few things are worse than watching your project record to a DVD-R, only to realize it's called "Untitled Disc." While you're in the Property Inspector, make sure that DVD Studio Pro knows what type of disc media you're authoring for, and verify that the proper video standard and aspect ratio are selected for your menus.

To name the disc:

1. In the Disc area of the Disc Property Inspector, highlight the text in the Name text box.

   The default name (Untitled Disc) is highlighted.

2. Type a new name for the disc (**Figure 6.2**).

   When DVD Studio Pro builds and formats your project on a DVD disc, this name becomes the disc's name (**Figure 6.3**).

✔ Tip

- If the Property Inspector does not show disc properties, click the Graphical View's background, which is the same as selecting the disc.

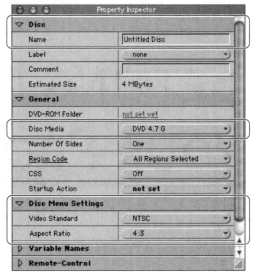

Figure 6.1 First things first! Supply all new projects with a disc name, media type, and appropriate menu settings.

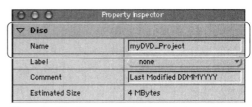

Figure 6.2 The Disc area of the Property Inspector contains the Name text box, which sets the name of your final DVD-Video disc.

Figure 6.3 The DVD-Video icon that appears on the desktop in Mac OS X. Note that the name matches the one specified in the previous figure.

SETTING DISC PROPERTIES

─Disc Space indicator
  ─Graphical View   ─Property Inspector

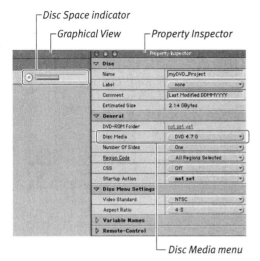

─ Disc Media menu

Figure 6.4 For the Graphical View's Disc Space indicator to accurately reflect your project's size, you must choose the correct media size from the Disc Media menu.

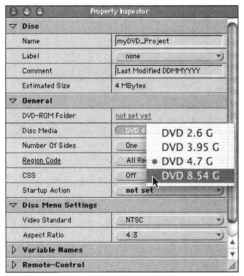

Figure 6.5 The Disc Media menu tells DVD Studio Pro what type of DVD disc your DVD-Video will be written to.

Defining disc media

As you add assets to tiles in the Graphical View, your DVD-Video's file size grows. DVD Studio Pro keeps track of how much space you have available for your project (**Figure 6.4**), but only if you correctly set the Disc Media property (to learn more about DVD storage capacity, see Chapter 2, "DVD Basics").

To specify the disc media:

◆ In the General area of the Disc Property Inspector, select a disc media type (**Figure 6.5**).

✔ Tip

■ Selecting DVD 8.54 G from the Disc Media menu tells DVD Studio Pro that you're working on a dual-layer DVD-9 disc. When you later build and format a DLT tape, DVD Studio Pro will place a break in the program that tells the reading laser where to change layers. To learn more about building your project to DLT, see Chapter 13, "Finishing the DVD."

SETTING DISC PROPERTIES

Setting disc menu properties

A DVD-Video project must be either NTSC or PAL—not both. When you begin a project, select the correct video standard for your menus. If you select the incorrect format, your menus either will not fill the screen (NTSC) or will be cut off (PAL), as shown in **Figure 6.6**.

To set the menu video standard:

1. In the Disc Menu Settings area of the Disc Property Inspector, click the Video Standard drop-down menu (**Figure 6.7**).

2. Choose the correct video standard for your project.

✔ Tip

- The DVD Studio Pro Preferences dialog box contains a section titled Default TV-System (**Figure 6.8**). This section sets the default video standard for your menus. If you work with one standard more than another (and let's face it, you do) set this preference and DVD Studio Pro will always start a new project using the correct video standard.

Figure 6.6 If you're working on a PAL project, make sure you choose the correct video standard from the Disc Menu Settings area of the Property Inspector, or your menus will appear cropped.

Figure 6.7 The Video Standard property sets the resolution for your project's menus. All menus on your DVD must be either NTSC or PAL; they can't be both.

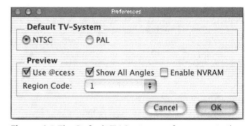

Figure 6.8 The Default TV-System preference sets the default video standard for your projects' menus.

SETTING DISC PROPERTIES

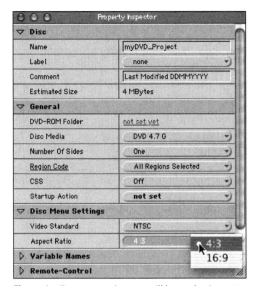

Figure 6.9 For most projects, you'll leave the Aspect Ratio menu property set to 4:3.

To set the menu aspect ratio:

1. In the Disc Menu Settings area of the Disc Property Inspector, click the Aspect Ratio drop-down menu (**Figure 6.9**).

2. Choose the aspect ratio for your menus.

   Unless you're working on a widescreen 16:9 project, leave this menu set to the default value of 4:3 (see Chapter 14, "Widescreen: 16:9").

SETTING DISC PROPERTIES

Importing Assets

Assets anchor source files to your project. When you import a new source file into DVD Studio Pro, the file itself does not come into the program. Instead, an asset is created that shows DVD Studio Pro how to locate the source file. When DVD Studio Pro needs this source file it follows the path set by the asset, and grabs the source file from your hard disks.

While this setup may initially seem confusing, it provides great flexibility. You can, for example, easily change an asset's source file, which comes in handy if you discover a source file has been encoded incorrectly or is otherwise unsuitable for your project (to learn more, see "Replacing Source Files" later in this chapter).

For each source file that you import into DVD Studio Pro, a new asset is added at the bottom of the Assets container. Not every file is fit to be an asset, and DVD Studio Pro is very selective about the type of files it accepts. **Table 6.1** lists the file types that DVD Studio Pro understands, along with their corresponding file extensions.

To add an asset:

1. Click the Assets container to make it active.

2. Choose Item > New Asset (**Figure 6.10**), or press Command-K.

   The Open File dialog box appears (**Figure 6.11**).

3. Navigate to a source media file and click Choose.

   A new asset is created at the bottom of the Assets container.

Table 6.1

Asset Source Files	
FILE TYPE	FILE EXTENSION
AC-3	.ac3
AIFF	.aif
MPEG-1 video	.mpg
MPEG-1 audio	.mp2
MPEG-2 video	.m2v, .mpg, .mpv
Photoshop	.psd
PICT file	.pct
Wave	.wav
SoundDesigner	.sd2
Subtitles	.spu

Figure 6.10 To add a new asset, select the Assets container and choose Item > New Asset.

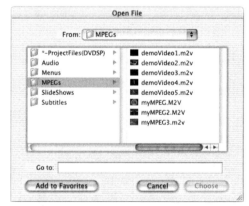

Figure 6.11 The Open File dialog box lets you add individual assets to the Assets container.

Figure 6.12 To expedite asset import, drag multiple files from the Finder straight into DVD Studio Pro's Assets container.

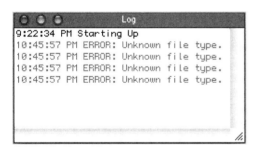

Figure 6.13 If you accidentally drag an unrecognizable file into DVD Studio Pro, the Log window opens and displays an error message (printed in red).

To drag files into the Assets container:

1. In the Finder, select a source media file. If you want to add more than one source file at a time, hold down the Shift key while selecting multiple files.

2. Drag the files directly into the Assets container and release the mouse (**Figure 6.12**).

✔ Tip

- If you drag a file that DVD Studio Pro doesn't recognize into the Assets container, the Log window opens to alert you that an error has occurred (**Figure 6.13**).

Figure 6.14 Keep all of your source media well organized! This figure shows a folder hierarchy that has one separate folder for each type of source file used in a DVD-Video project (including a folder for the project files themselves).

Asset File Management

DVD-Video projects can get very complex and may use several dozen (or more) source files. Before you begin authoring, gather all of your source files in one folder, with each file placed in an appropriately named subdirectory, as shown in **Figure 6.14**. This keeps all of your source media organized and in a central location, saving you innumerable headaches when it comes time to archive your project and delete the source files after you've finished authoring.

To add multiple assets in Mac OS X:

1. Choose File > Import (**Figure 6.15**), or press Command-I.

   The Import Files dialog box opens (**Figure 6.16**).

2. Navigate to the directory that contains the source media files. Select a file and *do one of the following:*

   ▲ To select multiple sequential files, hold down the Shift key and select a second file (**Figure 6.17**).

   or

   ▲ To select noncontiguous files, hold down the Command key and select one or more new files (**Figure 6.18**).

3. Click Import.

   The Import Files dialog box closes. For every selected file, a new asset is created at the bottom of the Assets container.

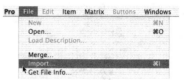

Figure 6.15 To import multiple source files into DVD Studio Pro 1.5 for Mac OS X, choose File > Import.

Figure 6.16 The Import Files dialog box.

Figure 6.17 Select multiple sequential files by holding down the Shift key as you click file names.

Figure 6.18 Select noncontiguous files by holding down the Command key as you click file names.

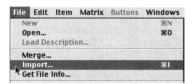

Figure 6.19 To import multiple source files into DVD Studio Pro 1.5 for Mac OS 9, choose File > Import.

— Source Files list   *Import Assets list —*

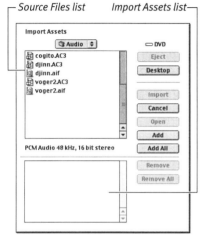

Figure 6.20 The Import Assets dialog box shows source files in the top list and files to be imported in the Import Assets list at the bottom. The buttons down the side let you add one or all source files to the Import Assets list, or remove them.

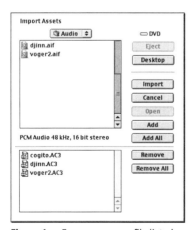

Figure 6.21 For every source file listed in the bottom pane of the Import Assets dialog box, a new asset is created in the Assets container.

To add multiple assets in Mac OS 9:

1. Choose File > Import (**Figure 6.19**), or press Command-I.

   The Import Assets dialog box opens (**Figure 6.20**).

2. Navigate to the directory that contains the source media files. Select a file and *do one of the following:*

   ▲ To add the file to the Import Assets list, click Add.

   or

   ▲ To add all files from the folder to the Import Assets list, click Add All.

   The added files appear in the Import Assets list of the Import Assets dialog box (**Figure 6.21**).

3. Click Import.

   For every selected file, a new asset is created at the bottom of the Assets container.

✔ Tips

- Mac OS 9 allows you to import source files from many different folders at one time. If need be, you may navigate to new folders and add as many assets as desired to the Import Assets list.

- If you add a file to the Import Assets list, but then decide you don't want to import it, select the file and click Remove. In a similar fashion, you can remove all assets from the Import Assets list by clicking the Remove All button.

IMPORTING ASSETS

129

Renaming Assets

Each asset is automatically named after its source file, and in most situations you won't change this name. If you do decide your assets need different names, re-label them using the Property Inspector's Name text box.

To change an asset's name:

1. Select the asset from either the Assets container or the Project View.

   The asset is highlighted, and the Property Inspector updates to display the asset's properties.

2. In the Asset area at the top of the Property Inspector, enter a new name in the Name text box (**Figure 6.22**).

   In the Assets container, the asset's name changes.

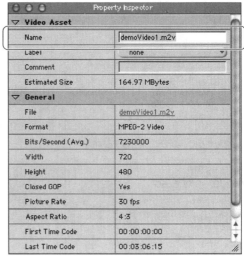

Figure 6.22 To change an asset's name, select it in the Assets container and then enter a new name into the Property Inspector's Name text box.

Replacing Source Files

Occasionally while authoring in DVD Studio Pro, you will need to replace an asset's source file. For example, you may notice an AC-3 file was encoded using incorrect dialog normalization settings, or that an MPEG asset displays compression artifacts. To correct the problem, re-encode the files and then replace the asset's old source file with the properly encoded one.

Look out for two things when replacing an asset's source file:

◆ If you're adding an MPEG or audio file with a higher bit rate than the old one, recalculate the total bit rate of any Track or Slideshow tiles containing the asset and ensure that the total bit rate stays below 10.08 Mbps.

◆ If you switch the source file of an MPEG asset that belongs to a track with markers, the markers break away from their anchor points (I-frames) in the original file and will need to be reattached. To learn more, see the sidebar "Reattaching Markers."

Reattaching Markers

If you switch the source file of an MPEG asset that belongs to a track with markers, the track's name becomes italicized, and you cannot preview or build the project (see Chapter 10, "Creating Markers and Stories"). The problem rests with the track's markers, which are attached to specific I-frames from the original source file. Assigning a new source file removes these I-frames, and the markers get confused. To fix this problem, open the Marker editor and wiggle the markers back and forth. The markers will *snap* onto new I-frames and you'll now be able to preview and build your project.

To replace an asset's source file:

1. Select the asset in the Assets container. The asset is highlighted.

2. In the General section of the Property Inspector, locate the File property (**Figure 6.23**).

   The File property indicates the name of the asset's source file. This file name is blue and underlined.

3. Click the underlined file name.

   The Open File dialog box appears. Use this dialog box to find a new source file for the selected asset (**Figure 6.24**).

4. Navigate to a new source file and click Choose.

   The selected source file is assigned to the asset.

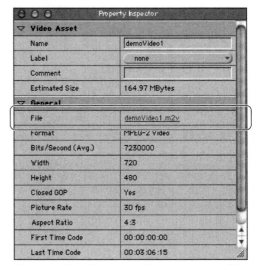

Figure 6.23 The File property displays the name of the asset's source file. To change the source file associated with an asset, click the underlined file name.

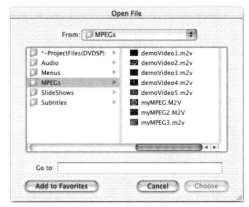

Figure 6.24 The Open File dialog box lets you choose a new asset source file.

Using the Asset Files Window

The Asset Files window lists all of your project's assets and also shows you their locations on your hard disks (**Figure 6.25**). This window is primarily used for two purposes:

◆ Assigning new source files to several assets at one time

◆ Locating missing assets (usually upon opening a project)

Figure 6.25 The Asset Files window lets you choose new source files for your project's assets.

Using Placeholders

The Asset Files window is particularly useful for replacing *placeholders* (low-bit-rate representations of the project's final source files). Placeholders lighten your project's overall data rate, which is particularly important when previewing menus and DVD-9 projects:

Previewing menus. If you're testing your menus' interactivity, you won't want to sit through a long MPEG stream after each menu button is clicked. Develop your menus using 5- or 10-second placeholders instead of the final MPEG streams. When you have the menu working correctly, use the Asset Files window to assign the proper source file to each asset.

Previewing DVD-9 projects. One problem with DVD-9 projects is that you can't write them to a DVD-5 DVD-R disc. Here's where placeholders really come to the rescue. Encode your source files twice, the first time at normal bit rates and the second time using severely lowered bit rates (for example, a bit rate of 2 Mbps for MPEGs). Author the project with the low-bit-rate placeholders. Build the project to a DVD-R disc and watch it on a DVD player attached to a TV. It will look terrible, but if everything works, you can confidently return to DVD Studio Pro and replace the placeholders with the properly encoded source files.

To open the Asset Files window:

◆ Choose Item > Asset Files (**Figure 6.26**). The Asset Files window opens (refer to Figure 6.25).

To assign a new source file to an asset:

1. Choose Item > Asset Files to open the Asset Files window.

2. Select an asset from the Asset List (**Figure 6.27**).
   The asset is highlighted.

3. Click the Assign button.
   The Open File dialog box appears.

4. Locate the new source file and click Choose.
   The selected asset's old source file is replaced with the new one.

✔ Tip

■ If you click the Locate button instead of the Assign button, the Locate File dialog box opens. This dialog box performs similarly to the Assign File dialog box, but is used only to locate a missing source file. As a result, it only displays files with exactly the same name as the missing one.

Figure 6.26 To open the Asset Files window, choose Item > Asset Files.

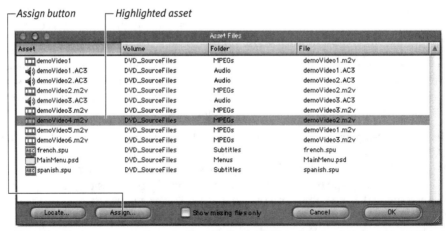

Figure 6.27 To change an asset's source file using the Asset Files window, select an asset and click the Assign button.

USING TRACKS

Tracks are used to synchronize video and audio streams. In a basic configuration, a Track tile holds one video and one audio stream—sort of like a VHS video. In conjunction with one or two menus, this is often all you need (indeed, many commercial DVD-Videos use little more than one video and audio track). The beautiful thing about DVD-Video, however, is that it provides choices. With DVD Studio Pro, you can go beyond no-frills VHS-like presentations. In fact, each track can hold up to nine video and eight audio streams that viewers can cycle through simply by clicking buttons on their remote controls.

When you supply a track with alternate video streams, you create *alternate angles*. Alternate angles were originally designed to show the same scene from different vantage points, but they can also be used for more creative purposes. A DVD-Video of a live DJ set, for example, could have the main stream showing the DJ spinning records while several other angles play computer-generated graphics.

Alternate audio tracks work much the same way. Although designed to hold alternate-language versions of the same audio program, they are equally as effective at supplying entirely different audio programs. Think of a meditation DVD-Video. A viewer may eventually get tired of listening to the sound of a trickling brook. In this case, wouldn't it be nice to also supply the sounds of an alpine forest or tropical seashore? Don't you feel relaxed already? Using alternate audio tracks, viewers can choose the audio streams that match their moods, and this adds a lot of value to your DVD-Video.

But alternate video and audio streams do consume bandwidth and disc space, so you must plan accordingly. Also, if you're using alternate video angles, you must encode the MPEG streams following specific rules or they will not work properly. This chapter tells you what those rules are, so read on to begin confidently adding alternate video and audio streams to your projects.

About Track Tiles

Track tiles have a thumbnail area and five container icons (**Figure 7.1**). The thumbnail area provides a visual clue to the track's content, and the container icons, when clicked, open containers used to organize the track's audio streams, subtitles, markers, stories, and alternate angles.

To create a Track tile:

1. In the lower left corner of the Graphical View, click the Add Track button (**Figure 7.2**).

   A new Track tile is created in the Graphical View, and the Property Inspector updates to display the track's properties.

2. From the Track Property Inspector's Asset menu, choose an MPEG asset (**Figure 7.3**).

   The MPEG asset is assigned as the main video stream for that track.

✔ Tips

■ All DVD-Video titles must have at least one Track tile, or some DVD-Video players will not play the disc.

■ Some DVD-Video players have a counter that displays a number corresponding to the currently playing track. These numbers are assigned to tracks in the same order the tracks are created.

■ If you create your tracks in the wrong order, you can rearrange them in the Project View. Tracks are written to the DVD disc in the same order as they appear in the Project View's Tracks tab. The first track is track 1, the second is track 2, and so on.

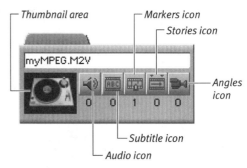

Figure 7.1 The Track tile.

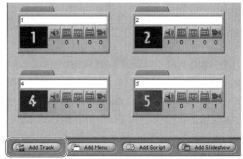

Figure 7.2 The Add Track button adds an unnamed Track tile to the Graphical View.

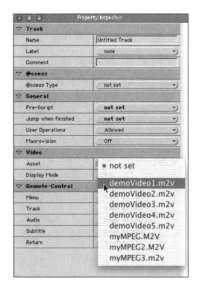

Figure 7.3 Use the Track Property Inspector's Asset menu to assign a track's MPEG asset.

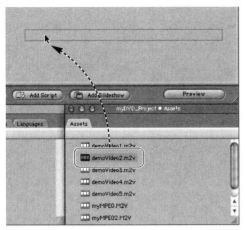

Figure 7.4 To quickly create a Track tile, drag an MPEG asset from the Assets container directly into the Graphical View.

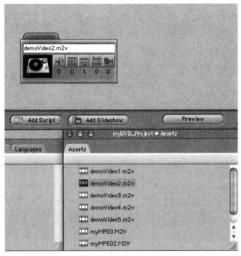

Figure 7.5 When you drop an MPEG asset into the Graphical View, the newly created Track tile assumes the same name as the MPEG asset.

To create a Track tile using drag and drop:

◆ From the Assets container, drag an MPEG asset into the Graphical View (**Figure 7.4**).

A new Track tile is created with the MPEG video assigned as its asset (**Figure 7.5**).

✔ Tip

■ When you drag an MPEG asset into the Graphical View, the new Track tile is given the same name as its MPEG asset. To change a track's name, type a new name in the Name text box at the top of the tile.

ABOUT TRACK TILES

Changing thumbnails

By default, the Track tile's thumbnail area displays the first frame of its primary MPEG asset. Unfortunately, sticking with the default often results in a non-descript black thumbnail because videos tend to fade in from black. To give your thumbnail more meaning, use DVD Studio Pro's Change Thumbnail option.

To change a track's thumbnail:

1. In the Graphical View, select a Track tile.

2. Choose Item > Change Thumbnail (**Figure 7.6**).

   The Thumbnail editor opens (**Figure 7.7**). Along the bottom of this editor is a thumbnail marker.

3. Drag the thumbnail marker along the slider until the editor displays the video frame you want to have represent your track.

4. Click OK.

   The track's thumbnail area updates to show the selected frame.

✔ Tip

- The QuickTime MPEG Encoder automatically makes thumbnail images for your MPEG-2 streams. If you've created a track out of an MPEG-1 video or an MPEG-2 video that was not compressed by the QuickTime MPEG Encoder, the track's thumbnail area may be blank. To fix this, choose Item > Update Thumbnails.

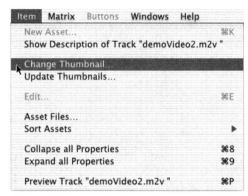

Figure 7.6 To change the picture displayed in a tile's thumbnail area, choose Item > Change Thumbnail.

└─*Thumbnail marker* └─*Slider*

Figure 7.7 Drag the Thumbnail editor's thumbnail marker along the slider until you find the frame that you want to have visually represent the track.

Figure 7.8 The Preview button launches DVD Studio Pro's Preview mode.

Previewing tracks

After creating a track and assigning it an MPEG asset, use DVD Studio Pro's Preview mode to see how it looks.

To preview a track:

1. In the Graphical View, select a Track tile. The Track tile is highlighted.

2. In the lower right corner of the Graphical View, click the Preview button (**Figure 7.8**).

   DVD Studio Pro's Preview mode launches and plays the track.

Troubleshooting Preview Mode

If the Preview mode does not launch, there is a problem with your track. To verify this, look at the track's Name text box. If the name is printed in italics, something is not right (**Figure 7.9**). First, check to see that an MPEG asset has been assigned to the track. Next, click the container icons to open them, checking for any items printed in italics (9 out of 10 times, the problem will be in the Marker container). If you see an italicized item, you've found the source of the problem. Fix the item, and you can then preview the track.

Figure 7.9 Uh, oh; this track's name is printed in italics. This means that there is a problem with the track, and it cannot be previewed.

Linking Tracks

DVD Studio Pro links each newly created track to the one that was created just before it, with the final track linked back to the first. This rarely reflects the way your project actually flows. For example, if you've jumped into the track from a menu, you'll most likely want to jump back to that menu after the track has finished playing. To do so, use the Jump When Finished track property (**Figure 7.10**).

To set the Jump When Finished property:

1. In the Graphical View (or the Project View), select a Track tile.

   The Track tile is highlighted, and the Property Inspector updates to show the track's properties.

2. From the Property Inspector's Jump When Finished menu, choose an item (refer to Figure 7.10).

   When the track finishes playing, the DVD-Video jumps to the selected project item.

✔ Tip

■ When finished playing, tracks can jump to menus, scripts, slideshows, or even chapters in other tracks.

Figure 7.10 The Jump When Finished track property tells the DVD-Video where to go once the track has finished playing.

Figure 7.11 The Wait After Playback track property appears only if you've supplied the track with a Jump When Finished value.

Figure 7.12 To set a delay after the track finishes playing, choose Wait x Seconds from the Wait After Playback menu.

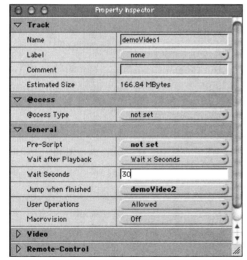

Figure 7.13 In the Wait Seconds text box, enter a value between 1 and 254.

Using Wait After Playback

If you've provided a track with a Jump When Finished property, the Wait After Playback track property appears in the Property Inspector (**Figure 7.11**). After the track has finished playing, the Wait After Playback property causes your DVD-Video to pause for a certain number of seconds before it jumps to the assigned item. How long does it wait? Well, that's up to you, but the time cannot exceed 254 seconds (just over four minutes).

To set a Wait After Playback value:

1. Assign a track a Jump When Finished value as described in the previous task, "To set the Jump When Finished property."

   The Wait After Playback track property appears in the Property Inspector (refer to Figure 7.11).

2. From the Wait After Playback menu, choose Wait x Seconds (**Figure 7.12**).

   The Wait Seconds track property appears in the Property Inspector.

3. Enter a value in the Wait Seconds text box (**Figure 7.13**).

   When the track finishes playing, the DVD-Video waits the specified number of seconds before jumping to the item specified by the Jump When Finished property.

✔ Tip

- The Wait After Playback property is particularly useful if you string several tracks together. It's good to provide your viewers with a few seconds to digest what they've just watched. By setting the Wait After Playback property, you provide this time by creating a pause between the fade out at the end of the first video and the fade in at the beginning of the second.

LINKING TRACKS

141

Alternate Angle Tracks

As their name implies, alternate angles provide alternate views of sporting events, instructional videos, live concert footage, or any other visual display where you might want to see an object from different vantage points. Each track can hold up to eight alternate angles on top of the main MPEG video stream—that's a total of nine separate MPEG video streams per track.

Encoding multi-angle MPEGs

For multi-angle tracks to work properly, the GOPs from each MPEG stream must line up. Consequently, all MPEG streams destined for multi-angle playback should be encoded *exactly* the same way.

Here are a few rules to keep in mind as you encode your multi-angle MPEG video streams:

◆ Each alternate angle must be exactly the same length as the track's primary MPEG video stream.

◆ Each alternate angle should be compressed using exactly the same bit rate settings. You can mix bit rate settings, but doing so is generally not recommended.

◆ Each alternate angle must have the same resolution and frame rate. If you're trying to mix MPEG-1 and MPEG-2 video angles, it's just not going to work (MPEG-1 is usually 352 x 240 pixels, whereas MPEG-2 is 720 x 480 pixels).

◆ Each alternate angle must be encoded with closed GOPs. The QuickTime MPEG Encoder automatically creates closed GOPs. If you're using a different MPEG compression utility, such as Cleaner 5 with MPEG Charger, make sure you don't create open GOPs.

◆ Each alternate angle must have GOPs of corresponding lengths so that all I-frames line up in exactly the same places (see the sidebar titled "Final Cut Pro Markers and Multi-Angle MPEGs").

About multi-angle bit rates

As mentioned earlier, all multi-angle MPEG streams must be compressed at exactly the same bit rate. To make sure your DVD-Video plays back on the widest range of DVD-Video players, you should encode all angles at less than 7 Mbps (see Chapter 3, "Encoding Video Streams"). If you're the type who insists your MPEG streams be compressed at the highest possible bit rate, be warned that multi-angle MPEGs face a few extra limitations. Apple suggests that you do not exceed the following bit rates for MPEGs used in multi-angle tracks:

Five angles or less. 8 Mbps maximum for each multi-angle MPEG stream.

Six to eight angles. 7.5 Mbps maximum for each multi-angle MPEG stream.

Nine angles. 7 Mbps maximum for each multi-angle MPEG stream.

Final Cut Pro Markers and Multi-Angle MPEGs

If you've used Final Cut Pro to set your own chapter and/or compression markers, you must be sure to place markers on the same frames of *all* multi-angle MPEG streams (Chapter 3, "Encoding Video Streams," discusses setting compression and chapter markers using Final Cut Pro). If you don't set markers on exactly the same frames, the I-frames in the various multi-angle MPEG streams will not match, and you will be unable to preview the track or build your final DVD-Video project. Attempting to do so causes an error (**Figure 7.14**).

As you can see, encoding multi-angle MPEG streams directly from Final Cut Pro can be difficult. Consequently, it's usually easier to render a Final Cut reference movie with *no* markers and then use the QuickTime MPEG Encoder to compress your multi-angle MPEG-2 streams (Final Cut Pro reference movies are discussed at the end of Chapter 3).

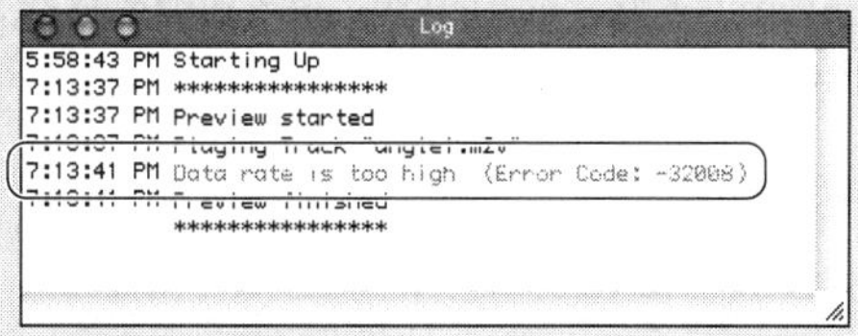

Figure 7.14 If the GOPs in your alternate angles don't align, this "Data rate is too high" error occurs, and you will be unable to preview or build your project.

Creating multi-angle tracks

The hard part of creating multi-angle tracks is remembering all the do's and don'ts while encoding your MPEG streams. Once you import those streams into DVD Studio Pro, creating a multi-angle track is as easy as dragging MPEG assets into a track's Angles container.

Figure 7.15 Click the Angles icon to open the track's Angles container.

To create a multi-angle track:

1. On a Track tile, click the Angles icon (**Figure 7.15**).

   The Angles container opens.

2. Drag an MPEG asset from the Assets container and drop it into the Angles container (**Figure 7.16**).

   A new angle is added to the track.

✔ Tip

- If you can't get the MPEG asset to drop in the Angles container, you've encoded the asset incorrectly. For example, the angle may be a different length than the track's primary MPEG asset, or its GOPs may not line up or may be of a different size.

To change an angle's MPEG asset:

1. On a Track tile, click the Angles icon.

   The Angles container opens.

2. In the Angles container, select an angle (**Figure 7.17**).

   The Property Inspector updates to show the angle's properties.

3. From the Angle Property Inspector's Asset menu, select a new MPEG asset (**Figure 7.18**).

   The new MPEG asset is assigned to the angle.

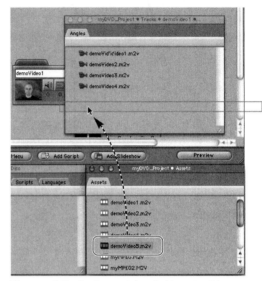

Figure 7.16 The Angles container holds up to eight alternate angles. To create a new angle, drag an MPEG asset from the Assets container into the Angles container.

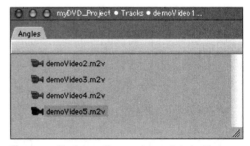

Figure 7.17 To change the asset associated with an angle, first select the angle in the Angles container.

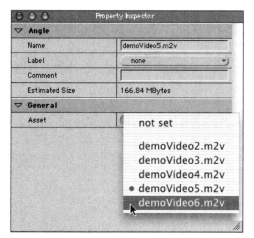

Figure 7.18 Next, use the Property Inspector's Asset menu to choose a new MPEG asset.

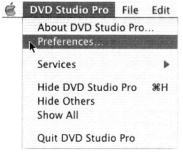

Figure 7.19 Open the Preferences window by choosing DVD Studio Pro > Preferences...

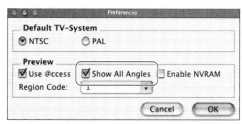

Figure 7.20 ...Then select the Show All Angles check box. The Preview mode will now play all angles.

Previewing multi-angle tracks

To preview multi-angle tracks you must make sure you've set DVD Studio Pro's preferences to allow multi-angle playback.

To enable the Show All Angles preference:

1. In Mac OS X, choose DVD Studio Pro > Preferences (**Figure 7.19**).

   or

   In Mac OS 9, choose Edit > Preferences.

2. In the Preview section of the Preferences window, select the Show All Angles check box (**Figure 7.20**).

   The Preview mode allows the display of alternate angles.

ALTERNATE ANGLE TRACKS

To preview a multi-angle track:

1. In the Graphical View, select the multi-angle track that you want to preview.

2. In the lower right corner of the Graphical View, click the Preview button.
   DVD Studio Pro's Preview mode launches.

3. To switch angles while previewing the track, click the Angle button (**Figure 7.21**).
   The Preview mode switches angles.
   In the upper right corner of the Preview mode, the Angle counter updates to show you which angle you are viewing (**Figure 7.22**).

✔ Tips

- Tracks change angles at GOP headers, or I-frames. If you notice a slight pause between when you hit the Angle button and when the track changes angles, it's because the current GOP must finish playing before the next one is swapped in (this is also the reason why GOPs from all the track's alternate angles must line up).

- If you experience problems while previewing a multi-angle track, it's most likely due to unaligned GOPs in your MPEG streams. Unfortunately, you'll need to go back and re-encode each MPEG stream, making sure that you use the same settings for each one.

Figure 7.21 If you've supplied a track with alternate angles, click the Angle button to cycle through them in the Preview mode.

Preview mode's angle counter

Figure 7.22 The Preview mode's angle counter shows you which angle you are currently watching.

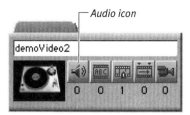

Figure 7.23 Click the Audio icon to open the track's Audio Streams container.

Figure 7.24 With the track's Audio Streams container open, create a new audio stream by choosing Item > New Audio Stream.

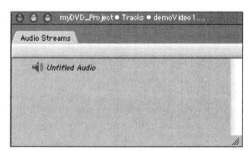

Figure 7.25 A newly created, untitled audio stream. This audio stream does not have an audio asset assigned to it, so its name is printed in italics.

Adding Audio Streams

If you haven't read Chapter 4, "Encoding Audio Streams," go there now. There are many things you need to know to create audio that plays smoothly, and all of them are covered in that chapter. If you've already memorized Chapter 4, then it's time to add audio to your tracks.

To add an audio stream to a track (using the Audio Stream container):

1. In the Graphical View, click the track's Audio icon (**Figure 7.23**).

   The Audio container opens.

2. Choose Item > New Audio Stream (**Figure 7.24**), or press Command-K.

   An untitled audio stream is added to the Audio Streams container (**Figure 7.25**). At this point, there is no audio asset attached to the stream, which causes the stream's name to appear italicized. Until you assign an asset to the stream, you will not be able to preview the track or build your final project.

3. In the Audio Streams container, select the untitled audio stream.

   The untitled audio stream is highlighted, and the Property Inspector updates to show the untitled audio stream's properties.

   continues on next page

ADDING AUDIO STREAMS

4. From the Property Inspector's Asset menu, select an audio asset for the audio stream (**Figure 7.26**).

The audio asset is assigned to the stream, and you can now preview the track or build your final project. Back in the Audio Streams container, the untitled audio stream is no longer italicized.

✔ Tips

■ Make sure that you name all of your audio streams. In the Audio Streams container, select an audio stream and use the Property Inspector's Name text box to name it.

■ You can also add audio streams by dragging them from the Assets container and dropping them in the Audio container.

To add an audio stream to a track (using the Project View):

1. In the Project View, select the Tracks tab.

2. Find the track to which you want to add an audio stream and click its disclosure triangle.

The track expands to display its subcontainers.

3. From the Assets container, drag an audio asset into the Project View and drop it on the track's Audio Streams subcontainer (**Figure 7.27**).

The number under the Audio Stream button increases by one, and the audio stream is added to the Track tile.

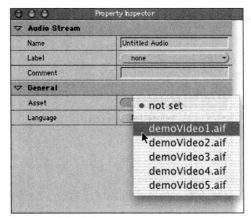

Figure 7.26 The Audio Stream Property Inspector's Asset menu.

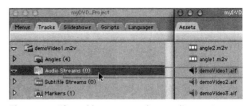

Figure 7.27 If need be, you can drag audio assets from the Assets container and drop them onto a track's Audio Streams container in the Project View.

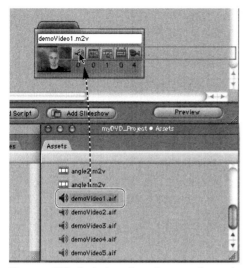

Figure 7.28 The fastest way to assign an audio asset to a track is to simply drag it from the Assets container and drop it directly onto the tile's Audio icon.

To add an audio stream to a track (using the Audio icon):

1. In the Graphical View, locate the Track tile to which you want to add an audio stream.

2. From the Assets container, drag an audio asset and drop it directly onto the Track tile's Audio icon (**Figure 7.28**).

   The number under the Audio Stream button increases by one, and the audio stream is added to the Track tile.

Alternate Audio Streams

You can add up to eight audio streams to each Track tile, creating *alternate audio streams*. Alternate audio streams are primarily used to supply alternate languages for DVD-Video projects (see the sidebar titled "Using Multiple Languages"), but there are also plenty of other, more creative uses for alternate audio streams. Any DVD-Video, for example, could let viewers select among background soundscapes that match their moods or that contain bonus commentary adding insight into the topic at hand.

Using alternate audio streams

Unlike alternate angle streams, all alternate audio streams are multiplexed together with the track's primary MPEG video stream. This decreases the seek time needed to switch between audio streams, but increases the DVD's data rate. If you use alternate audio streams, you must budget them into the track's overall bit rate.

Here's an example: DVD-Video titles have a maximum bit rate of 10.08 Mbps. If your MPEG video is compressed at 8 Mbps, this leaves only 2.08 Mbps for the audio (and sub-picture) streams associated with that track. That's enough room for only four 5.1 surround AC-3 streams encoded at 448 kbps.

Problems will arise if you use multiple linear PCM audio streams. PCM audio is uncompressed and suffers from extremely high data rates. For example, a stereo, 16-bit, 48 kHz AIFF has a bit rate of 1,500 kbps! That's higher than three 5.1 AC-3 streams combined. If you're using alternate audio streams, use A.Pack to convert your PCM files to more efficient AC-3 audio streams (to learn more about A.Pack, see Chapter 4, "Encoding Audio Streams").

Using Multiple Languages

Using alternate language tracks, you can easily incorporate English, French, Spanish, and any other language into your project. Viewers can switch between language tracks by pressing the Audio button on their remote controls. Even better, depending on how the DVD-Video player has been set up, the player can dynamically select the correct language. To learn more about working with languages, see Chapter 15, "Working with Multiple Languages."

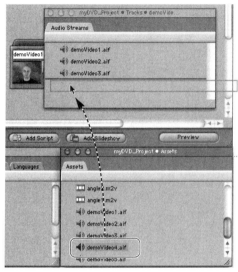

Figure 7.29 If you use too many audio streams, you will exceed the maximum DVD-Video data rate of 10.08 Mbps. This is most likely to happen when you are using multiple linear PCM audio streams.

Figure 7.30 Creating alternate audio streams is as easy as dragging audio assets into a track's Audio Streams container.

✔ Tips

■ Alternate audio streams can cause a track's data rate to exceed the 10.08 Mbps limit for DVD-Video. Should this occur, you will be unable to preview the track or build the final DVD-Video (**Figure 7.29**).

■ Ensure that you have enough bandwidth for all of your alternate audio streams by creating a bit budget. To learn more, see Appendix B, "Making a Bit Budget."

To add an alternate audio stream to a track:

1. Click the track's Audio icon.

   The Audio Streams container opens.

2. From the Assets container, drag one or more audio assets into the Audio Streams container (**Figure 7.30**).

   For each audio asset that you drag into the Audio Streams container, a new audio stream is added to the track.

To preview alternate audio streams:

1. In the Graphical View, select a track with alternate audio streams.

2. In the lower right corner of the Graphical View, click the Preview button.

   DVD Studio Pro's Preview mode launches.

3. To switch audio streams while previewing the track, click the Audio button (**Figure 7.31**).

   The Preview mode switches audio streams. In the upper right corner of the Preview mode, the Audio counter updates to show you which audio stream you are currently listening to (**Figure 7.32**).

✔ Tip

- To change the order of alternate audio streams, open the Audio Streams container and drag audio streams up or down the list.

Figure 7.31 To cycle through alternate audio streams in the Preview mode, click the Audio button.

Audio counter ⌐

Figure 7.32 The Preview mode's Audio counter shows you which audio stream is currently playing.

PHOTOSHOP LAYER MENUS

Your DVD-Video is only as good as its worst menu; after all, without menus there's little difference between a DVD-Video and its VHS counterpart. Because so much rides on how your menus look, you must make sure they look as good as possible. There are a few tricks, however, to getting still images designed on a computer to look right on a television. The first part of this chapter explains those tricks and shows you how to accomplish them in Adobe Photoshop.

If you don't have Photoshop, don't worry. The DVD Studio Pro DVD-ROM disc contains Corel PhotoPaint 10, which is perfectly capable of creating multilayer Photoshop files that DVD Studio Pro understands. Although some of the steps in this chapter work differently in PhotoPaint than in Photoshop, you should have little trouble making the translation.

By their very nature, Photoshop layer menus cannot include video clips or audio, but if that's what you want in a menu, you're not entirely out of luck. DVD Studio Pro lets you create two types of menus: Photoshop layer menus and highlight menus. Highlight menus, while not as graphically engaging as Photoshop layer menus, react more quickly and accept both audio and MPEG-2 video clips. If your menu is crying out for sound or motion, jump straight to Chapter 9, "Highlight Menus." Otherwise, flip the page and get acquainted with layers.

Using Photoshop

DVD Studio Pro imports Photoshop files, but that's as far as the Photoshop file goes. When DVD Studio Pro compiles your project, it takes your menus and turns them into *MPEG-2 stills*, which are encoded much like I-frames.

Consequently, you must treat Photoshop documents as if they were video frames. All of the same rules apply, including title safe areas and color saturation requirements (these rules are discussed in Chapter 3, "Encoding Video Streams"). However, there is one big difference between Photoshop files and video frames: Photoshop uses square pixels to represent images, while the pixels in an NTSC video frame are slightly taller than they are wide. Unless you compensate for this difference in pixel aspect ratio, stills from Photoshop will look thin on a television.

Understanding pixels

Computers use perfectly square pixels (with an aspect ratio of 1:1), while televisions use non-square pixels (with an aspect ratio of 0.9:1 for NTSC and 1.07:1 for PAL). If you show square pixels on a television set, the TV stretches the pixels, making them taller than they are wide. Graphics designed in Photoshop will appear slightly anorexic when displayed on a television, unless you do something to compensate for the slimming effect (**Figure 8.1**).

The difference between the aspect ratio of square and nonsquare pixels remains constant, so you can compensate by designing Photoshop graphics at a larger resolution and then resizing them to the dimensions of the video standard you are working with (NTSC or PAL). The files will look squashed in Photoshop, but when you play them on a television, the TV will stretch them back to their original proportions.

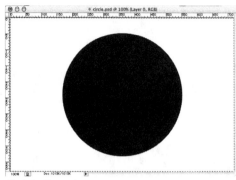

Circle in Photoshop

Circle in DVD Studio Pro's Preview mode

Figure 8.1 The difference between square and nonsquare pixels is best demonstrated by circles. In this figure, the circle looks perfect in Photoshop, but appears stretched in DVD Studio Pro's Preview mode.

USING PHOTOSHOP

Preset Sizes menu

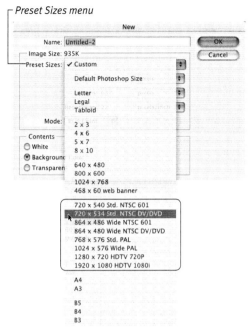

Figure 8.2 Photoshop 7's new video document presets. For your DVD-Video menus, you usually choose 720 x 534 Std. NTSC DV/DVD.

In Photoshop, design your menus as follows:

◆ For NTSC, create the Photoshop menu at 720 x 534 pixels and resize it to 720 x 480 pixels.

◆ For PAL, create the Photoshop menu at 768 x 576 pixels and resize it to 720 x 576 pixels.

✔ Tip

■ Many people begin their Photoshop documents at 720 x 540 and then resize to 720 x 480. While this works, it's not recommended. Although 720 x 540 is the correct square pixel dimensions for D1 NTSC video, DVD uses DV NTSC video. There's a slight difference between the frame size of the two. To learn more, see the sidebar "D1 vs. DV NTSC."

D1 vs. DV NTSC

As if all of the various dimensions, resolutions, and aspect ratios aren't enough to worry about, you must also contend with two forms of NTSC video, each using different dimensions. DV NTSC, the format used for DVD-Video, measures 720 x 480 pixels. D1 NTSC, the other type of NTSC video, measures 720 x 486 pixels—an extra 6 pixels taller! If you're working with D1 NTSC video, create your Photoshop documents at 720 x 540 and then resize them to 720 x 486. Before you bring the documents into DVD Studio Pro, crop off the top six lines to make them 720 x 480.

For those of you who like math and are wondering what the difference is, think of it this way: NTSC televisions use pixels with an aspect ratio of 0.9:1. Multiplying 540 by 0.9 equals 486—that's D1 NTSC. Multiplying 534 by 0.9 gets you 480, which is DV NTSC (well, it's actually equal to 480.6, but what's a few tenths among friends?).

To help you keep everything straight, Photoshop 7 has introduced several new preset document sizes in the New Document dialog box's Preset Sizes menu (**Figure 8.2**). Use these presets to ensure that you always create new documents with the correct dimensions.

To resize a Photoshop file:

1. Create a 720 x 534 pixel Photoshop file.

2. Choose Image > Image Size (**Figure 8.3**). The Image Size dialog box opens.

3. From the lower left corner of the Image Size dialog box, deselect the Constrain Proportions check box (**Figure 8.4**).

4. In the Pixel Dimensions section at the top of the dialog box, enter 480 in the Height text box.

5. Click OK.

   The Photoshop document resizes to 720 x 480.

✔ Tip

- Computer DVD players, including the Apple DVD Player, compensate for rectangular television pixels by resizing the 720 x 480 NTSC frame to 640 x 480.

About pixel density

If you're coming to DVD Studio Pro from a print background, you're used to designing still images at 300 pixels per inch (ppi), or perhaps even higher. If you're from a video or Web background, you're probably more comfortable designing at 72 ppi. Either way, DVD Studio Pro caters to you.

DVD Studio Pro imports Photoshop files of any resolution, so your Photoshop documents can be 72 ppi, 300 ppi, or whatever resolution you feel is needed for your designs (**Figure 8.5**). But this applies only to Photoshop documents. PICT files, the only other still image format accepted by DVD Studio Pro, must be designed at 72 ppi for DVD Studio Pro to display them correctly.

Figure 8.3
To resize a Photoshop document, from within Photoshop choose Image > Image Size.

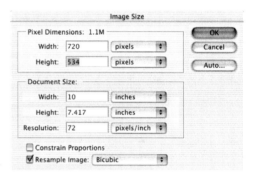

Figure 8.4 The Image Size dialog box lets you change a Photoshop document's dimensions.

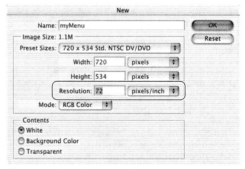

Figure 8.5 Photoshop's New dialog box lets you create new documents at any resolution (ppi) you want. As long as you save the document as a Photoshop file, DVD Studio Pro doesn't care what resolution you choose (PICT files must be 72 ppi only).

Creating title safe areas

The title safe area, used to prevent your video or graphics from getting cropped when played on a TV, is defined by a rectangle set 10 percent in from each edge of the video frame. In NTSC terms, that's 72 pixels from the left and right edges, and 48 pixels from the top and bottom. In Photoshop terms, where you're designing menus at 720 x 534, the title safe area is actually 54 pixels in from the top and bottom edges of the document (**Figure 8.6**). Later, when you resize the document to 720 x 480, the title safe area is reduced to its proper dimensions.

✔ Tips

■ To help you remember what's in bounds and what's out, set up Photoshop guides to define the title safe area. Keeping all text and buttons inside these guides will ensure that they won't be cut off by the edge of a television set.

■ To drag guides onto your Photoshop document, you must be able to see its rulers. Choosing View > Rulers causes rulers to appear along your document's top and left edges. Click and drag a pointer off a ruler to create a guideline for your document.

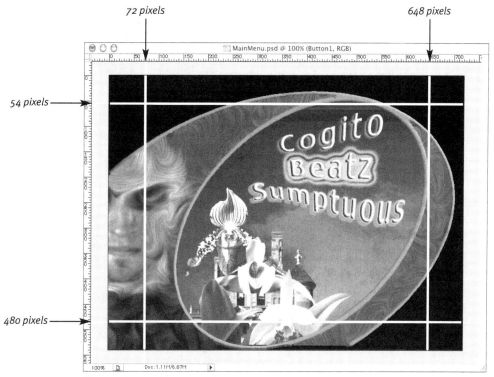

Figure 8.6 Use guides as you design your menus to ensure that all important imagery remains where viewers can see it.

Using layer styles

Photoshop layer styles (drop shadows, embossing, and glows) are not represented as pixels on a Photoshop layer, but are *generated* by Photoshop while the document is open. DVD Studio Pro cannot generate layer styles, so all Photoshop layer styles must be flattened before they are brought into DVD Studio Pro.

Flattening a layer style is not the same as flattening the document. When you flatten a Photoshop document, all layers are collapsed into the document's background. Flattening a layer style, on the other hand, merges the layer style into the layer it is applied to—the rest of the layers remain just as they were. To learn more, see the sidebar "Flattening Photoshop Documents" on the next page.

To flatten a Photoshop layer style:

1. In Photoshop, if the Layers palette isn't already open, choose Windows > Layers.

   The Layers palette opens on your screen, revealing a strip of icons along the bottom of the palette (**Figure 8.7**). The folded page icon beside the Trash is the New Layer icon.

2. Click the New Layer icon.

   A new layer is created in the Layers palette.

3. Drag the new layer underneath the layer containing the layer style (**Figure 8.8**).

   The new layer must be the one on the bottom. For layer styles to flatten, they need to merge down into the layer below.

4. Select the layer with the layer style.

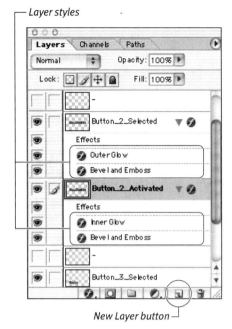

Layer styles

New Layer button

Figure 8.7 Photoshop's Layers palette, displaying a few layers that use layer styles, such as glows and embossing.

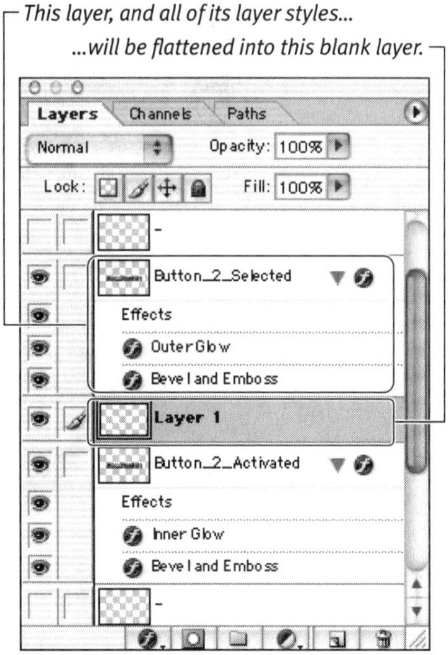

This layer, and all of its layer styles...

...will be flattened into this blank layer.

Figure 8.8 Create a new layer and drag it under the layer that you want to flatten.

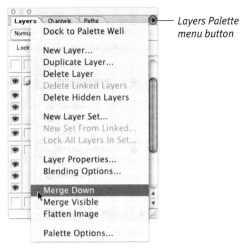

Layers Palette menu button

Figure 8.9 To flatten the layer, click the Layers Palette menu button and choose Merge Down.

5. From the Layers palette menu, choose Merge Down (**Figure 8.9**).

The layer style is flattened into the new layer below. When you bring this Photoshop document into DVD Studio Pro, the layer's drop shadows, embossing, and glows will now be visible.

✔ Tip

■ When you flatten a layer, it assumes the name of the layer it merges into, so be sure to rename the new layer.

Flattening Photoshop Documents

A *flattened layer* is not the same as a *flattened document*. When you flatten a Photoshop document, you merge all of its layers into the *background*. The background, however, is not a layer (**Figure 8.10**), and DVD Studio Pro requires all Photoshop files to have at least one (**Figure 8.11**) layer.

If you flatten a document, you'll need to convert the background to a layer before you can import the document into DVD Studio Pro. To convert the background, go to Photoshop's Layers palette and double-click the background's name. The New Layer dialog box opens to convert the background into a layer.

Figure 8.10 A Photoshop document with only a background actually has no layers.

Figure 8.11 If you try to import a Photoshop file with only a background (no layers) into DVD Studio Pro, the Log window opens to alert you to your error.

Preventing menu flicker

Televisions display interlaced images, in which each video frame is divided into two sets of one-pixel horizontal lines. As the picture flicks by on the television, one set of lines is displayed, then the second, and so on. The result is that at any one time, only half of the lines in your video frame are showing. This has an unfortunate side effect: If any of the horizontal lines in your Photoshop file are one pixel high, they'll appear to flicker on and off. By making all horizontal lines a minimum of three pixels high, you ensure that part of the line is always on the screen, preventing menu flicker.

✔ Tips

- If your still image depends on thin horizontal lines, instead of designing it at 720 x 534 pixels, use 640 x 480 and resize it to 720 x 480 before importing the still image into DVD Studio Pro.

- Flicker can also creep into small text. In general, serif fonts are more prone to flicker than sans-serif fonts, but applying a drop shadow or stroke can help reduce the effect.

About broadcast safe colors

Televisions reproduce millions fewer colors than are available to Photoshop. Saturated colors, such as reds, fluorescent colors, and even pure white and black (super white and super black) cause colors to *bleed* into each other, creating a mushy-looking image (see **Table 8.1**).

Photoshop contains a filter that adjusts colors to fit within the range that can be safely displayed on televisions. This filter is called the NTSC Colors filter. After you finish designing your menu graphics, apply the NTSC Colors filter to each layer in your Photoshop document.

Table 8.1

Broadcast Safe Colors

Color	Standard RGB Value	Broadcast Safe RGB Value
Red	255, 0, 0	204, 0, 0
Green	0, 255, 0	0, 204, 0
Yellow	255, 255, 0	153, 153, 0
Black	0, 0, 0	15, 15, 15
White	255, 255, 255	235, 235, 235

USING PHOTOSHOP

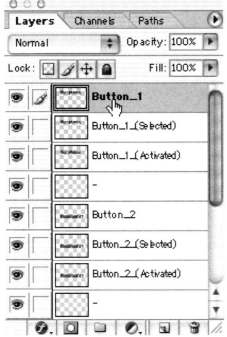

Figure 8.12 Photoshop's filters work on only one layer at a time, so you'll have to apply the NTSC Colors filter to each layer in your document. To ensure that you don't miss a layer, start at the top and work your way down.

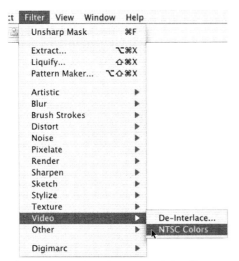

Figure 8.13 Use Photoshop's NTSC Colors filter to ensure that the colors in your Photoshop document are not too saturated for display on a television.

To apply the Photoshop NTSC Colors filter:

1. From the Layers palette, choose the top layer in your Photoshop document (**Figure 8.12**).

2. Choose Select > All (Command-A). The Photoshop layer is selected.

3. Choose Filter > Video > NTSC Colors (**Figure 8.13**).
   The colors on the selected layer become noticeably less saturated.

4. Working down the Layers palette, select each layer in turn and apply the NTSC Colors filter as demonstrated in steps 2 and 3. The NTSC Colors filter works on one layer at a time, so you must apply it to each layer individually.

✔ Tip

- Photoshop's NTSC Colors filter does not adjust the document's black and white areas, so you must do so by hand. White should have RGB values no higher than 235, 235, 235 and black should have RGB values no lower than 15, 15, 15.

- If your menu uses whites and blacks, use the Photoshop Levels dialog box to adjust the color saturation in your documents. In Photoshop, press Command-L to open the Levels dialog box. Near the bottom of the dialog box are two text boxes labeled Output Levels. Set the first box to 15 and the second to 235 and you can rest assured that your colors, including whites and blacks, will all fall within the acceptable broadcast range.

USING PHOTOSHOP

161

About Photoshop Layers

Photoshop layer menus use the layers in a Photoshop document to represent each menu button's three physical states: normal, selected, and activated (**Figure 8.14**). Creating Photoshop layer menus is a fairly straightforward process. In Photoshop, you place all menu graphics (such as the shapes that sit behind the buttons) on the background or bottommost layer of the file. Next, create all of the normal, selected, and activated button states, putting each on its own layer. After you bring the file into DVD Studio Pro, turning these layers on and off creates the effect of changing button states.

✔ Tips

■ Selected and activated button states appear *on top* of the normal state and usually hide the normal state from view. This allows you to merge your normal button states into the background, resulting in fewer layers to deal with in DVD Studio Pro.

■ As you can see, you're going to have a lot of layers. Don't feel like you need to ration them. Photoshop gives you 100 layers to play with, so it's unlikely you'll run out.

■ More than one menu can access the same Photoshop document. If it suits your purposes, you can keep all of the menus for a single project in one Photoshop file.

■ Do not use parentheses in Photoshop layer names or you will be unable to select those layers from DVD Studio Pro's Layers menus (**Figure 8.15**).

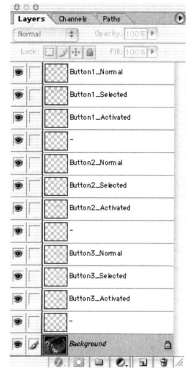

Figure 8.14 Take a moment to look at the layers on this Photoshop Layers palette. Notice how the document's background contains the menu background, while each layer above the background holds a single button state.

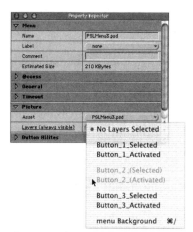

Figure 8.15 If you include parentheses in your layer names, you will not be able to select the layer inside DVD Studio Pro.

Understanding buttons

In Photoshop, you can preview each menu's action by turning layers on and off to see how buttons look when selected and activated. Your DVD-Video does more or less the same thing, except that the viewer turns layers on and off by selecting and activating buttons.

Well, actually, nothing gets turned on or off. In fact, menus work in a rather deceptive way. In Chapter 3, "Encoding Video Streams," you learned that an MPEG I-frame is compressed like a JPEG still image. DVD Studio Pro takes advantage of this fact by turning each button state into an I-frame in the final DVD-Video. Multiplexing the project transforms the menu from a series of layers to a series of I-frames. So when a viewer selects a button, the DVD-Video jumps to the I-frame representing the button's selected state; when the viewer activates the button, the DVD-Video jumps to the activated I-frame, and so on.

✔ Tip

■ Photoshop layer menus constantly jump back and forth among different MPEG-2 stills (similar to I-frames) as you select and activate menu buttons. Whenever the DVD-Video player's laser is forced to refocus on another part of the disc, playback briefly pauses. All of this jumping around makes Photoshop layer menus seem sluggish, or slow to respond. Highlight menus do not suffer from this problem. To learn more, see Chapter 9, "Highlight Menus."

Where's That Button?

How you group the Photoshop layers representing your button states is up to you. You may decide to group each button's selected and activated states together, or you may prefer to group the selected states of all buttons at the top of the Layers palette, and all activated states at the bottom. Just be sure to use a logical method that lets you quickly find the necessary button state once the document lands in DVD Studio Pro.

For similar reasons, you should give each layer a name that reflects its contents. It's also a good idea to use an empty layer named "-" as a spacer between each group of layers (refer to Figure 8.14). Back in DVD Studio Pro, you can then quickly locate layers in either the List window or the Layers menus (**Figure 8.16**).

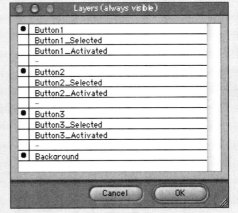

Figure 8.16 Logically organizing your Photoshop layers makes it easier to use DVD Studio Pro's List window.

About Menu Tiles

Each Menu tile has a large thumbnail area and a single icon called the Button icon (**Figure 8.17**). Double-click the thumbnail area to open the Menu editor and add buttons to the menu; double-click the Button icon to open the Button container—an alternate means of accessing your menu buttons' properties (**Figure 8.18**).

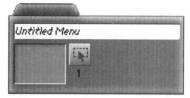

Figure 8.17 An empty Menu tile.

To add a Menu tile:

1. At the bottom of the Graphical View, click the Add Menu button.

   An untitled Menu tile is added to the Graphical View (**Figure 8.19**).

2. From the Menu Property Inspector's Asset drop-down menu, choose a picture asset (**Figure 8.20**).

   Setting a picture asset causes a new menu property to appear in the Property Inspector's Picture area: the Layers (Always Visible) property.

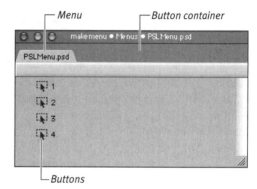

Figure 8.18 The Button container provides easy access to the menu's buttons. From here, you can select a button and alter its properties in the Property Inspector.

Figure 8.19 The Add Menu button creates a new, empty Menu tile.

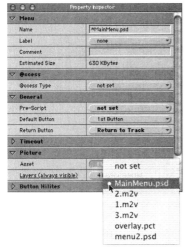

Figure 8.20 Each menu can have only one picture asset, and that picture asset must contain all of the layers needed to construct the menu.

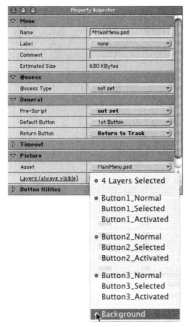

Figure 8.21 From the Layers (Always Visible) menu, choose the layers that form the menu's background.

3. From the Layers (Always Visible) property, choose the layer (or layers) that forms the background for your menu (**Figure 8.21**).

Normally, all of your background graphics, including the normal states of all buttons, are merged onto one layer. But if you prefer to leave your button normal states on their own layers, it's not a problem. The DVD Studio Pro's Layers (Always Visible) property lets you assign multiple Photoshop layers to the menu background.

✔ Tips

■ Menus can access only a single picture asset, so all of a menu's Photoshop layers must be present in the picture asset that you choose.

■ Dragging a picture asset from the Assets container into the Graphical View automatically creates a Menu tile with the same name as the picture asset.

About the Menu Editor

With its ability to paste buttons on a menu background, the *Menu editor* is your project's interactivity construction yard. When you open the Menu editor, the first thing you see is a menu (background). All menus must have at least one button (or DVD Studio Pro will not let you build your project), so you'll also see one default button in the Menu editor's upper left corner. You can reposition this first button anywhere on the menu and then add up to 35 more, for a total of 36 buttons per menu.

To open the Menu editor:

◆ In the Graphical View, double-click the Menu tile's thumbnail area (**Figure 8.22**).

The Menu editor opens displaying the menu background and one default button (**Figure 8.23**). If you can't see the menu background (for example, if the Menu editor is white or black with no images displayed), you need to assign the menu a picture asset; see "To add a Menu tile" earlier in this chapter.

✔ Tip

■ To change a button's name, select the button and type a new name in the Property Inspector's Name text box.

Thumbnail area

Figure 8.22 Click a Menu tile's thumbnail area to open the Menu editor.

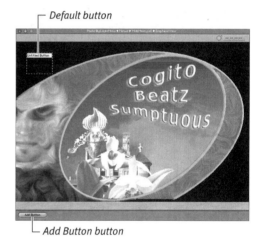

Default button

Add Button button

Figure 8.23 When you open the Menu editor for the first time, you'll find a default button waiting in the editor's upper left corner.

Figure 8.24 Reposition buttons by dragging them to a new spot in the Menu editor.

Figure 8.25 Place the pointer over the edge or corner of a button to display a double-headed pointer.

Figure 8.26 Simply drag to resize the button.

Working with buttons

In the Menu editor, a button's rectangular footprint represents its "hot," or active, area (also known as its *hotspot*). When the DVD-Video is played on a computer, viewers can interact with buttons by moving the pointer over hotspots and clicking, so make sure that all hotspots completely cover their buttons.

To reposition a button:

◆ In the Menu editor, drag the button to a different position (**Figure 8.24**).

To change a button's size:

1. In the Menu editor, place the pointer over the edge or corner of the button hotspot.

   The pointer turns into a double-headed arrow (**Figure 8.25**).

2. Drag the button's edge until the hotspot is the correct size (**Figure 8.26**).

continues on next page

ABOUT THE MENU EDITOR

✔ Tips

- To create a hotspot at a specific size, use the Dimensions area of the Button Property Inspector (**Figure 8.27**).

- Don't confuse the DVD-Video player; avoid overlapping your button hotspots.

To add a button:

1. In the Menu editor, place the pointer at the upper left corner of the area that you want the button to cover in the menu.

2. Drag to create a box over the entire area of the button (**Figure 8.28**).

To delete a button:

1. In the Menu editor, select a button.

2. Press the Delete key on your keyboard. The button is deleted from the Menu editor.

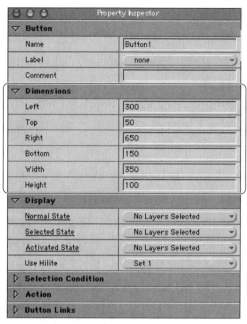

Figure 8.27 With a button selected, the Property Inspector displays the Dimensions area. Use this area to make pixel-accurate adjustments to your button's position and dimensions.

Figure 8.28 To create a new button in the Menu editor, click anywhere there isn't already a button and drag out a new one.

Figure 8.29 The Button Property Inspector's Display area holds properties that set Photoshop layers for the button's normal, selected, and activated states.

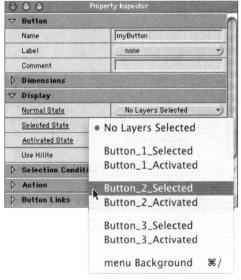

Figure 8.30 The Selected State button property lets you choose the Photoshop layers that hold the button's selected graphics.

Setting Button States

If you've designed your Photoshop document correctly, you have the menu graphics on the background and each button state on a separate layer of the document (see "About Photoshop Layers" earlier in this chapter). After creating button hotspots, finish the button by assigning each button state to a layer in the Photoshop document (**Figure 8.29**).

To assign layers to button states:

1. In the Menu editor (or the Button container), select a button.

   The Property Inspector updates to display the button's properties.

2. From the Property Inspector's Selected State menu, choose the Photoshop layer that represents the button's selected state (**Figure 8.30**).

   Each time the button is selected, this layer appears on top of the menu background.

   continues on next page

3. From the Property Inspector's Activated State menu, choose the Photoshop layer that represents the button's activated state image (**Figure 8.31**).

Each time the button is selected, this layer appears on top of the menu background.

✔ Tips

■ The button states in the Button Property Inspector's Display area are underlined, indicating that they hide a List window. Click the underlined name to open this window (**Figure 8.32**).

■ The Layer matrix speeds up the process of assigning Photoshop layers to buttons (**Figure 8.33**). To open the Layer matrix, select a Menu tile and choose Matrix > Layers.

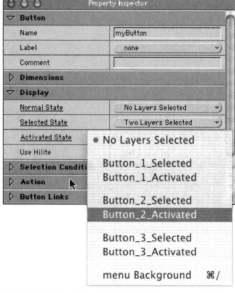

Figure 8.31 The Activated State button property lets you choose the Photoshop layers that hold the button's activated graphics.

Figure 8.32 The Selected State list window provides a convenient means of assigning multiple Photoshop layers to the same button.

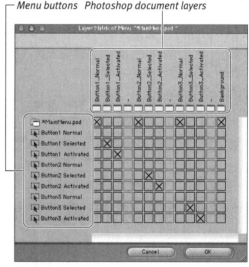

Figure 8.33 The Layer matrix lets you conveniently assign Photoshop layers to buttons.

Figure 8.34 When you select a button in the Menu editor, you can use DVD Studio Pro's Buttons menu to check its selected and activated states without launching the Preview mode.

Displaying button states

The Menu editor can show you the selected and activated button states as you design your menus. Enable the Show options to see how your buttons look as you assign Photoshop layers and to quickly spot any errors, such as when you've assigned a layer to the wrong button state.

To display button states:

1. In the Menu editor, select a button.

2. From the Buttons menu, choose Show Selected State (**Figure 8.34**).

   The button's selected state is displayed.

3. From the Button menu, choose Show Activated State (refer to Figure 8.34).

   The button's activated state is displayed.

Setting Button Actions

Buttons need to *do* something once they are activated, such as play a track or cause a menu to appear on the screen. You can drum up all kinds of action by linking buttons to scripts, slideshows, and track chapters (for more on track chapters, see Chapter 10, "Markers and Stories") using the Button Property Inspector's Jump When Activated property.

To set the Jump When Activated action:

1. In the Menu editor (or the Button container), select a button.

    The Property Inspector updates to display the button's properties.

2. From the Property Inspector's Jump When Activated menu, choose an item (**Figure 8.35**).

    In your DVD-Video, activating the button causes the selected item to play.

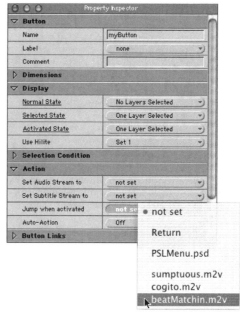

Figure 8.35 The Jump When Activated button property links the button to a project item such as a track, slideshow, or a different menu.

Other Button Actions

Although you'll use the Jump When Activated property most frequently, the Button Property Inspector's Action area holds three other properties that may occasionally prove handy (**Figure 8.36**):

Set Audio Stream To. If the Jump When Activated property links to a track or slideshow with alternate audio streams, use this property to specify which audio stream should play. This property is particularly useful for menus that let viewers choose among audio programs in multiple languages.

Set Subtitle Stream To. This property works the same way as the Set Audio Stream To property, but instead is used to choose among alternate subtitle streams.

Auto-Action. If you turn on Auto-Action, the button automatically activates as soon as it's selected.

Figure 8.36 The Button Property Inspector's Action area has four menus that tell your button what to do when it is clicked.

Linking Buttons

Linking buttons creates a button navigation pattern that the viewer moves through by pushing the arrow keys on the remote control. How you link your buttons is up to you. DVD Studio Pro lets you link any button to any other button on the menu. You should, however, try to use common sense when setting up links so as not to confuse the viewer. Pressing the up arrow key should select the button above the one currently selected, pressing the right arrow should select the button to the right, and so on.

Most of the time, you won't have to do anything at all; DVD Studio Pro lends a helping hand by automatically linking each new button to the last. If this default link order doesn't suit your purposes, use the Property Inspector's Button Links area to create a button navigation pattern that works for your menu.

Numbering Buttons

DVD-Video players let you select buttons by pressing the number keys on the remote control. This works for menus created in DVD Studio Pro, but only if you set up your buttons correctly.

Numbers are assigned to buttons as they are created. The first button created for the menu is given the number 1, the second is given the number 2, and so on.

If you later decide to change the button order, open the Button container and drag buttons up or down the list until they are numbered appropriately (**Figure 8.37**).

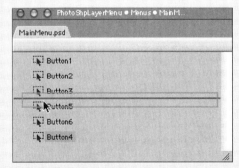

Figure 8.37 Viewers use the number keys on a DVD-Video player's remote control to select buttons on your menu. The order in which the buttons are listed in the Button container determines which button corresponds to which number key. The top button is key 1, the next button down corresponds to key 2, and so on.

To set links between buttons:

1. In the Menu editor (or the Button container), select a button.

   The Property Inspector updates to display the button's properties. At the bottom of the Property Inspector is a Button Links area (**Figure 8.38**). This area has four menus, each corresponding to one of the arrow keys on the remote control.

2. From the menus in the Button Links area, choose buttons for each of the remote control's arrow keys (**Figure 8.39**).

✔ Tip

- Setting button links can be tedious. To speed the process, DVD Studio Pro has a special power tool called the Button Navigation tool. You learn how to use it in Chapter 9, "Highlight Menus."

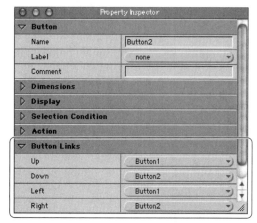

Figure 8.38 The Button Links area defines how the remote control's arrow keys navigate menu buttons.

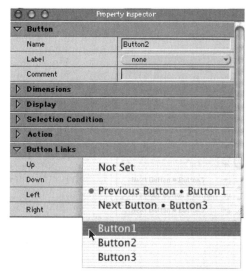

Figure 8.39 Select appropriate buttons from the Up, Down, Left, and Right button property menus.

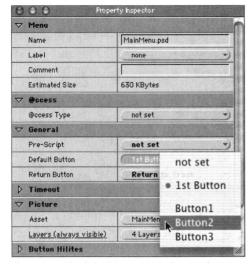

Figure 8.40 The default button is the button that is automatically selected when the menu is first displayed on the screen.

Setting the Default Button

The default button is the button that is automatically selected each time the menu comes onscreen, customarily the button that the viewer is most likely to choose. The DVD-Video's main menu, for example, might have a Play Movie button and an Extra Features button. In this case, the viewer is more likely to select the Play Movie button, so that button should be set as the default.

To set a menu's default button:

1. In the Graphical View, select a Menu tile.
   The Property Inspector updates to show the menu's properties.

2. From the Property Inspector's Default Button menu, select a button (**Figure 8.40**).
   As your DVD-Video plays, each time it returns to this menu, the default button is automatically selected.

✔ Tip

■ To have no buttons selected by default, choose Not Set from the Default Button menu.

About Selection Conditions

Setting a selection condition adds a bit of finesse to your menus. If the viewer returns to a menu after watching a track, the menu should automatically select the button that corresponds to the last track played. In other words, the button that jumped the viewer out of the menu should be the button selected by default when the viewer returns to the menu. By setting up a simple button selection condition, you can easily program this menu behavior (**Figure 8.41**).

To set a button selection condition:

1. In the Menu editor (or the Button container), select a button.

   The Property Inspector updates to display the button's properties.

2. From the Property Inspector's Selection Type menu, choose the type of item the button should watch for (**Figure 8.42**).

   A new property appears under the Selection Type menu, called the Current Track Is property (**Figure 8.43**).

3. From the Current Track Is property, select a project item.

   When the menu returns onscreen, it automatically selects the button corresponding to the last item played.

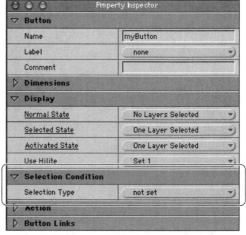

Figure 8.41 The Selection Condition area tells the button to watch for a specific project item. If that item was the last thing playing before the menu came onscreen, the button will be automatically selected.

Figure 8.42 The Selection Type property sets the *type* of item to look for (track, audio stream, or subtitle stream).

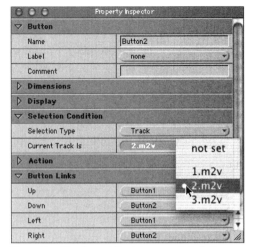

Figure 8.43 The Current Track Is property tells the button *exactly* which item to watch for.

✔ Tips

- Selection conditions are set on a button-by-button basis, so you must be sure to go through all of the menu's buttons and assign each a selection condition.

- If you assign a selection condition to a button, don't use the Auto-Action property, or the DVD-Video will jump straight back to the track without giving the viewer a chance to make a new menu selection.

- You can also write a prescript that allows your menu to dynamically decide which button should be selected when the menu appears on the screen. To learn more, see Chapter 17, "Scripting!"

Previewing Menus

In Preview mode, you can navigate among buttons to check their selected states as well as trigger buttons to check their activated states and Jump When Activated properties. If you've provided your buttons with selection conditions, the Preview mode also lets you check to see that the correct button is selected when the menu comes onscreen.

To preview a menu:

1. In the Graphical View, select a Menu tile.

2. In the lower right corner of the Graphical View, click the Preview button.

   The Preview mode opens, displaying the menu.

3. From the Preview mode's Pixel Aspect ratio menu, choose Square (**Figure 8.44**).

   The Pixel Aspect Ratio menu's square setting causes Preview mode to correctly display your DVD-Video when viewed on the square pixels of a computer monitor.

4. Select buttons using the Preview mode's arrow buttons (**Figure 8.45**).

   As you select a button, the Preview mode displays its selected state.

5. Activate a button by clicking the Preview mode's OK button.

   The button's activated state appears briefly before the Preview mode jumps to play the new item (as defined by the button's Jump When Activated property).

Figure 8.44 Computers use square pixels, and DVD Studio Pro's Preview mode is on a computer. Select Square from the Preview mode's Pixel Aspect Ratio menu, and DVD Studio Pro resizes the preview so it looks proportionally correct on your computer monitor.

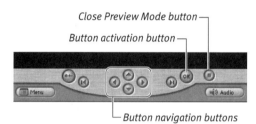

Figure 8.45 To navigate your menu buttons, use the Preview mode's arrow buttons. To activate a button, click the OK button.

HIGHLIGHT MENUS

Similar to the way a highlight pen marks text in a book, a highlight menu uses a strip of color to indicate button states. The chief benefit? Speed. Although highlight menus don't have the graphical depth of a Photoshop layer menu, they are quick to react to viewer input and, as a result, don't feel as sluggish as Photoshop layer menus. When you're navigating menu buttons on a computer, highlights turn on as soon as you place the pointer over button hotspots, whereas a Photoshop layer menu would have you waiting for up to a second—or more!

While Photoshop layer menus must remain silent, highlight menus can have sound, such as background music or, say, a narrative track that describes the menu choices. And while Photoshop menus are restricted to still images, a highlight menu can also use an MPEG-2 video stream as a background, creating a *motion menu*.

Highlight menus are initially daunting, but after a bit of practice you'll find them much easier to create than their Photoshop counterparts. This chapter shows you how to use an overlay image to give your highlights distinct shapes, add single and multicolor highlights, attach sound to a menu, and create motion menus that give any Hollywood DVD-Video a run for its money. This chapter does *not*, however, cover menu basics such as designing still images that look good on a television or using DVD Studio Pro's Menu editor. If you're new to menus, you should backtrack to Chapter 8, "Photoshop Layer Menus," and solidify your menu-making skills before continuing.

Highlight Basics

Basic highlights make your video screen look like it was attacked by a three-year-old with a giant highlight pen. In its most basic form, a highlight menu is simply a strip of color pasted over text, or some other button art on a menu (**Figure 9.1**). What basic highlights lack in shape or excitement, they make up for in convenience. It's not uncommon, even today, to rent Hollywood-produced DVD-Videos that contain nothing more complex than basic highlights. If you're in a rush, basic highlights are your best friend.

To make a basic highlight menu:

1. Create a Photoshop document containing your menu background (**Figure 9.2**) and import that document into DVD Studio Pro.

   The Photoshop document appears as a picture asset in DVD Studio Pro's Assets Container.

2. Drag the picture asset into the Graphical View (**Figure 9.3**).

   A new Menu tile is created, and the Property Inspector updates to display the new menu's properties. When a Photoshop picture asset is dragged directly into the Graphical View, the picture asset is automatically assigned to the new Menu tile. If the picture asset is a single-layer Photoshop document or a PICT file, skip to step 4. If it is a multilayer Photoshop document, read on.

Figure 9.1 A basic highlight is a strip of color rendered over some button art, such as the text in this menu.

Figure 9.2 A Photoshop document containing the graphics for a highlight menu. Here, the button art is simply text placed over the menu background.

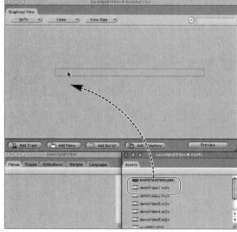

Figure 9.3 Create a Menu tile by dragging the picture asset directly into the Graphical View.

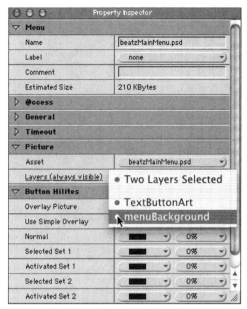

Figure 9.4 If the Photoshop document containing the graphics for your menu has more than one layer, you will need to choose each layer from the Menu Property Inspector's Layers (Always Visible) menu.

Button Hilites area   Highlight set

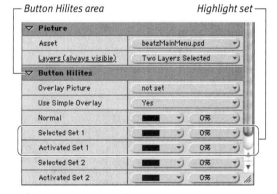

Figure 9.5 The Button Hilites area contains several menus that define the selected and activated colors for your menu's highlights. Together, the selected and activated colors are called a *highlight set*.

3. From the Property Inspector's Layers (Always Visible) menu, select the Photoshop layers that make up your menu's background, as shown in **Figure 9.4** (this menu is not available to single-layer Photoshop or PICT files).

The layers you select will form the menu background over which your button highlights will be placed.

Before opening the Menu editor and creating hotspots that define the highlight's position on the menu, you need to create a *highlight set* that specifies the color of the selected and activated highlights. To do this you'll use the Button Hilites area at the bottom of the Menu Property Inspector (**Figure 9.5**).

continues on next page

HIGHLIGHT BASICS

4. From the Button Hilite area's Selected Set 1 color menu, choose a color (**Figure 9.6**).

This will be the color of your menu's selected highlights. But choosing a color is only half the battle. By default, the highlight's opacity is set to 0 percent, which is completely transparent and cannot be seen. To fix this, you must assign the highlight an opacity value.

5. From the Button Hilite area's Selected Set 1 opacity menu, choose an opacity value (**Figure 9.7**).

You may need to come back and modify this opacity value once you've defined button hotspots (which you'll do in the next several steps). For now, choose a value that allows some of the button art to shine through the menu, but also still clearly defines the highlight itself. Usually, 66 percent is a good place to start.

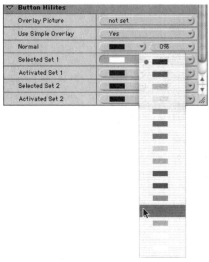

Figure 9.6 Choose a selected state highlight color from the Selected Set 1 color menu.

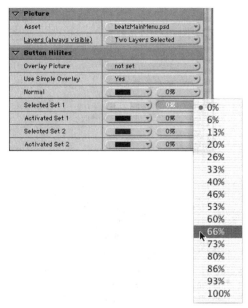

Figure 9.7 By default, the highlight is completely transparent. Give the highlight some substance by choosing an opacity value from the Selected Set 1 opacity menu.

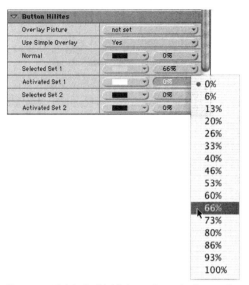

Figure 9.8 Finish the highlight set by assigning a color and opacity value for the menu button's activated states using the Activated Set 1 menus.

6. From the Button Hilite area's Activated Set 1 color and opacity menus, choose a color and provide the color with an opacity value (**Figure 9.8**).

This sets the color and opacity value for the menu's activated highlights.

7. In the Graphical View, double-click the Menu tile's Thumbnail area (**Figure 9.9**).

The Menu editor opens.

8. Choose Buttons > Show Selected Hilites (**Figure 9.10**).

Showing your button's selected highlights helps ensure that your button hotspots fully cover their button art and are correctly positioned on the menu.

continues on next page

Figure 9.9 Click the Menu tile's thumbnail area to open the Menu editor.

Figure 9.10 With the Menu editor open, choose Buttons > Show Selected Hilites so you can see your highlights as you drag out button hotspots.

HIGHLIGHT BASICS

9. In the Menu editor, drag out rectangles to define the button hotspots (**Figure 9.11**).

As you drag out your hotspots, the Menu editor displays their selected highlight color (if you'd like to see the activated color, choose Buttons > Show Activated Hilites).

Congratulations! You've created your first highlight menu. Click the Preview button in the lower right corner of the Graphical View to check out your highlights. Finish your menu by linking the buttons to other project items, as described in "Using the Jump Matrix" later in this chapter.

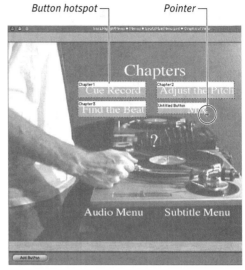

Button hotspot   Pointer

Figure 9.11 In the Menu editor, drag out button hotspots.

Menu Transitions

Menus typically *pop* onto the screen. When the viewer activates a button, the menu then disappears as suddenly as it arrived. To provide a more seamless integration, provide transitions that ease the viewer into, and out of, the menu.

Transitions into the menu are particularly easy to make. Start by importing the menu's Photoshop document into Apple's Final Cut Pro or Adobe After Effects. Create a video sequence that fades from black into your menu graphics; then use the QuickTime MPEG Encoder to encode the transition into an MPEG-2 video stream. Next, import the transition into DVD Studio Pro and place it in a Track tile. Set the transition Track tile's Jump When Finished action to the Menu tile, and make sure that the transition always plays before the menu (for example, the Menu button on the DVD-Video player's remote control should jump to the transition track and not straight to the menu). Transitions out of the menu work exactly the same way, but in reverse.

NTSC video uses a slightly different color space than MPEG-2 video. If you are exporting your transitions and then using the QuickTime MPEG Encoder to convert them to MPEG-2 streams, *do not use the NTSC codec.* Doing so will make your transitions appear lighter than the menu graphics, which causes a noticeable change when the video stream jumps to the menu. Instead, render your transitions using the Animation codec, which preserves all color and makes the transition appear smooth. If you are using Final Cut Pro, avoid this step by exporting the MPEG-2 video stream directly from Final Cut Pro.

HIGHLIGHT BASICS

Menu

Overlay image

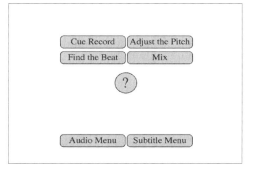

Selected button in final DVD-Video

Figure 9.12 A highlight menu uses an overlay image to create colored buttons that are placed on top of the menu.

Shaping Up Highlights

The basic highlights explored so far are nothing more than rectangles of color pasted over button art. But highlights don't have to be rectangular. They can be round, oval, or even shaped like text. To make these shapes, you create an *overlay image*, which acts like a template that shows DVD Studio Pro where to stamp the highlight graphics on the menu (**Figure 9.12**).

About overlay images

You create overlay images the same way you create any still image for DVD Studio Pro. If you're not quite sure how to do that, Chapter 8, "Photoshop Layer Menus," contains a section called "Using Photoshop" that you should read before continuing.

DVD Studio Pro uses two different overlay modes: *simple overlay* and *multicolor overlay*. Simple overlay mode provides a fast way to create single-color highlights (to learn more, see "Using Simple Overlays" later in this chapter). For most circumstances, simple overlay mode works well. But there will be times when you need more colors in your highlights. Using the multicolor overlay mode, you can create highlight buttons with up to three different colors (to learn more, see "Using Multicolor Highlights" later in this chapter).

✔ Tips

■ Highlights are not anti-aliased, which can lead to jagged-looking edges on complex shapes with small, rounded corners. To guard against this, use simple shapes with square edges whenever possible.

■ If your overlay image uses squares, circles, or any other shape that must remain proportionally correct in the final DVD-Video, don't forget to design the overlay at 720 x 534 (NTSC) and then resize it to 720 x 480.

■ A multilayer Photoshop file can hold both the menu and overlay image. But if you assign a multilayer Photoshop file as a Menu tile's picture asset, you will not be able to attach audio to the menu (see "Adding Audio to Menus" later in this chapter). If your menu needs audio, you'll need to save two single-layer Photoshop or PICT files: one containing the menu graphics and one containing the overlay image.

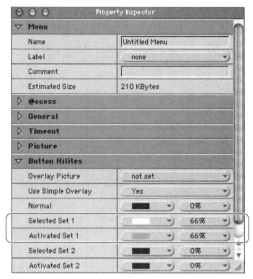

Figure 9.13 A highlight set defines the colors (and opacity value) of the menu's selected and activated highlights.

100 percent black   66 percent black

Figure 9.14 The square on the left is 100 percent black, and the square on the right is 66 percent black. This slight difference in color can make it difficult to distinguish between the two when designing overlay images. In the overlay image, you can substitute 100 percent red for 66 percent black. Your highlights will work fine, and you'll be able to easily tell the difference between the two colors.

Table 9.1

Overlay Color Values

Color	RGB Value
100% black	0, 0, 0
66% black	84, 84, 84
33% black	168, 168, 168
0% black	255, 255, 255

Mapping overlay colors

A *highlight set* defines the selected and activated colors for the menu's highlights (**Figure 9.13**). All overlay images use highlights created with just four colors (also known as 2-bit color): 100 percent black, 66 percent black, 33 percent black, and 0 percent black, which of course is white (**Table 9.1**). In DVD Studio Pro, each of the overlay's four shades of gray are translated into a distinct color from the highlight set. For example, in multicolor overlay mode, where the overlay is 100 percent black, the highlight might be blue. Where it's 66 percent black, the highlight might be red, and where it's 33 percent black, the highlight might be yellow. DVD Studio Pro turns the grayscale overlay into a highlight with vibrant color!

✔ Tips

- While DVD Studio Pro clearly sees the difference between 100 percent black and 66 percent black, the naked eye has to work a little harder to see the slight difference (**Figure 9.14**). Because it can be difficult to tell these two colors apart, you may prefer to design your overlay image in color. DVD Studio Pro will let you substitute 100 percent red, green, or blue for 66 percent black, and 100 percent yellow for 33 percent black. DVD Studio Pro understands these colors and translates them into the correct highlight colors.

- Any part of the overlay image that's outside the button hotspot will not be shown when the button is selected or activated.

- DVD Studio Pro quantizes the color value of all overlay images to the colors in Table 9.1. If your overlay contains other colors, they will be shifted to the nearest acceptable color.

Using Simple Overlays

Simple overlays use a single color for each button's selected and activated states. In simple overlay mode, highlight opacity is defined by the overlay image's four grayscale values. For example, if you choose yellow as a highlight color and assign it an opacity value of 100 percent, where the overlay image is 100 percent black, the highlight is 100 percent yellow. Where the overlay is 66 percent black, the highlight is 66 percent yellow, and so on.

The highlight's four opacity values are mapped to the 2-bit overlay image as follows:

◆ **100 percent black.** Selected color is displayed at the selected opacity.

◆ **66 percent black.** Selected color is displayed at 66 percent of the selected opacity.

◆ **33 percent black.** Selected color is displayed at 33 percent of the selected opacity.

◆ **0 percent black.** Selected color is displayed at 0 percent of the selected opacity, or in other words, becomes transparent.

To create a simple overlay menu:

1. Create an overlay image (**Figure 9.15**).

2. Make a basic highlight menu, as described in "Highlight Basics" earlier in this chapter. A basic highlight menu creates solid rectangular highlights. In the next step, you will assign the overlay image to the menu, magically transforming the rectangular highlights into new shapes.

3. From the Menu Property Inspector's Overlay Picture menu, select the picture asset that contains your overlay image (**Figure 9.16**).

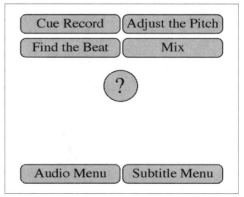

Figure 9.15 An overlay image contains nothing but grayscale graphics that define the shapes for your button highlights.

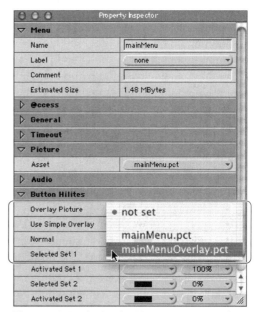

Figure 9.16 Use the Overlay Picture property to select the overlay picture asset.

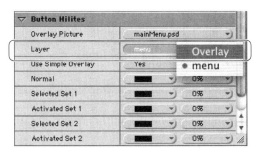

Figure 9.17 If your overlay is part of a multilayer Photoshop file, select the layer that contains the overlay graphics from the Button Hilites area's Layer menu.

Figure 9.18 If you select Yes from the Use Simple Overlay menu, DVD Studio Pro provides the menu's buttons with simple, single-color highlights.

Figure 9.19 Back in the Menu editor, your highlights now have shape!

If you selected a multilayer Photoshop file, a new property named Layer appears under the Overlay Picture property (**Figure 9.17**). From this menu, select the Photoshop layer that contains your overlay graphics.

4. From the Menu Property Inspector's Use Simple Overlay menu, select Yes (**Figure 9.18**).

   DVD Studio Pro's simple overlay mode is now enabled.

5. In the Graphical View, double-click the Menu tile's thumbnail area.

   The Menu editor opens (**Figure 9.19**). Presto! Your highlights now have shape (if you can't see the highlight shapes in the open Menu editor, choose Buttons > Show Selected Hilites).

6. Adjust your button hotspots so that they completely cover the shapes defined in the overlay image.

   Make any other cosmetic tweaks necessary to ensure that everything looks good, and your simple overlay menu is ready for action. You may, however, still need to link the buttons together so that they synch up correctly with a remote control, and you'll also want to assign a jump action to each button so that the button does something when activated. To learn more, see "The Button Navigation Tool" and "Using the Jump Matrix" later in this chapter.

USING SIMPLE OVERLAYS

Choosing Highlight Sets

A highlight set is a group of two colors that represent a button's selected and activated states. The Menu Property Inspector lets you define two highlight sets, enabling you to have different-colored buttons on the same menu (**Figure 9.20**). One highlight set, for example, might use green as the selected color, while the other highlight set uses red. Back on the menu, you can make some buttons with green selected states, and others with red (just remember that each menu button may use only one highlight set).

To select a highlight set:

1. In the Menu editor, select a button.

   The Property Inspector updates to display the selected button's properties.

2. From the Button Property Inspector's Use Hilite menu, choose a highlight set (**Figure 9.21**).

   The colors from the chosen highlight set are used for the button's selected and activated states.

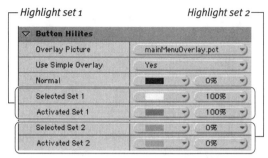

Highlight set 1 Highlight set 2

Figure 9.20 The Button Hilites area lets you create two highlight sets.

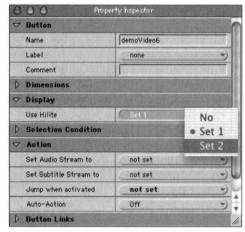

Figure 9.21 Choose the button's highlight set from the Button Property Inspector's Use Hilite menu.

Button Navigation tool —

Figure 9.22 With the pointer directly over the edge of a selected button hotspot, press Control to call up the Button Navigation tool.

The Button Navigation Tool

Although linking menu buttons is a pain at best, nothing frustrates viewers more than hitting keys on a remote control and having seemingly random buttons activate unexpectedly. People expect their remote controls to just work, and it's your job to ensure that they do by making all of your buttons link correctly. Thank goodness for the Button Navigation tool!

The Button Navigation tool makes linking buttons drastically easier than the alternative: Instead of selecting a button and setting values in the Property Inspector's Button Link's area, simply use the Button Navigation tool to drag links between hotspots in the Menu editor.

To use the Button Navigation tool:

1. In the Menu editor, select a button hotspot.

2. Move the pointer over the right edge of the selected hotspot and press the Control key.

   The pointer turns into a one-sided arrow (**Figure 9.22**). This is the Button Navigation tool.

   continues on next page

3. Drag from the selected hotspot to a second hotspot.

A line is drawn from the selected hotspot to the second hotspot. When the pointer passes over a button hotspot that can accept links, it turns into a check mark (**Figure 9.23**).

4. Release the pointer.

The first button is now linked to the second. However, you're far from finished. Each hotspot has four sides that correspond to the four arrow keys on the remote control, so you'll have to go around the hotspot and set the links for each side individually.

5. Work your way around the sides of the hotspot repeating steps 2 to 4.

In the final DVD-Video, the remote control's arrow keys correctly navigate the menu's buttons.

✔ Tip

■ There are no hard and fast rules for button navigation; the best way to link your buttons is through common sense. If a hotspot is up and to the left of the currently selected hotspot, perhaps both the up and the left arrows should jump to that button. But then again, maybe only the up or only the left arrow should move to it. The choice is up to you, but make sure that you use the Preview mode to test your links from the viewer's perspective.

Figure 9.23 The Button Navigation tool turns into a check mark when it passes over a button.

Figure 9.24 The Jump When Activated property tells buttons what to do when selected.

Using the Jump Matrix

Buttons need to *do* something, and you provide that thing by supplying the button with a *jump action*. There are two ways to assign a button's jump action: the slow way and the fast way. The slow method uses the Jump When Activated property, which was described in Chapter 8, "Photoshop Layer Menus" (**Figure 9.24**). Setting the Jump When Activated property works, but it's a time-consuming process that involves moving between each button and the Property Inspector to assign the button's jump action. To expedite the process of setting button actions, use the Jump matrix.

The Jump matrix lets you set the jump actions for all of your menu's buttons in one convenient place. Each button is listed along the left edge of the Jump matrix, and project items (tracks, scripts, slideshows, and so on) are listed across the top. To link a button to a project item, click the box shared by both the button and the project item (**Figure 9.25**).

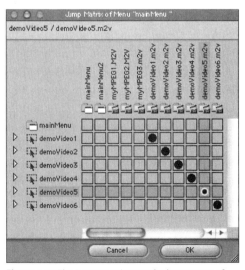

Figure 9.25 The Jump matrix speeds the process of assigning button jumps by letting you set them all in one convenient window.

To assign button actions using the Jump matrix:

1. In the Graphical View, select a Menu tile.

2. Choose Matrix > Jumps of Menu "myMenu," where myMenu equals the name of the selected Menu tile (**Figure 9.26**).

   The Jump matrix opens.

3. Click the boxes that link each button with the project item to which you want it to jump (refer to Figure 9.25).

✔ Tips

■ Selecting the Menu tile causes only that menu's jumps to be displayed in the Jump matrix. If you don't select a Menu tile, the Jump matrix displays the jumps of every item in your project.

■ Matrix views display patterns that can often help you spot errors in your project. But the patterns can be difficult to spot if project items are disorganized. To change the way items are displayed in the Matrix View, reorder them in the Project View.

Figure 9.26 Open the Jump matrix by choosing Matrix > Jumps of Menu "myMenu," where myMenu is the name of your Menu tile.

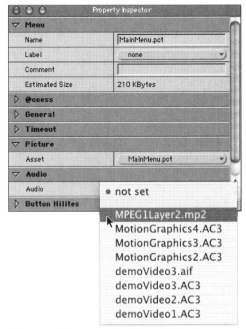

Figure 9.27 If you use a single-layer Photoshop or PICT file as the picture asset for your menu, the Menu Property Inspector's Audio area lets you assign an audio stream to the menu.

Adding Audio to Menus

Unlike Photoshop layer menus, highlight menus can contain audio. But there's a bit of a trick to it: the Menu tile's picture asset must be a PICT, single-layer Photoshop, or MPEG-2 file. If you set a multilayer Photoshop image as the Menu tile's picture asset, DVD Studio Pro assumes that you want to make a Photoshop layer menu. You can add highlight buttons to the menu, but you will not be able to attach an audio asset.

To add sound to a menu:

1. In the Graphical View, select a Menu tile.

    The Property Inspector updates to display the selected Menu tile's properties.

2. From the Property Inspector's Audio menu, select an audio asset (**Figure 9.27**).

    The audio file plays when the menu is displayed.

✔ Tips

- Sounds add ambiance to menus, but are not meant to distract. To give the main audio programs more emphasis, make the menu audio slightly quieter.

- When you add audio to a still highlight menu, the audio stream's length determines the menu's length. For example, if you use a one-minute audio stream, the menu will play for one minute before either looping (see "Looping Menus," next) or executing a timeout action (see "Setting Timeout Actions" later in this chapter).

Looping Menus

When you attach an audio file or MPEG-2 video stream to a highlight menu, the Loop property appears in the Menu Property Inspector's Timeout area (**Figure 9.28**). The Loop property sets the menu to loop, causing it to continue playing until the viewer selects a menu button.

To loop a menu:

1. In the Graphical View, select the Menu tile.

   If the menu has an audio asset attached to it or uses an MPEG-2 video as the picture asset, the Timeout area expands to include the Loop property.

2. In the Property Inspector, set the Loop property's menu to On (refer to Figure 9.28).

   The menu plays to the end of its attached audio file, jumps back to the beginning, and plays again.

✔ Tips

- When a menu loops, its highlights flicker off and on. Unfortunately, there's nothing you can do to fix this.

- If you set a motion menu to loop, it plays to the end of either the attached audio file or its MPEG-2 video stream (whichever is longer) before looping back to the start.

- Preview mode sometimes loops menus before they reach the end of the audio file, but this does not affect your finished video project. After you build the project, the menus play correctly.

- If you want a menu to loop only a certain number of times, you will need to write a script. See Chapter 17, "Scripting!" for more information on how to do that.

Figure 9.28 Turning on the Loop property sets the menu to loop indefinitely.

Figure 9.29 The Timeout section's Action property tells the menu to automatically jump to a different project item after a certain amount of time has passed.

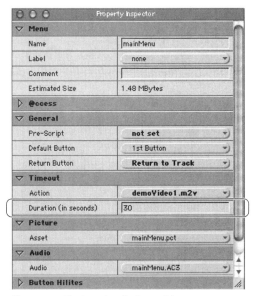

Figure 9.30 The Duration (in Seconds) property sets the interval between the time when the menu finishes playing and the time when the timeout action starts.

Setting Timeout Actions

A timeout action causes a menu to play for a specific amount of time before jumping to a different project item. Timeout actions are made of two parts: the timeout action itself (**Figure 9.29**) and the period of time between when the menu finishes playing and when the timeout action is triggered (**Figure 9.30**).

If the menu doesn't use an audio or MPEG-2 asset, the Duration (in Seconds) property begins counting down as soon as the menu appears on the screen. Otherwise, the menu plays to the end of its audio or MPEG-2 asset (whichever is longer) and then pauses for the amount of time set by the Duration (in Seconds) property.

To set a timeout action:

1. In the Graphical View, select a Menu tile.

   The Property Inspector updates to display the Menu tile's properties.

2. From the Property Inspector's Action menu, choose a project item (refer to Figure 9.29).

   The Property Inspector's Timeout area expands to display a Duration (in Seconds) property (refer to Figure 9.30).

3. Type a value in the Duration (in Seconds) text box.

   The menu waits for the specified amount of time before moving on to play the project item selected in step 2.

✔ Tips

- You cannot set a timeout action and also loop your menu. It's one or the other.

- The Duration (in Seconds) text box accepts any value between (and including) 1 and 254, which is just over 4 minutes.

SETTING TIMEOUT ACTIONS

Using Multicolor Highlights

Simple overlay highlights are, well, simple. Stylistically they don't offer much, but they're easy to make, which is probably why they're used in most commercial DVDs. You can, however, expect multicolor highlights to become more common once DVD authors get their hands on DVD Studio Pro, which makes creating multicolor highlights extremely easy.

A multicolor highlight assigns up to three colors to the grayscale shades in the overlay image. But before you can use multicolor highlights, you have to turn them on (by turning simple overlays *off*). Doing so expands the Property Inspector's Button Hilites area, providing each selected and activated state in a highlight set with four percentage values: 0 percent, 33 percent, 66 percent, and 100 percent (**Figure 9.31**).

These four percentage values should look familiar, and indeed, they are the four grayscale colors from the overlay image (0 percent black, 33 percent black, 66 percent black, and 100 percent black). Beside each value sits a color and an opacity menu. The choices you make from those menus determine the color that is mapped to the corresponding grayscale color in the overlay image.

Sound confusing? It's actually a very easy process, and walking through it once will show you exactly what's going on. The best way to learn how to make multicolor highlights is to start with a simple overlay menu that uses a 2-bit overlay image. Make sure the simple overlay menu is fully functional, including all button hotspots and links. Once you have a 2-bit simple overlay menu ready to go, move on to the steps that follow to turn it into a highlight menu with vibrant color.

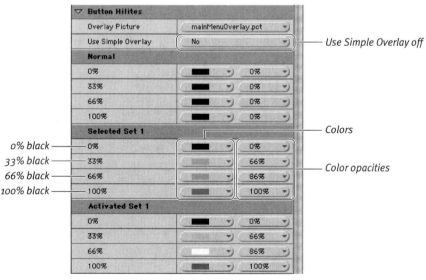

Figure 9.31 Using multicolor highlights, the four grayscale colors in an overlay image correspond to the four highlight colors in DVD Studio Pro.

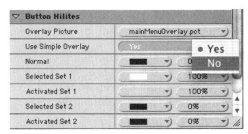

Figure 9.32 To create multicolor highlights, you must turn off simple overlays.

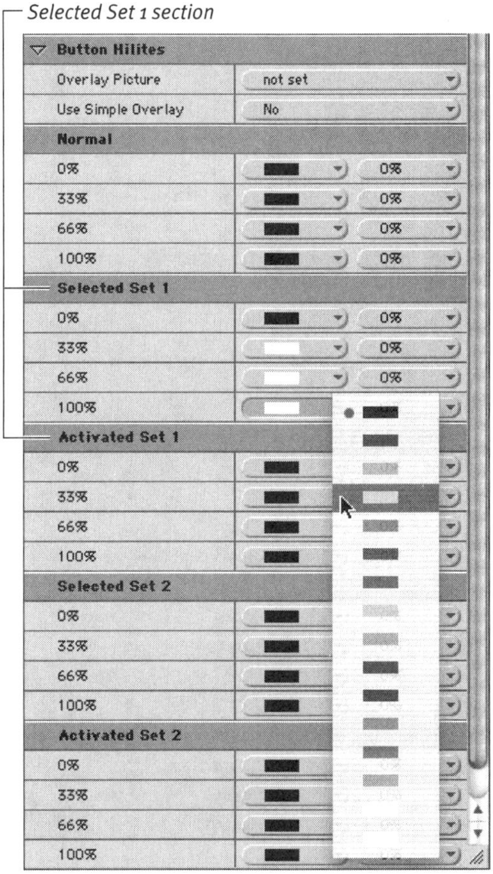

Selected Set 1 section

Figure 9.33 The Selected Set 1 section is used to specify colors that will be mapped to the grayscale colors in the overlay image.

To create multicolor highlights:

1. Create a simple overlay menu using a four-color greyscale overlay image.

   To learn more about simple overlay menus, see the previous section in this chapter, "Using Simple Overlays."

2. In the Graphical View, select the Menu tile containing your menu.

   The Property Inspector updates to display the Menu tile's properties.

3. From the Property Inspector's Use Simple Overlay menu, choose No (**Figure 9.32**).

   The Property Inspector's Button Hilites area expands (refer to Figure 9.31).

4. From the Button Hilites area's Selected Set 1 section, select colors for each of the overlay image's four grayscale colors (**Figure 9.33**).

continues on next page

USING MULTICOLOR HIGHLIGHTS

5. From the Button Hilites area's Selected Set 1 section, select opacity values for each highlight color (**Figure 9.34**).

Make sure to set these opacity values. By default, opacity is set to 0 percent, which is completely transparent (your highlight will not be visible).

6. Set color and opacity values in the Menu Property Inspector's Activated Set 1 section (**Figure 9.35**).

7. In the lower right corner of the Graphical View, click the Preview button.

The Preview mode opens. Check your multicolor highlights to make sure that they are displayed as expected.

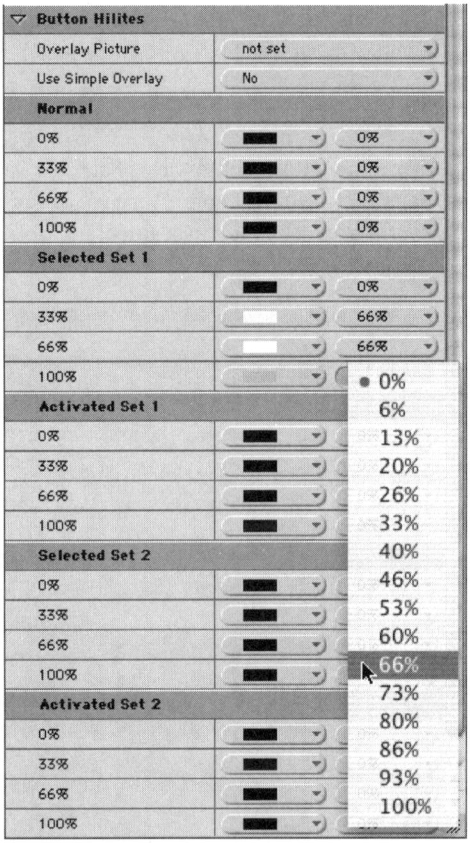

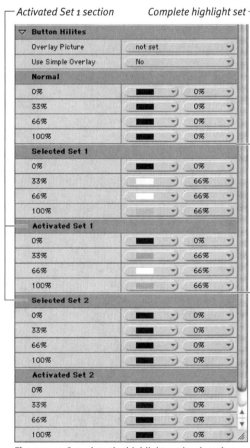

Figure 9.34 Don't forget to choose opacity values for your highlight colors, or your highlights will be zero percent opaque, which is transparent.

Figure 9.35 Complete the highlight set by choosing colors and opacity values from the Activated Set 1 section.

USING MULTICOLOR HIGHLIGHTS

Video clips used as button art   _Menu_

Figure 9.36 The best way to figure out how a motion menu works is to actually look at one. The DVD Studio Pro program DVD-ROM contains a tutorial that uses this motion menu. If you open the completed tutorial and check out this motion menu, you'll notice that the four rectangles are actually moving video clips.

Figure 9.37 Unlike with still menus, where you can simply drag the picture asset into the Graphical View to create a Menu tile, dragging an MPEG-2 asset into the Graphical View automatically creates a Track tile. To make a motion menu, you must start by clicking the Add Menu button in the lower left corner of the Graphical View.

About Motion Menus

A motion menu uses an MPEG-2 file as the menu background. As with a still highlight menu, the motion menu's MPEG-2 stream usually contains all of the button art. Unlike with a still highlight menu, the button art on a motion menu can be made of moving images composited on top of a still _or_ moving background. Each button on a motion menu, for example, might be a single video clip representing the video stream that the button links to (**Figure 9.36**). Or the button could be a spinning 3D logo that is circled by a highlight when selected.

If you've mastered still highlight menus, you'll have no problem creating motion menus, because they are created exactly the same way as their sedentary cousins. Motion menus can use both simple overlays and multicolor highlights, they can have audio, and they can even loop just like a regular highlight menu (see the sidebar later in this chapter, "Looping Motion Menus").

To create a motion menu:

1. In the lower left corner of the Graphical View, click the Add Menu button (**Figure 9.37**).

   A Menu tile is created in the Graphical View, and the Property Inspector updates to display the Menu tile's properties.

   continues on next page

2. From the Property Inspector's Asset menu, choose an MPEG-2 asset (**Figure 9.38**).

The MPEG-2 asset becomes the menu's background.

3. Add highlights and hotspots to the menu in the exact same way you add highlights and hotspots to a still highlight menu.

To add single-color highlights, see "Using Simple Overlays" earlier in this chapter. To add multicolor highlights, see "Using Multicolor Highlights" earlier in this chapter.

4. In the lower right corner of the Graphical View, click the Preview button.

The menu moves!

✔ Tip

■ Motion menu MPEG-2 streams are created the same way as any other MPEG-2 stream. For more information, refer to Chapter 3, "Encoding Video Streams."

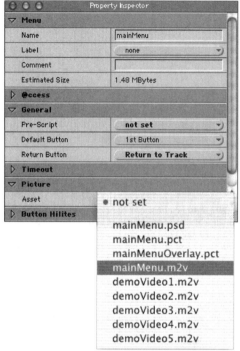

Figure 9.38 The only difference between a motion menu and a still highlight menu is that a motion menu uses an MPEG-2 asset instead of a still picture asset for the menu's background.

Looping Motion Menus

If your motion menu is set to loop (see "Looping Menus" earlier in this chapter), you must ensure a smooth transition between its end and its beginning. To do this, create your motion menu's source video file with an extra second of footage at the point just *before* you want the menu to begin. Next, cut this extra second of footage off the front of the file and fade it into the last second of the motion menu. Now the frame at the end of the menu blends directly into the frame at the beginning, creating a clean cut between the point where the motion menu ends and the point where it begins.

Alternately, if you have plenty of free space on your DVD disc, you can simply create a very long motion menu. The loop between its end and its beginning may not be seamless, but the loop comes around so infrequently that it doesn't detract much from the menu's display.

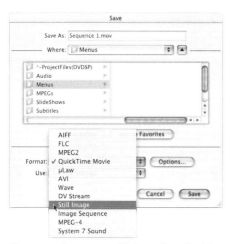

Figure 9.39 To export a still picture from Final Cut Pro, choose File > Export > QuickTime and then select Still Image from the Format menu.

Figure 9.40 To export a still picture from QuickTime Pro Player, choose File > Export and then select Movie to Picture from the Export menu.

Figure 9.41 To export a still picture from Adobe After Effects, choose Composition > Save Frame As > File.

Using overlay images with motion menus

Motion menus are composited with video editing applications such as Final Cut Pro, Adobe After Effects, or even QuickTime Pro Player. Overlay images, on the other hand, are created in Photoshop or Corel PhotoPaint (Corel PhotoPaint is located on the DVD Studio Pro DVD-ROM disc). To make sure that your highlight buttons are positioned correctly in the final DVD-Video, export a frame of the motion menu source file, import it into Photoshop, and use that frame as a template for the overlay image.

To create an overlay image for a motion menu:

1. In your video editing application, move the playhead to the frame you want to export.

2. Turn this frame into a PICT file by doing one of the following:

   ▲ In Final Cut Pro, choose File > Export > QuickTime and then choose Still Image from the Format menu (**Figure 9.39**).

   ▲ In QuickTime Pro, choose File > Export and then choose Movie to Picture from the Export menu (**Figure 9.40**).

   ▲ In Adobe After Effects, choose Composition > Save Frame As > File (**Figure 9.41**).

3. Open the PICT file in Photoshop.
   To account for the difference between the square pixels in Photoshop and the nonsquare pixels in your video, you must resize this new Photoshop document to 720 x 534 pixels for NTSC video (768 x 576 pixels for PAL video) before designing the overlay graphics. (For more information, see Chapter 8, "Photoshop Layer Menus.")

continues on next page

4. In Photoshop, choose Image > Image Size (**Figure 9.42**).

The Image Size dialog box opens.

5. Uncheck the Constrain Proportions check box; then in the Pixel Dimensions section at the top of the dialog box, enter 720 in the Width text box and 534 in the Height text box (**Figure 9.43**). Then click OK to close the Image Size dialog box.

The document resizes to 720 x 534.

6. Design your overlay graphics.

7. Resize the overlay image back to 720 x 480 pixels (720 x 576 pixels for PAL).

The shapes on the overlay image look proportionally correct in the final DVD-Video, and they line up with the button art in the motion menu's MPEG-2 stream.

Figure 9.42 To resize a Photoshop document, from inside Photoshop choose Image > Image Size.

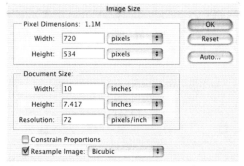

Figure 9.43 Photoshop's Image Size dialog box.

D1 NTSC and Overlays

D1 NTSC is a very common format that uses a frame dimension of 720 x 486. When D1 NTSC video is compressed using the QuickTime MPEG Encoder, the top six lines of the D1 video are cut off to produce a 720 x 480 MPEG-2 video stream. (Note: Some MPEG-2 encoders crop D1 NTSC video streams differently.) While 6 pixels may not seem like much, it's enough to throw your overlay graphics out of position, which means that your highlights won't match up with the button art in the MPEG-2 stream.

To cure this problem, in Photoshop design your overlay at 720 x 540 (yes, that's 540, not 534), resize the document to 720 x 486, and then crop the top 6 pixels off the document. The result is a 720 x 480 overlay image that perfectly lines up with the button art in the MPEG-2 stream.

CREATING MARKERS AND STORIES

10

Trying to find a specific scene on a VHS video almost always involves a time-consuming and frustrating workout with the remote control. Fast forward. Play. Oops, went too far. Rewind. Play. Darn it! Forward...just...a...bit...more. DVD-Video takes all this monotonous haggling out of scene selection by letting viewers jump right to specific points in the video using the Previous or Next buttons on the remote control (sort of like skipping through the songs on an audio CD). As the DVD-Video author, you set those key points using reference points in tracks called *markers*.

Markers, also called chapter markers, divide the video into chunks, or *chapters*, that are typically used to define sections of unique content, such as a particular scene in a movie or a group of similar exercises in a workout video. You can use markers to slice up your DVD-Video in whatever way you want—there are no rules. Well, maybe one. You're limited to 99 markers per track, which should be enough for all but the most complex presentations.

DVD Studio Pro also lets you string together sequences of chapter markers to create *stories*, much like a story you would find in a typical book. However, unlike in a book, where chapter progress linearly from beginning to end, there are no hard rules about chapter order in a DVD Studio Pro story. For example, you might have one video stream that contains six music videos, each assigned to a chapter on the track. If you want to change the videos' playback order, simply create a story with the chapters in a different order. Each track can hold up to 99 stories, giving your DVD-Video 99 unique ways to proceed through a track's chapters.

About Markers

You do all your work with markers using the Marker editor, which you open by double-clicking a Track tile's thumbnail area. The Marker editor consists of a preview area that displays the track's MPEG video stream, a marker menu, a New Marker button, a slider used to scrub (drag) markers along the MPEG video, and a Time Code button that jumps markers to exact points in the MPEG stream (**Figure 10.1**).

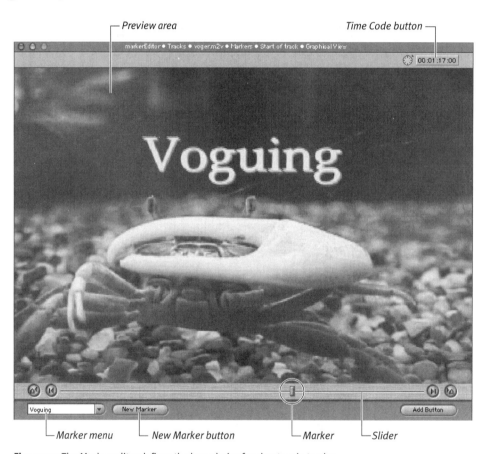

Figure 10.1 The Marker editor defines the boundaries for chapters in tracks.

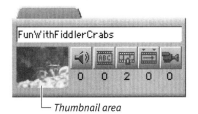

Thumbnail area

Figure 10.2 To open the Marker editor, click the Track tile's thumbnail area.

To open the Marker editor:

◆ In the Graphical View, double-click a Track tile's thumbnail area (**Figure 10.2**).
The Marker editor opens, and the Property Inspector updates to display marker properties.

Creating markers

Creating markers is easy—just click the New Marker button located in the Marker editor's lower left corner. The Marker editor displays only one marker at a time, and each newly added marker is created in exactly the same position on the slider as the last marker displayed. DVD Studio Pro will not let you build a project that has two (or more) markers in exactly the same spot, so you must move each new marker to a new home in the MPEG stream immediately after the marker is created.

You'll eventually be working with enough markers to become confused unless you name each one, so assign each marker a descriptive name from the start. If you later need to skip to a specific marker, you can then select it by name from the Marker menu. Names are also very important when it comes to creating stories, so keep this in mind when you read the "About Stories" section later in this chapter.

To create a marker:

◆ In the lower left corner of the Marker editor, click the New Marker button (**Figure 10.3**).

A new marker is created on the slider at the bottom of the Marker editor.

✔ Tips

■ Markers can be placed only on I-frames, which are also called group of pictures (GOP) headers.

■ You cannot delete markers from the Marker editor itself. Instead, you must use the Marker container. To learn more, see "About the Marker Container" later in this chapter.

Figure 10.3 To create a new marker, click the New Marker button.

Setting Markers in Final Cut Pro

Final Cut Pro 3.0.2 introduced a new feature that lets you set DVD Studio Pro chapter markers right in the Final Cut Pro timeline. When you encode your Final Cut Pro project to MPEG-2, these markers are encoded in the MPEG-2 stream. In DVD Studio Pro, the markers show up in the Marker editor, named and ready to go.

This new Final Cut Pro feature allows frame-accurate marker placement. Although you can usually get close enough using DVD Studio Pro's Marker editor, there will be times when the Marker editor doesn't let you set markers exactly where you need them. With Final Cut Pro 3.0.2, this is no longer a problem. (For more information on how to set markers in Final Cut Pro, see the end of Chapter 3, "Encoding Video Streams.")

Registered users of Final Cut Pro 3.0 can download version 3.0.2 for free from Apple's Web site: www.apple.com/software/.

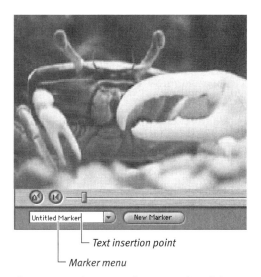

Figure 10.4 To change a marker's name, first click inside the Marker menu's text box to create a text insertion point.

Figure 10.5 Then press Command-A to highlight the Marker menu's text, type in a new name, and press Return.

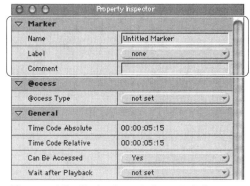

Figure 10.6 The Marker Property Inspector's Name text box is another way to name markers.

To name a marker:

1. In the Marker editor, click inside the Marker menu's text box (**Figure 10.4**).

   An insertion point appears.

2. Select all of the text in the box, or simply press Command-A.

   The text in the Marker menu's text box is highlighted (**Figure 10.5**).

3. Type a new name. Then press the Return key on your keyboard.

   DVD Studio Pro may not register the new name unless you press Return after typing it in the Marker menu's text box. To be safe, always press Return after naming a marker.

✔ Tip

■ You can also rename a marker by selecting it and typing a name in the Marker Property Inspector's Name text box (**Figure 10.6**).

Positioning Markers

Markers can be attached only to I-frames, which head up the first frame in an MPEG GOP. You'll usually position markers by dragging them along the slider at the bottom of the Marker editor, but in long tracks it's hard to find specific I-frames using the slider alone. Once you have the marker close to where you want it, use the nudge buttons on the right and left of the slider to jump the marker to the previous or next I-frame in the MPEG stream.

To set the marker position:

◆ In the Marker editor, select a marker and drag it along the slider (**Figure 10.7**).

✔ Tips

■ Because markers can be attached only to I-frames, that's all the Marker editor displays. For more information on I-frames, see Chapter 3, "Encoding Video Streams."

■ If you need a marker on a specific frame, but the Marker editor does not give you access to it, you'll need to set the marker in Final Cut Pro 3.0.2 (or higher) and then re-encode your MPEG-2 stream.

To nudge a marker to an I-frame:

◆ Click the Previous or Next marker button located at either end of the Marker editor's slider (**Figure 10.8**).

Depending on which button you've clicked, the marker jumps backward or forward by one I-frame.

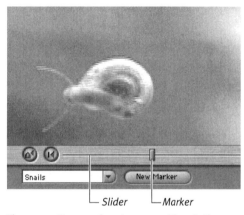

Figure 10.7 Move markers to new positions in the MPEG stream by dragging them along the slider at the bottom of the Marker editor.

Nudge marker backward　　　　　*Nudge marker forward*

Figure 10.8 The buttons directly to the left and right of the slider nudge markers backward or forward by one I-frame.

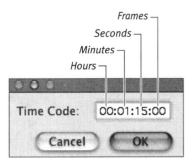

Frames —
Seconds —
Minutes —
Hours —

Time Code: 00:01:15:00

Cancel   OK

Figure 10.9 Time code values are measured in hours, minutes, seconds, and frames.

The Time Code button

The Marker editor's Time Code button opens a dialog box that lets you position markers at predetermined points in an MPEG stream. This is the easiest way to set markers if you know exactly where they need to go. Well, "exactly" may be a bit misleading. Markers can be attached only to I-frames, and it's difficult (if not impossible) to know exactly where those I-frames are located. When you click the OK button to close the Time Code dialog box, however, DVD Studio Pro automatically positions the marker on the I-frame nearest the entered time code value.

Time code values are listed using hours, minutes, seconds, and frames, separated by colons (:) (**Figure 10.9**). To save time, however, you can substitute a period for the colon, or if you're really in a hurry, you can just type part of the time code. If you want the marker set to 1 second, for example, type 1.00 into the dialog box. For 1 minute, type 1.00.00, and so on.

Marker Errors

If the File menu's Build Disc options are dimmed, you cannot multiplex your project. The problem is usually the result of marker errors, which are easily fixed. First, check the Graphical View to see if any of your Track tiles have names that are printed in italics. If so, you've found the problem. To fix it, open the Marker editor and use the buttons at either end of the slider to nudge markers forward or backward to the next I-frame.

Alternately, you can select markers and click the Time Code button in the Marker editor's right corner. Immediately after the Time Code dialog box opens, click OK, and DVD Studio Pro will search the MPEG stream, locating the nearest I-frame. When the track's name no longer appears in italics, you know your problem is solved.

You can also quickly find offending markers by opening the Marker container, as described in the section "The Marker Container" later in this chapter.

To use the Time Code button:

1. In the upper right corner of the Marker editor, click the Time Code button (**Figure 10.10**).

   The Time Code dialog box appears (**Figure 10.11**).

2. Type a time value in the Time Code dialog box.

3. Click OK.

   The marker jumps to the I-frame closest to the time code that you've entered.

✔ Tip

■ The QuickTime MPEG Encoder uses a GOP size of 15 frames. If you haven't used Final Cut Pro to encode chapter or compression markers in your MPEG-2 stream, the QuickTime MPEG Encoder always places I-frames on either frame :00 or :15. So when you use the Time Code dialog box to enter your marker positions, end with :00 or :15.

Time Code button

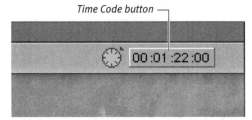

Figure 10.10 If you already know a marker's time code value, click the Time Code button in the upper right corner of the Marker editor to open the Time Code dialog box.

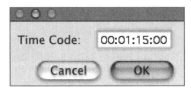

Figure 10.11 Type a time value into the Time Code dialog box. The marker will jump to the I-frame nearest the value that you enter.

Figure 10.12 The Marker menu displays all of the track's markers. To jump straight to a specific marker, select it from the Marker menu.

Navigating markers

To check your markers or reposition them after they are set, you need a quick way to find specific markers in the Marker editor. DVD Studio Pro provides the Marker menu and buttons at either end of the Marker editor's slider for just this purpose.

To navigate markers:

◆ Select a marker by name from the Marker menu (**Figure 10.12**).

  or

◆ Use the Next and Previous marker buttons at either end of the Marker editor's slider to jump from marker to marker (**Figure 10.13**).

  The selected marker appears in the Marker editor.

✔ Tip

■ Make sure you don't accidentally click a nudge marker button instead of the Previous or Next marker button, or you'll move the current marker instead of jumping to the next marker.

— *Previous marker*   *Next marker* —

Figure 10.13 To cycle through your markers, use the Previous and Next marker buttons located at either end of the Marker editor's slider.

The Marker Container

The Marker container lets you easily change marker properties, such as the marker's name, without bothering to open the Marker editor. The Marker container also lets you delete markers, which can't be done in the Marker editor.

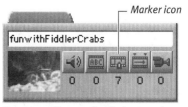

Marker icon

Figure 10.14 To open the Marker container, click the Track tile's Marker icon.

To open the Marker container:

◆ In the Graphical View, click a Track tile's Marker icon (**Figure 10.14**).

The Marker container opens (**Figure 10.15**).

✔ Tip

■ You can also open the Marker container from the Project View (**Figure 10.16**).

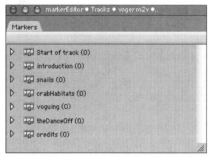

Figure 10.15 The Marker container lists all of the track's markers.

To delete a marker:

1. Open the Marker container.

2. Select a marker (**Figure 10.17**).

3. Press the Delete key on your keyboard.

Figure 10.16 To open the Marker container in the Project View, find the track in question and double-click its Markers folder.

Figure 10.17 To delete a marker, select it in the Marker container and press the Delete key on your keyboard.

About Stories

A story is a collection of chapters—whether in a novel or a DVD Studio Pro project. When you read a novel, however, you usually start with the first chapter and read to the last (unless you're the impatient type who likes to spoil the ending by reading it first). You never start in the middle and then read to the front before finishing off whatever chapters you missed at the end. The story would make no sense! In DVD Studio Pro, however, a story does not have to follow a novel's strict linear setup, leaving you free to organize your chapters in any order you like.

Each track can have up to 99 stories, which gives you 99 ways to move through the track's chapters. Once you've created a story, it appears in all of your project's Jump When Finished and Jump When activated menus, allowing you to link to the story from any other project item in the same way as you would link to a track, menu, chapter, or slideshow. For a concrete example of how stories come in handy, see the sidebar "Making Tracks Play" below.

continues on next page

Making Tracks Play

In some cases, such as a DVD-Video that contains music videos, you'll want to create a Play All button that plays each track in succession without returning to the main menu. You can do this with scripts (see Chapter 17, "Scripting!"), but if the thought of scripting fills you with dread, you can also create the effect using stories.

First, use Final Cut Pro to string the source video of each track together into one long video stream. Encode the new source file, import it into DVD Studio Pro, and create chapters for each video in the stream. Next, make a story for each chapter as well as a final story that includes every chapter. Back in the main menu, link each video's button to the correct story and link the Play All button to the story that holds every chapter.

If you don't have the source video files for the individual videos, you can combine MPEG-2 streams using a shareware application called MPEG Append. Download MPEG Append by pointing your Web browser at http://homepage.mac.com/DVD_SP_Helper/.

ABOUT STORIES

One thing to keep in mind about stories is that they are *track based*, which means that they can play chapters only within their own tracks. In other words, you can't mix and match chapters from different tracks. Also, story chapters always play completely through before moving on to the next chapter—that is, a chapter begins at its marker and plays to the next marker in the track before skipping to the next chapter in the story.

To create a story:

1. In the Project View, locate the track to which you want to add a story.

2. Click the track's Stories folder (**Figure 10.18**).

   The Stories container opens.

3. Choose Item > New Story (**Figure 10.19**).

   A new, untitled story is created in the Stories container (**Figure 10.20**).

Figure 10.18 In the Project View, click the track's Stories folder to open the Stories container.

Figure 10.19 To create a new story, choose Item > New Story.

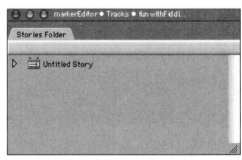

Figure 10.20 A new, untitled story appears in the Stories container.

Figure 10.21 In the Project View, click the track's Markers folder to open the Marker container.

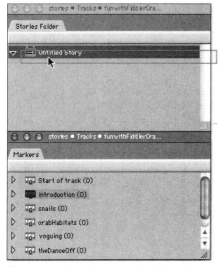

Figure 10.22 Drag chapter markers from the Marker container and drop them onto the story in the Stories container.

Figure 10.23 Stories appear in the button's Jump When Activated property.

4. In the Project View, click the track's Markers folder (**Figure 10.21**).

The Marker container opens.

5. Drag chapter markers out of the Marker container and drop them on the new story in the Stories container until you have as many chapters as you need (**Figure 10.22**).

✔ Tip

- Don't forget to name your stories so you'll recognize them when they're mixed in with other parts of your project, such as a Track tile's Jump When Finished action or a button's Jump When Activated property (**Figure 10.23**).

Using Wait after Playback

Viewers need time to digest what they're watching. In certain situations, you may want to create a period of reflection by inserting a pause after a chapter has finished playing. Say, for example, you have a track composed of several, short videos. Each of these videos fades in at the beginning and then fades out at the end. When you preview the track in DVD Studio Pro's Preview mode, you notice that new chapters begin too quickly after the last chapter has finished. Using the Wait after Playback property, you can give viewers ample time to ruminate upon what they've just seen by making the track pause for a few seconds before proceeding to the next chapter.

To set the Wait after Playback property:

1. In the Marker editor or the Marker container, select a marker.

    The Property Inspector updates to show the marker's properties.

2. From the Property Inspector's Wait after Playback menu, select Wait x Seconds (**Figure 10.24**).

    A new property, titled Wait Seconds, appears under the Wait after Playback property (**Figure 10.25**).

3. Enter a value in the Wait Seconds text box.

    The DVD-Video pauses on the last frame of the chapter for the specified amount of time.

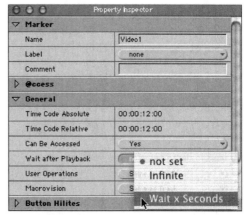

Figure 10.24 The Wait after Playback property creates a pause between chapters.

Figure 10.25 Enter a value (in seconds) for the pause in the Wait Seconds text box.

About Interactive Markers

If you're reading this book in a linear fashion, you know that Chapter 9, "Highlight Menus," covered the ins and outs of using button highlights to add interactivity to your DVD-Videos. Well, guess what? Menus are not the only path to interactivity. With interactive markers, you can place highlight buttons on top of MPEG streams right inside a Track tile!

Interactive markers turn the Marker editor into a Menu editor. What's more, each marker on the track can have its own buttons, complete with their own overlay images and highlight sets. Indeed, using interactive markers is like stringing several motion menus together in sequence (of course, you don't have to define buttons for every chapter marker in the track; it's perfectly fine to add buttons to some chapter markers and not to others).

To create an interactive marker:

1. In the Marker editor, select the marker to which you want to add buttons.

2. *Do one of the following:*
   Click the Add Button button.
   or
   Position the pointer anywhere inside the Marker editor; then drag out a new button (**Figure 10.26**).
   A new button is added to the Marker editor.

3. Finish the button by creating highlights according to the instructions in Chapter 9, "Highlight Menus."

✔ Tip

■ In the final DVD-Video, interactive marker buttons appear on the screen only when the chapter to which they're attached is playing. Once you enter a new chapter, the buttons disappear. If you want the new chapter to have the same buttons, you will have to re-create them for that chapter.

Figure 10.26 Adding buttons to the Marker editor creates an interactive marker.

Interactive marker button

Pointer

Using interactive markers

Interactive markers work exactly the same way as highlight menus. To learn how to create highlights for interactive markers, read Chapter 9, "Highlight Menus," and treat interactive marker buttons like the highlight buttons found on a motion menu.

Why not just use motion menus to begin with? Mainly because you can't have alternate angles or alternate audio streams in a motion menu, but with interactive markers, you can have both! Still, interactive markers are saddled with a few drawbacks. Although you can set an interactive marker's default button (**Figure 10.27**), for example, you cannot set a selection condition to dynamically choose the default button (**Figure 10.28**). Plus, markers can't use pre-scripts, and scripts can't target interactive marker buttons (to learn more about scripts, see Chapter 17, "Scripting!").

Figure 10.27 To set an interactive marker's default button, choose a button from the Marker Property Inspector's Default Button menu.

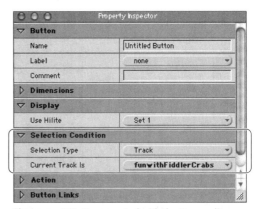

Figure 10.28 Buttons created with the Menu editor have this Selection Condition area in their Property Inspector. This area is not available in the Interactive Marker Property Inspector.

Interactive Markers and Subtitles

Highlight buttons use the subtitle feature to place buttons on top of tracks. Unfortunately, this means that tracks that use interactive markers cannot have subtitles, and vice versa. You can try to add a button to a track with subtitles, or subtitles to a track with interactive marker buttons, but DVD Studio Pro will refuse your attempts (which can be confusing because no alert box appears—in fact, nothing at all happens). To learn more about subtitle streams, see Chapter 16, "Subtitles."

ASSEMBLING SLIDESHOWS

Slideshows, generally used to show off a series of still images, are notoriously boring—but not in DVD Studio Pro! Using the Slideshow editor, you can liven up static picture shows by mixing in MPEG-2 video streams to create smooth transitions between slides. And you can attach up to eight audio tracks to each slide, enabling your images to literally speak for themselves in a number of languages—perfect for product catalogs and presentations destined for an international audience.

Slideshows also come in handy when you have audio, but no matching video. A DVD containing music videos, for example, can include bonus audio tracks, but the tracks must be attached to an image. Using a slideshow, you can create still placeholders that appear as the songs play.

As great as it sounds, DVD Studio Pro slideshows have one drawback: you can't run a continuous audio stream under *all* slides. In other DVD authoring programs, such as iDVD, you can create a slideshow that moves through a series of still images as a single audio stream plays, without interrupting the audio playback. DVD Studio Pro, however, can't and won't allow this type of behavior.

About Slideshows

A slideshow is a sequence of slides that plays from beginning to end in a linear order. When DVD Studio Pro multiplexes your project, it turns the slideshow into a track, with each slide treated similarly to a track chapter. Just as a track can have a maximum of 99 chapters, slideshows are limited to 99 slides. And as with a track, each slideshow is multiplexed into its own individual video title set (VTS; to learn more, see the section "DVD-Video Data Structure" at the end of Chapter 2, "DVD Basics"). Because each DVD-Video can have a maximum of 99 VTSs, your project can have a combined total of 99 tracks *and* slideshows; if you use slideshows, the number of available tracks is reduced, and vice versa.

Preparing source files

Still images in slideshows must be either single-layer Adobe Photoshop or PICT files. Although you can use a multilayer Photoshop document in a slideshow, only the document's first layer will be displayed. Moving images must be MPEG-2 video streams.

All slideshow slides must be 720 x 480 pixels for NTSC projects (or 720 x 576 for PAL). Unlike the Menu editor, which crops oversized pictures to the proper size, the Slideshow editor will not show an asset if it does not have the correct dimensions. This limitation doesn't normally present a problem, though it does mean that you can't use MPEG-1 video streams (MPEG-1 video is 352 x 240 pixels for NTSC, or 352 x 288 for PAL).

Other than these considerations, source files for slideshows are prepared exactly the same way as source files for tracks or menus. To learn how to prepare still images, see the section "Using Photoshop" in Chapter 8, "Photoshop Layer Menus." To learn how to prepare MPEG-2 video streams, see the section "Preparing Source Video Content" in Chapter 3, "Encoding Video Streams."

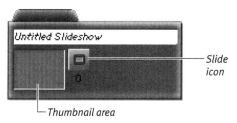

Slide icon

Thumbnail area

Figure 11.1 An empty, untitled Slideshow tile.

Figure 11.2 To create a slideshow, click the Graphical View's Add Slideshow button.

About Slideshow tiles

Of the four tiles you can create in the Graphical View, the Slideshow tile is perhaps the least complex (**Figure 11.1**). Like the other tile types, the Slideshow tile has a large thumbnail icon, which provides a visual clue to the tile's contents by displaying the first frame of the first slide in the slideshow (unlike with Track tiles, you can't change this thumbnail image). Beside the thumbnail image sits a single Slide icon that you double-click to open the Slide container.

To create a slideshow tile:

◆ In the Graphical View, click the Add Slideshow button (**Figure 11.2**).

An untitled Slideshow tile is created in the Graphical View (refer to Figure 11.1).

Using the Slideshow Editor

The Slideshow editor is composed of two lists: the Assets list, on the right, and the Slide list, on the left (**Figure 11.3**). The Assets list displays all of your project's MPEG-2, Photoshop, PICT, and audio assets, and the Slide list provides an area for you to create and organize the slides that make up the slideshow.

To open the Slideshow editor:

◆ In the Graphical View, double-click a Slideshow tile's thumbnail area.

The Slideshow editor opens (refer to Figure 11.3).

✔ Tip

■ If you are working with small tiles in the Graphical View, open the Slideshow editor by selecting a Slideshow tile and choosing Item > Edit, or simply double-click the small Slideshow tile.

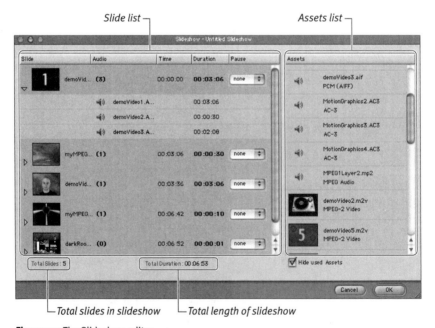

Figure 11.3 The Slideshow editor.

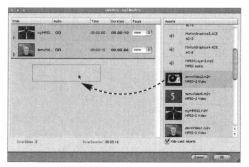

Figure 11.4 Add slides to slideshows by dragging assets from the Assets list to the Slide list.

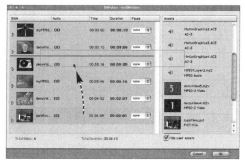

Figure 11.5 Drag slides up or down the Slide list to change their order in the slideshow.

To add an asset to the Slide list:

◆ Select an asset in the Assets list and drag it to the Slide list (**Figure 11.4**).

A new slide displaying the asset is created in the Slide list.

To reorder assets in the Slide list:

◆ Select the asset and drag it up or down the list (**Figure 11.5**).

Watch the Slide list closely. A thin black bar appears between slides, indicating the slide's new position after you release the mouse button.

To delete a slide from the Slide list:

1. Click a slide to select it.

The slide is highlighted (that is, barely highlighted; it changes color by only a shade).

2. On your keyboard, press the Delete key.

The slide is removed from the Slide list.

Setting slide durations

Slides play for a certain length of time before the show moves on to the next slide. By default, MPEG-2 slides appear for the full length of the MPEG-2 video stream. Still-picture slides, however, appear for *only one second*! One second isn't nearly long enough for the viewer to see and comprehend the slide's contents. Buy the viewer some time by setting a *pause interval* (or *wait state*) for all still-picture assets in your slideshow.

To pause a slide:

◆ In the Slide editor's Slide list, choose a value from the slide's Pause menu (**Figure 11.6**).

The slide pauses for the selected amount of time before the show moves on to the next slide.

✔ Tips

■ If a still-picture slide uses audio, it appears for the length of the audio stream. Attaching audio to slides is discussed later in this chapter, in the section "Adding Audio Streams."

■ If a slide uses an MPEG-2 asset, it plays to the end of the MPEG-2 stream and then pauses for the length of time set in the Pause menu.

Figure 11.6 Setting a Pause interval tells the slide to remain on the screen for the specified amount of time.

Creating Slide Transitions

With only still pictures in the slideshow, you'll experience a sudden, somewhat jarring change in imagery when you pass from one slide to the next. Fix these abrupt changes by using an MPEG-2 video stream to create smooth transitions between slides.

Here's how you do it: Import two back-to-back images from your slideshow into Final Cut Pro or Adobe After Effects. Now create a movie that fades the first slide into the second, making sure that the first frame of the new movie is exactly the same as the first slide, and the last frame is exactly the same as the second slide. Encode this new movie as MPEG-2, import it into DVD Studio Pro, and place it between the first and second slides for a smooth transition.

If you are using After Effects to create slide transitions, render out the final video clips using the Animation codec or there will be differences between the color of your slides and transitions.

Figure 11.7 Deselect the Hide Used Assets check box to see all of the assets available for use in the slideshow.

Figure 11.8 After you've added all of the necessary assets to your slideshow's Slide list, close the Slideshow editor by clicking OK.

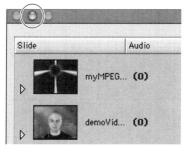

Figure 11.9 Be careful that you don't click the yellow circle in the upper left corner of the Slideshow editor. Doing so sends the Slideshow editor to your computer's dock, which effectively locks DVD Studio Pro so that you can't continue authoring.

Reusing Slideshow assets

When you drag an asset into the Slide list, it disappears from the Assets list. This is a problem if you want to use that asset more than once in your slideshow. The solution? The Hide Used Assets check box, which forces the Assets list to display all usable assets, all the time.

To show all assets:

◆ In the lower right corner of the Slideshow editor, uncheck the Hide Used Assets check box (**Figure 11.7**).

All assets remain visible in the Assets list.

To close the Slideshow editor:

◆ In the lower right corner of the Slideshow editor, click the OK button (**Figure 11.8**). The Slideshow editor closes.

✔ Tip

■ Do not click the yellow circle in the top left corner of the Slideshow editor (**Figure 11.9**). Doing so sends the Slideshow editor to your computer's dock (along the bottom or side of your computer). You will not be able to access other parts of your project until you reopen the Slideshow editor and close it by clicking its OK button.

Adding Audio Streams

As with tracks, each slide can have up to eight audio streams, which viewers can select using their remote controls. But slideshows do suffer one limitation not forced upon tracks: *all of the audio assets used in a slide-show must be the exact same type.* You can't mix AC-3 with PCM or MPEG-1 Layer 2 audio.

The first audio asset you add to a slide sets the default audio type for the entire slide-show. If you try to drag a different type of audio into the slideshow, DVD Studio Pro stares at you like a confused puppy and does nothing. This can be a bit perplexing at first, so if DVD Studio Pro doesn't let you add an audio asset to a slide, check to make sure you haven't added a different form of audio to any other slide in the show.

To add audio to a slide:

1. Drag an asset from the Assets list over a slide in the Slide list (**Figure 11.10**).

   A thin black line appears under the slide to which the audio asset will be attached.

2. Drop the audio asset on the slide.

✔ Tips

- If the slide's audio asset is longer than its picture or MPEG-2 asset, the slide plays for the duration of the audio asset.

- As you drag audio assets onto slides, watch the Slide list closely and make sure you don't accidentally drop the audio asset onto the wrong slide.

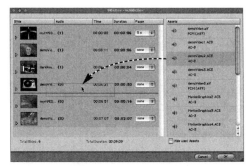

Figure 11.10 Add audio to slides by dragging an audio asset from the Assets list and dropping it on a slide.

Figure 11.11 Hold down the Command key to select multiple assets from the Assets list.

Figure 11.12 The slide's audio counter displays the number of audio streams attached to a slide.

Adding multiple audio streams

Slideshows offer one advantage you can't find anywhere else in DVD Studio Pro: they let you attach multiple audio streams to still pictures (menus can use only a single audio asset). In fact, you can attach up to eight audio streams to each slide, which is useful when authoring multilingual projects (to learn more, see Chapter 15, "Working with Multiple Languages").

To add multiple audio assets to a slide:

1. In the Slideshow editor's Assets list, hold down the Command key while selecting several audio assets (**Figure 11.11**). Each audio asset is highlighted.

2. Drag the audio assets onto a slide. The slide's Audio counter changes to show the number of audio assets attached to the slide (**Figure 11.12**).

✔ Tip

■ Do not attach multiple PCM audio assets to a slide. PCM audio is uncompressed, so using several PCM audio assets may surpass the data rate available to your DVD-Video.

ADDING AUDIO STREAMS

To view a slide's audio assets:

◆ In the Slide list, click the disclosure triangle to the left of the slide's name (**Figure 11.13**).

The slide expands to display its audio assets.

To delete an audio asset:

1. In the Slide list, click the disclosure triangle to the left of the slide's name.

The slide expands to display its audio assets.

2. Select an audio asset (**Figure 11.14**).

The audio asset is highlighted.

3. On your keyboard, press the Delete key.

The audio asset is deleted from the slide.

Disclosure triangle   *Slide audio streams*

Figure 11.13 To view the list of audio streams attached to a slide, click the disclosure triangle to the left of the slide's name.

Figure 11.14 To delete an audio stream, select the stream and press the Delete key on your keyboard.

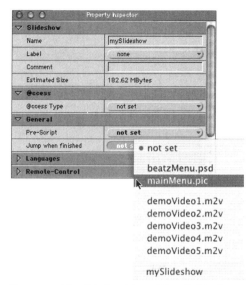

Figure 11.15 The slideshow's Jump When Finished property tells the DVD-Video what to do once the slideshow has finished playing.

Using Actions

Just like a track, a slideshow must be set to *do something* once it has finished playing, or else the DVD-Video stops. You tell the slideshow what to do by supplying it with a Jump When Finished action.

To set a Jump When Finished action:

1. In the Graphical View, select a Slideshow tile.

   The Property Inspector updates to display slideshow properties.

2. From the Property Inspector's Jump When Finished menu, select a project item (**Figure 11.15**).

   When the slideshow finishes playing, your DVD-Video jumps to the selected item.

Creating Interactive Slideshows

Rather than force viewers to skim through your DVD-Video slide by slide using the Previous and Next keys on the remote control, wouldn't it be nice to put buttons right on top of the slideshow so that viewers (especially those on a computer) could click onscreen buttons to move through slides? Or how about a product catalog with buttons that use DVD@ccess links to send the viewer straight to your Web site's ordering section! You can't add buttons to slideshows, but you *can* fake a slideshow-like presentation that has buttons by using a sequence of menus and/or tracks. Here's how:

◆ If your presentation uses still images, create a series of menus and link them together by setting each menu's timeout action so that the menu appears for an appropriate length of time. You can use either Photoshop layer or highlight menus, but if you want your slideshow to have audio, stick with highlight menus. For more information on setting a timeout action or using highlight menus, see Chapter 9, "Highlight Menus."

◆ If your presentation uses MPEG-2 video streams, create a series of tracks and link them together using the Jump When Finished track property. Use interactive markers to put buttons on top of each track (to learn more, see Chapter 10, "Creating Markers and Stories").

◆ If your presentation uses a mixture of still and MPEG-2 assets, use a combination of the preceding two methods and let your viewers click to their heart's content.

Previewing Slideshows

Previewing slideshows is easy work. After all, slideshows are not interactive; all you *can* do is jump back and forth between slides using the Preview mode's Previous and Next keys (**Figure 11.16**).

Nonetheless, previewing slideshows is important because you need to check that your Pause intervals are long (or short) enough, and that the slides play in the correct order. If you've supplied your slides with audio streams, listen to verify that the correct audio stream is attached to each slide, and cycle through all alternate audio streams. If everything works in the Preview mode, you can confidently build your project and burn it to a DVD disc.

To preview a slideshow:

1. In the Graphical View, select a Slideshow tile.

2. In the lower right corner of the Graphical View, click the Preview button.

   The Preview mode launches and plays the slideshow.

3. Use the Previous and Next keys to move backward or forward through slides (refer to Figure 11.16).

✔ Tip

■ Sometimes the Preview mode doesn't play through to the end of each slide. This was more of a problem in DVD Studio Pro 1.0 through 1.2, but it still occasionally occurs in version 1.5. If you notice this happening, don't worry. Once you build your project to a DVD disc, everything will work fine.

Previous key ⎯ ⎿ Next key

Figure 11.16 In DVD Studio Pro's Preview mode, move through the slideshow by pressing the Previous and Next keys.

12

DVD@ccess

DVD Studio Pro uses a proprietary system called DVD@ccess to launch URLs as your DVD-Video plays. URLs (also called DVD@ccess links in DVD Studio Pro) can launch Web pages, send e-mail, or even open files stored in a ROM folder on a hybrid DVD disc. But there is one catch: the DVD-Video must be played on a computer connected to the Internet, or DVD@ccess links will not work; the disc can also be played without fault on a television, but in this case, the DVD@ccess links will simply be ignored.

DVD@ccess does not load any content on the DVD-Video itself, but rather, opens each file in a separate application. If you provide a DVD@ccess link to a Web site, for example, your computer's default browser automatically launches to display the Web page. Similarly, if you add a DVD@ccess link to a PDF file on a hybrid DVD disc, Adobe Acrobat launches, and the PDF file appears on the screen.

About DVD@ccess

DVD@ccess intercepts a DVD-Video's call for a URL and then opens the URL in a Web browser or some other application. DVD@ccess itself is not part of the DVD-Video, but is rather a separate application that runs quietly in the background whenever a DVD-Video disc is placed into the computer's DVD drive. Because the URLs are encoded into the DVD-Video stream as tiny messages that only DVD@ccess understands, the viewer never sees the URLs, but only witnesses the results. Consequently, Web links in DVD Studio Pro projects work only on computers that have DVD@ccess installed.

DVD@ccess is not automatically installed when you put the disc into a DVD drive, so viewers must be proactive and install DVD@ccess before your project's DVD@ccess links will work. Fortunately, when you add DVD@ccess links to your DVD-Video, Windows and Macintosh DVD@ccess installers are automatically included in a folder named DVDccess on the final DVD-Video disc (**Figure 12.1**).

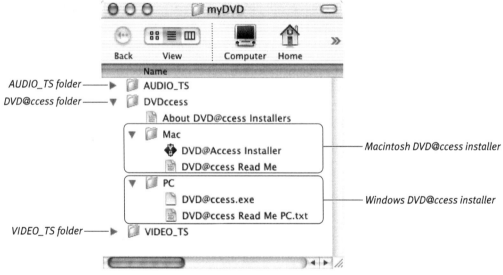

Figure 12.1 When you add Web links to your project, DVD Studio Pro includes both Windows and Macintosh DVD@ccess installers on the final DVD disc, in a folder named DVDccess.

Figure 12.2 Only the Build and Format Disc "myDVD" option builds a complete, final DVD-Video disc. If you want DVD@ccess installers on your finished DVD, be sure to choose this option.

Figure 12.3 If you use Toast Titanium 5 to write your finished DVD-Video disc, the DVD@ccess installers may not be included with your project. When needed, you can grab them from the Resources folder located in the DVD Studio Pro Mac OS 9 application folder.

✔ Tips

■ DVD Studio Pro does not include the DVD@ccess installers with projects you build directly on your hard disk (using the File > Build Disc option). The DVD@ccess installers are included only with projects multiplexed using the File > Build and Format Disc "myDVD" option (**Figure 12.2**). To learn more, see Chapter 13, "Finishing the DVD."

■ In Mac OS 9, the DVD@ccess installers are located in the DVD Studio Pro application folder, in a subfolder named Resources (**Figure 12.3**). If you are using Roxio's Toast Titanium 5 to burn your final DVD-Video, grab the DVD@ccess installers from this Resources folder and include them with your DVD-Video.

■ In Mac OS X, you can find the DVD@ccess installers inside the DVD Studio Pro application package. In the Finder, locate the DVD Studio Pro application icon, then hold the Control key while clicking the application icon one time. From the menu that appears, choose Show Package Contents, then navigate to the Contents > Resources > DVD@ccess folder.

ABOUT DVD@CCESS

235

Installing DVD@ccess on Windows

For your Web links to work on a Windows PC, the viewer must first install DVD@ccess. Most Windows users won't instinctively know this, so you'll need to tell them. A common way to do this is to include a text warning on the menu with the Web links, but you can also add an Info button that links to a menu with text instructions or a video segment that walks viewers through the installation process. Whatever method you choose, make sure it's obvious enough that Windows users understand that they must install DVD@ccess before the DVD-Video's Web links will work.

✔ Tips

- Even with proper warning, it's hard to convince some viewers to install new software on their computers. As a result, count on the fact that some people won't see your Web links.

- DVD@ccess is much improved for DVD Studio Pro 1.5. Past incantations had a few problems on Windows PCs, but most of those have been fixed in the newest release.

- You should take some satisfaction in getting Windows users to install DVD@ccess, because you're paving the way for all of your kindred DVD Studio Pro authors. Why? DVD@ccess needs to be installed only once. After that, it works fine for as long as it remains on the Windows PC, allowing all DVD-Videos authored with DVD Studio Pro to play without a hitch.

Figure 12.4 The Apple DVD Player works in tandem with DVD@ccess to show Web links, but only if the DVD@ccess preference is enabled.

Figure 12.5
To open DVD Player's preferences, choose DVD Player > Preferences.

Figure 12.6 At the bottom of DVD Player's Disc tab is a check box that turns DVD@ccess on or off.

Installing DVD@ccess on the Macintosh

Most Macintosh users will not need to install DVD@ccess; it's included with all copies of Apple DVD Player 2.4 or later. If your Web links don't work in Apple DVD Player, the problem is probably that DVD@ccess isn't turned on. A quick visit to DVD Player's Preferences dialog box fixes this.

To enable DVD@ccess:

1. Open Apple DVD Player (**Figure 12.4**).

2. Choose DVD Player > Preferences (**Figure 12.5**).
   The DVD Player Preferences dialog box opens.

3. Click the Disc tab (**Figure 12.6**).
   The Disc tab tells DVD Player how to play the disc, including settings for the disc's default languages and a check box at the bottom that turns on DVD@ccess.

4. Select the Enable DVD@ccess Web Links check box.

5. Click OK.
   The Preferences dialog box closes. Whenever DVD Player encounters a DVD@ccess Web link, DVD@ccess opens the corresponding Web page.

✔ Tip

- The Macintosh DVD@ccess installer works only on Mac OS 9. Mac OS X already has DVD@ccess installed and ready to go.

ABOUT DVD@CCESS

Using DVD@ccess

DVD@ccess links can be attached to several
types of project items, including tracks, menus,
slideshows, chapters, and slides. If an item
has a DVD@ccess link, the link's URL opens
as soon as the project item appears on the
screen.

Creating DVD@ccess links is usually as
simple as filling in the blanks. In most situations, you just select a project item, specify
the @ccess type, and provide a URL (**Figure
12.7**). When the project item plays, the Web
link launches. It's really that easy.

The only slight difficulty with DVD@ccess
lies in using the correct syntax. All links, for
example, use full path names only. For links
to the Internet, this means you must include
the http:// prefix: for example:

http://www.apple.com/dvd.

Without this prefix DVD@ccess will not
understand how to follow the link to the
Internet, and the link will not work.

DVD@ccess links can also launch the viewer's
e-mail application, link to an FTP server, or
even open files on the finished DVD disc
using pathnames similar to the following:

◆ mailto:myEmailAddress@myDomain.com

◆ ftp://myDomain.com/myMovie.mov

◆ file:///DiskName/Folder/
  FileName.extension

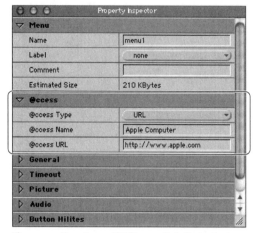

Figure 12.7 To set up a DVD@ccess link, first select
an item in the Graphical View. If the item supports
DVD@ccess, its Property Inspector will reveal an
@ccess area that you can use to specify a URL.

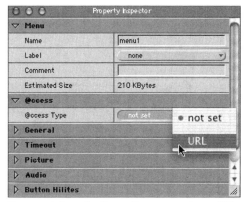

Figure 12.8 From the @ccess Type menu, choose URL.

Figure 12.9 The expanded @ccess area.

Figure 12.10 Enter the DVD@ccess link's full URL in the @ccess URL property field. For Internet links, use the http:// prefix; for FTP links, use the ftp:// prefix; and for links that point to the DVD disc itself, be sure to use the file:/// prefix.

To set a DVD@ccess Web link:

1. In either the Graphical View or Project View, select a track, menu, slideshow, chapter, or slide.

   The Property Inspector updates to display the item's properties. The second area from the top is the item's @ccess area (refer to Figure 12.7).

2. From the @ccess area's @ccess Type menu, choose URL (**Figure 12.8**).

   The @ccess area expands to show @ccess Name and @ccess URL properties (**Figure 12.9**).

3. In the @ccess Name text box, type a name for the link.

   This name serves only as a personal reminder about where the link points. It does not appear in the final DVD-Video, so you can enter whatever you want.

4. In the @ccess URL text box, type a URL (**Figure 12.10**).

   When the selected item appears on the screen, this URL is launched.

✔ Tip

■ Usually, DVD@ccess causes the Web browser to open directly on top of your DVD-Video. For specialized presentations that synchronize Web content to the video on the DVD disc, you may want the Web page to open in a smaller window off to the side of DVD Viewer. With some clever JavaScript work in the Web page's HTML document, you can position the Web browser anywhere on the screen, but you have little control over the screen location of DVD Player's viewer window. As a result, it's usually easier to just launch the Web page and let the user position the new window as needed.

USING DVD@CCESS

Linking to Buttons

Perhaps the most common use you will make of DVD@ccess is to add buttons that launch Web pages. For example, you've seen the Contact button found on most Web pages. Using DVD@ccess, you can add a Contact button to your DVD-Video. Viewers watching the disc on a computer can click the Contact button, and their default e-mail program will open with your e-mail address in the Send To field.

Interestingly, you can't create buttons with direct DVD@ccess links. Instead, you must use a workaround technique that jumps the button to a second menu with a DVD@ccess link attached to it. The second menu looks exactly like the first menu, but it has a very short timeout action that jumps the video back to the first menu after the second menu launches the URL. With all of the action that accompanies the opening of the browser, viewers will not even notice that they're jumping back and forth between the menus.

To open a URL from a button:

1. Create a menu that includes a DVD@ccess link button (**Figure 12.11**).

   Finish the menu by naming each button and assigning all button selected and activated states (for more information on creating menus, see Chapter 8, "Photoshop Layer Menus," and Chapter 9, "Highlight Menus").

2. In the Graphical View, select the Menu tile.

3. Choose Edit > Duplicate (**Figure 12.12**), or press Command-D.

   A copy of the Menu tile appears in the Graphical View with the word *copy* attached to its name (**Figure 12.13**). This new Menu tile is an exact copy of the first one, so both menus look identical.

DVD@ccess link button

Figure 12.11 A menu with a button that uses DVD@ccess to launch the viewer's e-mail program.

Figure 12.12 Choose Edit > Duplicate to make an exact copy of a menu (or any project item).

Figure 12.13 In the Graphical View, the menu copy appears on top of the original menu.

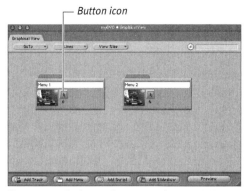

Button icon

Figure 12.14 The button icon opens the menu's Button container, which lets you select buttons and change their properties without opening the Menu editor.

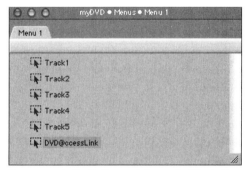

Figure 12.15 In the Button container, select the button that links to the URL...

Figure 12.16 ...And then set its Jump When Activated property to the second, duplicate menu.

4. Move the second menu off of the first one and give each menu an appropriate name.

You'll need to access both menus during the course of this exercise, so you don't want the first menu to be obstructed by the second. To avoid confusing the two menus, name the first menu Menu 1 and the second Menu 2.

5. On the Menu 1 tile, click the Button icon (**Figure 12.14**).

The Button container opens.

6. In the Button container, choose the DVD@ccess link button (**Figure 12.15**).

The Property Inspector updates to display the button's properties.

7. In the Property Inspector, set the button's Jump When Activated property so that it leads to Menu 2 (**Figure 12.16**).

8. In the Graphical View, select Menu 2.

The Property Inspector updates to display Menu 2's properties.

continues on next page

LINKING TO BUTTONS

9. In the @ccess area, set a DVD@ccess link by setting the @ccess Type, @ccess Name, and @ccess URL properties (**Figure 12.17**).

   Setting DVD@ccess links is described in the section "Using DVD@ccess" earlier in this chapter.

10. From the Timeout area's Action menu, choose Menu 1 (**Figure 12.18**).

    The Duration (in Seconds) property appears under the Timeout Action property.

Figure 12.17 Select the second menu and use its @ccess area to specify a DVD@ccess link.

Figure 12.18 The DVD@ccess link launches as soon as the second menu appears on the screen. After the link has been activated, you need to return to the first menu. To do this, use the second menu's Timeout Action property.

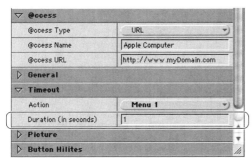

Figure 12.19 Enter a small number for the Duration (in Seconds) property. Unless your presentation requires something different, the default value of one second should work well.

Figure 12.20 Set Menu 2's default button to the DVD@ccess link button. Now the DVD@ccess link button is automatically selected when Menu 2 appears on the screen.

11. Set the Timeout Duration (in Seconds) property to one second (**Figure 12.19**).

This short timeout causes Menu 2 to quickly jump back to Menu 1, fooling the viewer into thinking that Menu 1 never left the screen. At this point the link will be opening, which also helps hide the jump back and forth between menus.

12. From the Property Inspector's General area, set Menu 2's default button to the Web link button (**Figure 12.20**).

Although Menu 2 flashes on the screen only briefly, it still has time to show the default button. Setting the Web link button as the default ensures that it is the button that's automatically highlighted.

For additional sleight of hand, make the button's selected state look like the activated state of the button in Menu 1. Now when Menu 2 comes on the screen, it looks the same as Menu 1 looked when leaving the screen, causing the transition between the two menus to appear seamless.

✔ Tips

■ If your menu uses audio, the audio stream will be interrupted when the DVD-Video jumps between menus. To make the interruption less jarring, turn off the audio for the second menu.

■ When Menu 1 comes back on the screen, its default button is automatically highlighted. This default button may not be the Web link button. To make sure that the proper button is highlighted, write a script. For more information on scripting, see Chapter 17, "Scripting!"

LINKING TO BUTTONS

Linking to the Disc

DVD@ccess can open files located on the finished DVD disc. This lets you create hybrid discs that include PDF files, HTML pages, high-resolution versions of slides in a slideshow, or even Macromedia Flash vector animations that launch as the DVD-Video plays (To learn more about hybrid DVDs, see Chapter 13, "Finishing the DVD").

To link to files on the DVD disc, use the following path as a URL:

```
file:///DiscName/Folder/
FileName.extension
```

Think carefully about how data folders will be written to your final DVD disc, because you must use exactly the same path in your URLs, or DVD@ccess will not be able to locate the files.

✔ Tips

- The `file:///` path prefix has three forward slashes (`///`), which is one more than the `http://` and `ftp://` path prefixes.

- If you're creating a hybrid DVD with a ROM folder, DVD Studio Pro takes all of the files out of the ROM folder and writes them alongside the VIDEO_TS and AUDIO_TS folders on the final DVD disc (**Figure 12.21**). The ROM folder itself is not included on the disc, so be careful that you don't include its name in the DVD@ccess link's pathname.

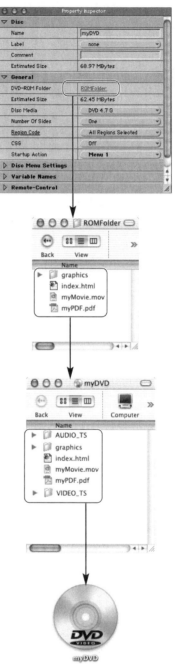

Figure 12.21 This figure traces the contents of the ROM folder as they move from your computer's hard disc to the hybrid DVD disc. Note that the ROM folder selected in DVD Studio Pro does not actually end up on the DVD disc.

Figure 12.22 To enable DVD@ccess links while previewing inside DVD Studio Pro, choose DVD Studio Pro > Preferences.

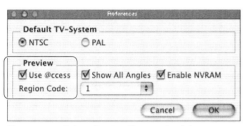

Figure 12.23 Select the Use @ccess check box to enable DVD@ccess links.

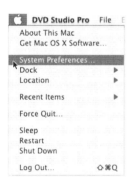

Figure 12.24 In Mac OS X, open the System Preferences window by choosing Apple menu > System Preferences.

Previewing DVD@ccess

The Preview mode launches DVD@ccess links, which let you verify that your links are pointing to the right files. If the Preview mode doesn't launch the links, it's because the DVD@ccess preference has been disabled. Turn it back on, and your links will work as expected.

To enable DVD@ccess previewing:

1. In DVD Studio Pro, choose DVD Studio Pro > Preferences (**Figure 12.22**).

   The Preferences window opens. At the bottom of the Preferences window is the Preview section.

2. In the Preferences window's Preview section, select the Use @ccess check box (**Figure 12.23**).

3. Click OK.

   The Preferences window closes. DVD@ccess is enabled during Preview mode, allowing you to test all of your Web links and verify that they work.

Setting the default browser

By default, all Web links open in Microsoft Internet Explorer. To use a different browser, such as the Omni Group's OmniWeb or Netscape Navigator, you will have to change your computer's default browser.

To set the default browser in Mac OS X:

1. In the Finder, choose Apple menu > System Preferences (**Figure 12.24**).

   The System Preferences window opens.

continues on next page

2. Double-click the Internet icon
(**Figure 12.25**).

The Internet Preferences Window opens.

3. Select the Web tab (**Figure 12.26**).

4. From the Default Web Browser menu,
choose the Web browser that you want to
set as the default browser (**Figure 12.27**).

When DVD@ccess encounters a Web link,
it opens the link in the selected browser.

Figure 12.25 In the System Preferences window,
double-click the Internet icon.

Figure 12.26 The Internet Preferences window's
Web tab.

Figure 12.27 Choose your preferred Web browser from
the Default Web Browser menu.

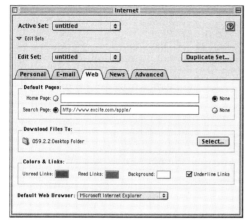

Figure 12.28 Mac OS 9's Internet Preferences window's Web tab.

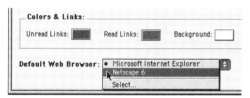

Figure 12.29 Choose your preferred Web browser from the Default Web Browser menu.

To set the default browser in Mac OS 9:

1. Choose Apple menu > Control Panels > Internet.

   The Internet Preferences Window opens.

2. Select the Web tab (**Figure 12.28**).

3. From the Default Web Browser menu, choose the Web browser that you want to set as the default browser (**Figure 12.29**).

   When DVD@ccess encounters a Web link, it opens the link in the selected browser.

PREVIEWING DVD@CCESS

13

FINISHING THE DVD

Finishing the DVD is a process that creates great excitement, but also some anxiety. On one hand, after all those creative hours, it's finally time to record your project on a DVD disc and watch it on TV! On the other hand, DVD-R discs are expensive, so you want to ensure that the project records correctly the first time, every time. This becomes very important if you intend to replicate the project in large quantities, because if you fail to notice a mistake in the DVD-Video, that mistake will be replicated hundreds, or even thousands, of times.

To guard against broken button links, improperly encoded assets, and other traumas, each project needs to pass rigorous quality assurance (QA) testing before it is recorded on a DVD-R disc (or DLT tape for projects going to a replication facility). QA begins in DVD Studio Pro's Preview mode. Preview mode is an excellent means for testing your project's interactivity as it faithfully plays all button links, jump actions, alternate angles, and alternate audio streams just like a DVD-Video player does. But Preview mode is not infallible and thus offers only a first line of defense. The next step of the QA process is building the project, which places a working copy of the DVD-Video on your computer's hard disks. Using Apple's DVD Player, you can open the project and play it just like a DVD-Video on a DVD disc. If everything checks out, you can record a DVD-R.

DVD Studio Pro can record a project straight to a DVD-R disc. You don't need any other applications or tools (although Roxio's Toast Titanium 5 is a welcome addition and is covered toward the end of this chapter). If you take a few simple precautions, such as quitting all other applications and setting your computer so that it doesn't fall asleep, DVD Studio Pro will successfully record a DVD-R every time. To help you get it right from the beginning, this chapter shows you how to preview, test, and record your project to disc. It also discusses startup actions, region codes, copy protection, and a few other settings designed to ensure that your DVD-Video plays the way that you want it to play.

Setting the Startup Action

The startup action is the DVD's autorun sequence. It tells the DVD-Video what to do once it's placed in a DVD-Video player. The startup action may be an introductory animation, an FBI warning, a transition that leads from black to a menu, or even a menu itself; in fact, any tile in your project's Graphical View makes an acceptable startup action.

Not setting the startup action leads to problems with your finished DVD-Video. In the best scenario, the DVD-Video will not autostart, and viewers will have to press Play to get the action rolling. The DVD-Video then starts playback at track 1, which may not be the first thing you want viewers to see. In the worst scenario, the DVD-Video player won't play the disc (Apple DVD Player won't play a disc if its startup action isn't set).

To set the startup action:

1. In the Graphical View, click anywhere there isn't a tile (**Figure 13.1**).

   Clicking the Graphical View's background selects the disc (in this case, the virtual disc, or the DVD Studio Pro project itself). The Property Inspector updates to show the disc's properties.

2. From the Property Inspector's Startup Action menu, select a project item (**Figure 13.2**).

   This menu lists every tile in your project, as well as all chapters and slides. Although there's a lot to choose from, the choice is simple. Think about which item you want your viewers to see first and select it. When the DVD-Video is inserted into a DVD-Video player, the selected item automatically begins playing.

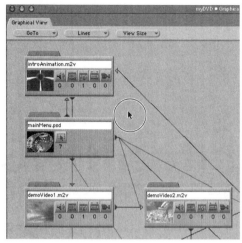

Figure 13.1 In the Graphical View, select the disc by clicking between tiles.

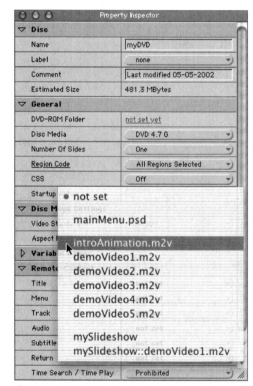

Figure 13.2 The startup action tells the DVD-Video player which project item to play first.

✔ Tips

■ If you forgot to set a startup action before multiplexing your project, DVD Studio Pro's Log window warns you of your mistake (**Figure 13.3**). For more information on the Log window, see "About the Log Window" later in this chapter.

■ Although increasingly rare, some DVD-Video players have problems displaying discs using a menu or script as a startup action. To guard against this, place a short (say 4-second) black MPEG-2 video stream in a track that plays just before the menu. Set the startup action to this *blank* track so that it plays before the menu appears on the screen.

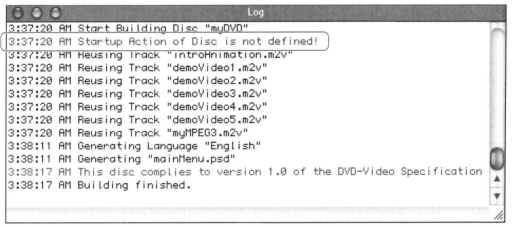

```
3:37:20 AM Start Building Disc "myDVD"
3:37:20 AM Startup Action of Disc is not defined!
3:37:20 AM Reusing Track "introAnimation.m2v"
3:37:20 AM Reusing Track "demoVideo1.m2v"
3:37:20 AM Reusing Track "demoVideo2.m2v"
3:37:20 AM Reusing Track "demoVideo3.m2v"
3:37:20 AM Reusing Track "demoVideo4.m2v"
3:37:20 AM Reusing Track "demoVideo5.m2v"
3:37:20 AM Reusing Track "myMPEG3.m2v"
3:38:11 AM Generating Language "English"
3:38:11 AM Generating "mainMenu.psd"
3:38:17 AM This disc complies to version 1.0 of the DVD-Video Specification
3:38:17 AM Building finished.
```

Figure 13.3 DVD Studio Pro's Log window warns you if you are multiplexing a project with no startup action.

Assigning Remote-Control Keys

The Remote-Control area at the bottom of the Disc Property Inspector sets the functions of several important remote-control keys, including the Title, Menu, Track, Audio, and Subtitle keys (**Figure 13.4**).

Figure 13.4 The Property Inspector's Remote-Control area sets the function of certain keys on a DVD-Video player's remote control.

Navigational Uniformity

As the DVD-Video's author, you have power over several remote-control keys and can set them to play whatever project item you want. It's possible to be very creative with the way the remote plays the DVD, but most of the time viewers expect their remote controls to work in a certain, logical way.

Navigational uniformity refers to the use of simple rules to ensure that the remote control always behaves as expected, regardless of the DVD-Video playing. For example, pressing the Title key should always bring the DVD-Video's main menu (or top menu) onto the screen, and pressing the Menu key should return viewers to the menu that jumped them to the currently playing track or slideshow.

The Track (also called Angle), Audio, and Subtitle keys are more of a challenge. By default, all remote controls use these keys to cycle through alternate angle, audio, and subtitle streams of tracks and slideshows. Imagine that you have a track with three audio streams: English, French, and Spanish. When the English audio stream is playing, pressing the Audio key swaps in the French stream. Pressing the Audio key a second time brings in the Spanish stream, and a third press brings back the English audio program.

But you may not always want the viewer to cycle through audio streams by clicking the Audio key. Instead, you may want to create an Audio menu that lists all three audio streams and assign that menu to the Audio button. In this case, pressing the remote control's audio key takes viewers straight to an Audio menu that they can use to select the correct stream instead of cycling through each audio stream.

Similar to the Audio key, the Track key may jump to a Scene menu listing the chapters on a track, and the Subtitle key may link to a Subtitle menu listing all available close-captioning options. Just remember one thing: if you set the Track, Audio, or Subtitle key, viewers lose the ability to cycle through alternate streams by pressing any of these keys.

Figure 13.5 The Title key should always link to the DVD-Video's main menu.

You can assign any tile from the Graphical View as the action of the remote keys listed in the Property Inspector's Remote-Control area. Although it's nice to have this level of control, most of the time you should follow simple rules that guarantee navigational uniformity across all DVD-Videos (to learn more, see the sidebar "Navigational Uniformity").

To set disc remote-control keys:

1. Click the background of the Graphical View to select the disc.

   The Property Inspector updates to display disc properties. At the bottom of the Property Inspector is a Remote-Control area that you use to set the actions for several remote keys.

2. From the Remote-Control area, assign project items to remote-control keys (**Figure 13.5**).

3. Preview your project and use the buttons along the bottom of the Preview mode screen to make sure that remote keys jump to the correct project items (**Figure 13.6**).

continues on next page

Title key — Menu key — Audio key — Subtitle key — Angle key —

Figure 13.6 The keys along the bottom of the Preview mode screen mimic the functions of the remote-control keys that you set using the Property Inspector's Remote-Control area.

ASSIGNING REMOTE-CONTROL KEYS

✔ Tips

- The Title key uses different names on different remote controls. Some call it "Top Menu," some label it "Main," but whatever the key's name, its action remains the same.

- The Track, Audio, and Subtitle keys usually switch through alternate track, audio and subtitle streams respectively (see the sidebar "Track and Slideshow Remote Settings"). Although DVD Studio Pro lets you assign them new actions, many remote controls will ignore the new settings in favor of the default actions.

Track and Slideshow Remote Settings

Each track and slideshow has its own Remote-Control area, located at the bottom of the Track or Slideshow Property Inspector (**Figure 13.7**). By default, these keys are set to Same As Disc and adopt the settings that you define in the Disc Property Inspector.

Depending on the complexity of your project, you may want to change these settings. The Menu key, for example, should always return viewers to the menu that jumped them to the currently playing track or slideshow. If your project has multiple menus linking to many different tracks and slideshows, you may need to set the Menu key on a track-by-track basis. In a similar fashion, the Track, Audio, and Subtitle keys should return viewers to the Scene, Audio, or Subtitle menu for the currently playing track or slideshow (see the sidebar "Navigational Uniformity" earlier in this chapter for more information on this topic).

Figure 13.7 Remote-control keys can behave differently depending on the track or slideshow being played by the DVD-Video player.

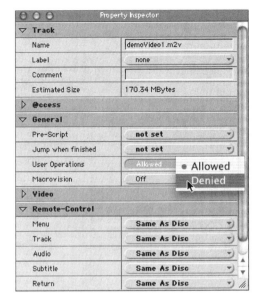

Figure 13.8 Denying User Operations disables the remote control so that viewers can't skip between tracks and chapters.

Disabling the remote control

There will be times when you don't want the remote keys to work. You may, for example, have an intro sequence (such as the FBI warning) that you want to force your viewers to sit through, no matter what. In this situation, you can disable the remote control by denying user operations.

To disable the remote control for an entire track:

1. In the Graphical View, select a Track tile.

2. From the Property Inspector's User Operations menu, select Denied (**Figure 13.8**). The viewer is unable to use the remote control while that track is playing.

✔ Tip

- Chapters can have user operation settings independent of the track to which they belong. This feature comes in handy if you've added buttons to one or more chapters on the track. If you don't disable the remote control, the viewer can skip right on to the next chapter by pressing the remote control's Next key, which defeats the navigational purpose of the interactive marker.

Hiding Easter Eggs

An *Easter egg* is a hidden track containing bonus content. Viewers are supposed to hunt for Easter eggs by finding hidden buttons, navigating tracks in a certain order, or activating a passcode from an onscreen keypad. Easter eggs should be hard to find, but if you don't plan ahead, viewers can jump straight to them by pressing the remote control's Next key to skip through tracks and chapters.

In this situation, denying user operations saves the day. Create a 4-second slug of black MPEG-2 video and drag it into the Graphical View to create a Track tile. Set the Track tile's jump value to the project's main menu (or any other project item) and set its User Operations property to Denied. On the Project View's Tracks tab, move the new track directly above the Easter egg track(s). This new track will be recorded to the DVD disc in front of the Easter eggs. If a viewer tries to scan the disc by pressing the Next key, the new track acts as a block, sending all trigger-happy viewers back to the project's main menu.

Protecting Your Content

DVDs hold digital data, and digital data is easy to copy. To keep your DVD-Video on the disc and out of the grip of those who might want to reproduce it, DVD Studio Pro offers three forms of content protection: region codes, the Content Scrambling System (CSS), and the Macrovision Analog Protection System (APS). For more on content protection see Chapter 2, "DVD Basics."

Region Codes

All DVD-Video players are hardwired with a certain region code when they are manufactured. Using DVD Studio Pro's Region Code property, you can set exactly where in the world your DVD-Video will play (see Chapter 2, "DVD Basics").

Region coding does not encrypt any of the files on the DVD; it simply tells the DVD-Video player to accept the disc, or not. But if you do decide to region code your disc, you must also CSS copy protect the project, or the region codes will not work.

To set the disc's region code:

1. Click the background of the Graphical View to select the disc.

   The Property Inspector updates to display the disc's properties.

2. From the Disc Property Inspector's Region Code menu, select the regions where you want your disc to be viewable (**Figure 13.9**).

   By default, all regions are selected, which means that your DVD-Video will play on any DVD-Video player, anywhere in the world (that is, any player that understands your DVD-Video's broadcast standard, as most NTSC players won't play PAL DVD-Videos regardless of the region code).

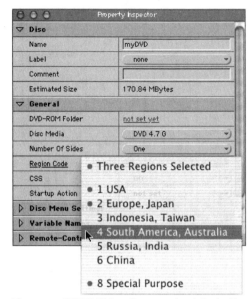

Figure 13.9 All DVD-Video players are hardwired with a region code. If you give your DVD-Video a region code, the final disc will play only in DVD-Video players that have a matching region code.

Figure 13.10 Turning on CSS tells the replicator to CSS encrypt your DVD-Video.

CSS copy protection

CSS is a data encryption system that prevents viewers from dragging your DVD-Video off of the DVD disc and onto their computers. CSS encrypts the DVD-Video's data by scrambling the audio and video in certain sectors on the disc (see the sidebar "CSS and Sector Sizes"). The keys used to put this data back together are stored in two places right on the DVD-Video disc. The first key, called the Title key, is stored in the header of each scrambled sector. The second key, the Disc key, is locked away in the disc's control area.

Computer DVD-ROM drives cannot harvest information from either sector headers or the disc's control area. Consequently, when someone drags your DVD-Video off of the disc and onto his or her computer, the person gets only the scrambled data—the keys to open that data are left behind on the DVD disc.

CSS encryption can be applied by qualified replicators only—you can't CSS protect your disc with DVD Studio Pro alone. However, you do need to tell the replicator to apply CSS copy protection, by turning on CSS to set a *flag*, or warning. Setting this flag doesn't automatically give you CSS; you must pay for it. If you intend to use CSS copy protection, discuss costs with the replicator before you send the DLT tapes.

To enable CSS copy protection:

1. Click the background of the Graphical View to select the disc.

   The Property Inspector updates to display the disc's properties.

2. From the Disc Property Inspector's CSS menu, choose On (**Figure 13.10**).

CSS and Sector Sizes

Data on DVD discs is stored in sectors. CSS copy-protected discs (including most Hollywood DVD-Videos) use a sector size of 2,054 bytes, whereas DVD-R discs use a sector size of 2,048 bytes. The replicator places encryption keys in the extra few bytes that DVD-R discs don't have, which makes it physically impossible for a DVD-R to hold a CSS-protected DVD-Video. DLT tapes, however, can record a sector size of 2,054 bytes, making them suitable for transporting your CSS-protected DVD-Video to the replicator.

Macrovision protection

Macrovision is an Analog Protection System (APS) that keeps people from recording your DVD-Videos onto VHS tapes. The system works by tricking the VHS recorder's Automatic Gain Control (AGC) circuit into thinking that the video stream is either brighter or darker than it actually is. To fix the problem, the VHS player's AGC circuit jumps in and increases or reduces the video's brightness. The result is a video stream that alternates between being too bright or too dark, making it unpleasant to watch. Some forms of Macrovision also *colorstripe* the video, which adds colored horizontal stripes across the video (see "What's Colorstripe?").

To use Macrovision copy protection, you must enter into a license agreement with Macrovision and have your project professionally replicated. In return for giving you access to its APS, Macrovision charges you a per-disc fee (usually around a few cents per disc; the higher the number of units, the lower the per-unit price). You can then activate Macrovision copy protection for certain tracks or chapters as you create the disc. After you deliver the disc to the replication facility, the replicator checks the disc to see which parts you want protected and reports this information to the folks at Macrovision, who complete the process by sending you a bill.

Before using Macrovision, contact the company to find out the cost for protecting your discs. For more information, either visit the company's Web site at www.macrovision.com, or send an e-mail directly to acp-na@macrovision.com.

What's Colorstripe?

Colorstripe modifies the colorburst signal, which is a reference contained within the analog video signal. Televisions and video monitors use this colorburst reference to decode and properly display color information. Although this modification is transparent to display devices, it dramatically upsets the VCR's color playback circuitry if it is recorded and played back.

Figure 13.11 Use the Macrovision property to enable Macrovision copy protection for entire tracks or specific chapters on a track.

To enable the Macrovision APS:

1. In DVD Studio Pro, select a Track tile or a marker.

   The Property Inspector updates to display the track or marker properties.

2. From the Property Inspector's Macrovision menu, choose a Macrovision type (**Figure 13.11**).

   When the disc is replicated, the replicator will add *trigger bits* that tell the DVD-Video player to turn on Macrovision copy protection.

✔ Tip

- DVD Studio Pro 1.5 has a bug that causes Macrovision copy protection to be applied incorrectly. If your project needs Macrovision copy protection, upgrade to DVD Studio Pro 1.5.1 or higher.

So Many Types, So Little Time

Macrovision-protected discs contain *trigger bits* that tell the DVD-Video player whether or not to enable the Macrovision APS. Macrovision copy protection comes in three types:

- Type 1: AGC protection only

- Type 2: AGC plus two-line colorstripe protection

- Type 3: AGC plus four-line colorstripe protection

Type 3 is the default, or standard, configuration; the two other types are available as alternatives in the event that problems with DVD playback occur on some televisions. (According to Macrovision, no problems have ever been reported.)

In authoring for NTSC video (U.S.), type 3 is recommended. For PAL video (Europe), type 2 is recommended, but with a catch: current PAL DVD-Video players use AGC copy protection *only* and at this time do not have colorstripe enabled. If you're working on a PAL project, hedge your bets by choosing type-2 protection, because if the decision is made to enable colorstripe in PAL, the discs will already be set to use it.

Previewing the Disc

Before building the final project, open the
Preview mode one last time and use it to
Preview the disc itself, checking that all menus,
tracks, and slideshows play as expected.

To preview the disc:

1. Click the background of the Graphical
   View to select the disc.

2. In the lower right corner of the Graphical
   View, click the Preview button
   (**Figure 13.12**).

   The Preview mode opens (**Figure 13.13**).

3. Play all project items in turn, making sure
   that each item works as it should.

✔ Tip

■ If Preview mode doesn't launch when the
   disc is selected, then you forgot to set a
   startup action. See "Setting the Startup
   Action" at the beginning of this chapter.

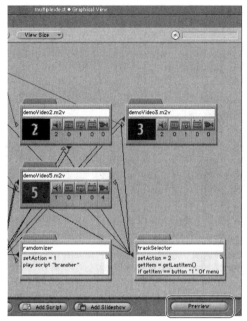

Figure 13.12 Click the Preview button to launch the
Preview mode.

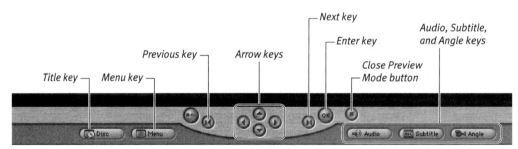

Figure 13.13 The buttons along the bottom of the Preview mode screen mimic keys on a DVD-Video player's
remote control.

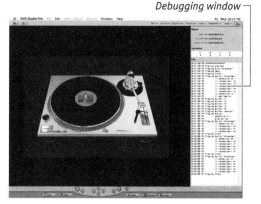

Debugging window

Figure 13.14 The Preview mode's debugging window keeps track of project items as you navigate and test the project.

Debugging button

Figure 13.15 To open the debugging window, click the Debugging button in the upper right corner of the Preview mode screen.

Debugging your project

The Preview mode has a debugging window that you can monitor as you preview your disc (**Figure 13.14**). The debugging window displays the last item played, the item that's currently playing, and the value of each variable used in a script. (See Chapter 17, "Scripting!" for more information on script variables.)

To open the debugging window:

◆ In the upper right corner of the Preview mode, click the Debugging button (**Figure 13.15**).

The debugging window opens to the right of the Preview mode pane (refer to Figure 13.14).

Quality Assured

Quality assurance (QA) is the process of testing a finished project to make sure that it plays as expected. There are three levels of QA testing:

Use the Preview mode—often. As you author your project, you should constantly use the Preview mode to discover and correct mistakes. By the time you're ready to record the project to disc, most problems will already be fixed.

Play the project in Apple DVD Player. When you build a project, you create a finished copy of the DVD-Video on your computer's hard disks. Using DVD Player, you can open the DVD-Video from your hard disks and watch it just like you would watch a DVD-Video placed in a set-top DVD-Video player. If your project plays correctly in DVD Player, it will also play correctly on a TV. Once you've tested all of your menus, watched the tracks, and cycled through all of the alternate angles and audio streams in DVD Player, you can record a DVD-R.

Create a test DVD-R disc. Recording your project onto a DVD-R disc lets you test it on a TV. If you're not replicating your project, this DVD-R is more than just a test disc—it's the final DVD-Video. But if you are sending your project to a replication facility, this DVD-R allows you to watch the project the way most other viewers will: on a television set. If the DVD-R works as it should, you can confidently send off your DLT tapes.

Creating a Hybrid DVD

Hybrid DVDs contain computer data alongside the VIDEO_TS and AUDIO_TS folders at the disc's root level. This data can be anything, including PDF files, QuickTime movies, and Power Point presentations; as long as a computer can understand the file, you can place it on a hybrid DVD. New to DVD Studio Pro 1.5, you can now specify a ROM folder, and the folder's contents will be included at the DVD disc's root level, beside the VIDEO_TS and AUDIO_TS folders (**Figure 13.16**).

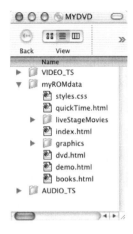

Figure 13.16
On a hybrid DVD, ROM data is recorded at the root level of the DVD disc, beside the VIDEO_TS and AUDIO_TS folders.

To select a ROM folder:

1. Click the background of the Graphical View to select the disc.

   The Property Inspector updates to display the disc's properties. In the General area, you'll find a DVD-ROM Folder property with the words "Not Set Yet" underlined and printed in blue (**Figure 13.17**).

Figure 13.17 The disc's DVD-ROM Folder property.

CREATING A HYBRID DVD

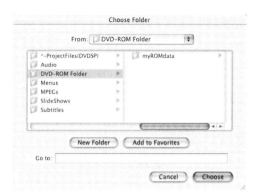

Figure 13.18 The Choose Folder dialog box lets you select a DVD-ROM folder from your hard disc to include on a hybrid DVD disc.

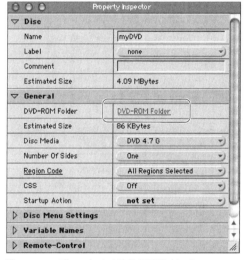

Figure 13.19 The selected DVD-ROM folder is set as the DVD-ROM Folder property.

2. In the DVD-ROM Folder property field, click the underlined words.

The Choose Folder dialog box opens (**Figure 13.18**).

3. Navigate to the folder containing the files that you want to include on the DVD disc and click Choose.

The Choose Folder dialog box closes. In the Property Inspector, the DVD-ROM Folder property now shows the DVD-ROM folder you selected (**Figure 13.19**). When you later choose the Build and Format Disc File option, the contents of the selected folder will be recorded at the root level of the final DVD disc (to learn more about recording a DVD disc, see "Recording a DVD-R Disc" later in this chapter).

continues on next page

✔ Tips

- Return the DVD-ROM Folder property to Not Set Yet by pressing Option and clicking the DVD-ROM Folder property's blue, underlined name.

- The DVD-ROM Folder's content contributes to the size of your DVD-Video project, as reflected by the disc space indicator in the upper right corner of the Graphical View (**Figure 13.20**). When adding DVD-ROM content, keep a careful eye on the disc space indicator to make sure that you don't go into the red and exceed your target DVD disc's capacity.

- DVD@ccess links can open data files stored in ROM folders on a hybrid DVD. To learn more, see Chapter 12, "DVD@ccess."

Disc space indicator

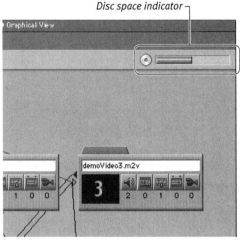

Figure 13.20 After adding a DVD-ROM folder, check the disc space indicator to make sure that the extra ROM content fits on the disc.

Hybrid DVD Tricks

The DVD-ROM Folder property is new in DVD Studio Pro 1.5. If you are using a previous version of DVD Studio Pro, you can still include a ROM folder on your DVD disc by using the following trick:

1. On your hard disk, create a folder to hold the project's multiplexed files.

2. Inside this new folder, create a folder named DVD-ROM Data. Make sure to use this exact name, including the space between *DVD-ROM* and *Data*.

3. Place all ROM files into the DVD-ROM Data folder.

4. Build and format your project to a DVD disc.

5. When DVD Studio Pro asks you to specify the build location, choose the folder containing the DVD-ROM Data folder.

DVD Studio Pro now formats the disc with your project, and it includes the DVD-ROM Data folder, along with all of the data files that it contains.

And one final tip: Before recording the DVD-R disc, make sure that the disc has enough space to hold both your project and the ROM content. The file size of the ROM folder used in this trick does not add to the size shown by the disc space indicator, so if you're not careful, you can easily exceed the capacity of your target DVD disc.

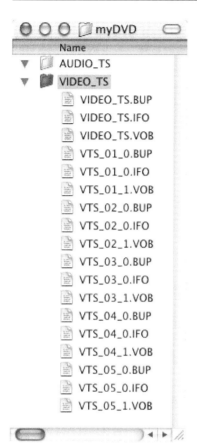

Figure 13.21 Multiplexing a project creates an AUDIO_TS folder and a VIDEO_TS folder. The AUDIO_TS folder is empty, but the VIDEO_TS folder contains vital DVD-Video data files.

Building the Project

Multiplexing combines all project items into a VIDEO_TS folder, which contains information that a DVD-Video player can read and display (**Figure 13.21**). The VIDEO_TS folder holds files with three file extensions: .vob, .ifo, and .bup. VOB files contain the video, audio, subtitles, and other media that comprise your DVD-Video, and IFO files contain button definitions, jumps, Wait After Playback values, and other navigation information that the DVD-Video player needs to assemble and play the media in the VOB files.

IFO files are usually less than 20 kilobytes. In DVD terms, this is microscopic, and indeed, every byte of that information is important to the correct display of your project. Should an IFO file become corrupted by a scratch or some other trauma to the disc's surface, the BUP file is a backup copy that provides the exact same information as the IFO file. To minimize the chance that a scratch might corrupt both files, the IFO file is written on the inside of the disc, and the BUP file is written on the outside.

Multiplexing a project also creates an empty AUDIO_TS folder. AUDIO_TS folders hold information that DVD-Audio players understand, but that has no significance to your DVD-Video project. Some DVD-Video players, however, get confused if the DVD disc doesn't contain both a VIDEO_TS and an AUDIO_TS folder. Including an AUDIO_TS folder doesn't hurt anything, so DVD Studio Pro obligingly creates both when it multiplexes, or *builds*, the project.

To build a project to disk:

1. Choose File > Build Disc "myDVD," where "myDVD" is the name of your DVD Project (**Figure 13.22**), or press Command-B.

   DVD Studio Pro needs to know where you want to store the multiplexed files. To guide DVD Studio Pro to the correct location, the Specify Build Location dialog box opens (**Figure 13.23**).

2. Navigate to a folder on your hard disk and click Choose.

   The Progress window opens, and DVD Studio Pro begins multiplexing your project (**Figure 13.24**). Watching the Progress window lets you keep track of the action while multiplexing. To learn what the Progress window's graphs and values mean, see "About the Progress Window" later in this chapter.

Figure 13.22 The File menu offers two multiplexing options. The Build Disc option multiplexes the project to your computer's hard disk; the Build and Format Disc option multiplexes the project and records a DVD-R disc or DLT tape.

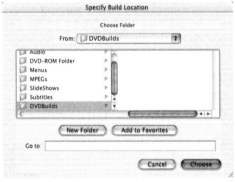

Figure 13.23 The Specify Build Location dialog box lets you choose a destination folder on your hard disks for your multiplexed project.

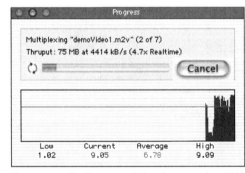

Figure 13.24 The Progress window keeps track as DVD Studio Pro multiplexes your project.

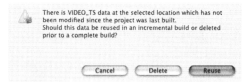

There is VIDEO_TS data at the selected location which has not been modified since the project was last built. Should this data be reused in an incremental build or deleted prior to a complete build?

Cancel   Delete   Reuse

Figure 13.25 DVD Studio Pro lets you reuse already-built IFO and VOB files, saving you time when building the project.

✔ Tips

■ If the folder that you choose as the target for multiplexing contains an old VIDEO_TS folder, the alert box shown in **Figure 13.25** may appear. If your project hasn't changed much from the last time you built it, select Reuse to speed the multiplexing process.

■ You can also decrease the time it takes to multiplex your project (as well as wear and tear on your hard disks) by building the project to a different disk than the one containing the source files.

BUILDING THE PROJECT

Building vs. Formatting

In DVD Studio Pro–speak, *building* a project is synonymous with multiplexing a project—they mean the exact same thing. In this case, the metaphor of *building* is well chosen, as multiplexing takes a lot of little parts (such as the video and audio streams) and snaps them together, building a solid stream of data.

The File menu offers two build options: Build Disc and Build and Format Disc (refer to Figure 13.22). The first option (Build Disc) multiplexes your project but leaves the multiplexed files sitting on your computer's hard disk. The second option (Build and Format Disc) multiplexes your project and then records, or *formats*, a DVD-R disc or DLT tape with the multiplexed files (see "Recording a DVD-R Disc" later in this chapter for more information).

About the Progress window

The Progress window displays values that help you spot errors as DVD Studio Pro multiplexes your project (**Figure 13.26**). The Progress window's prominent features are the progress meter in the top half and the data rate graph in the bottom half. The progress meter updates to show you how much of your project has been multiplexed, and the data rate graph presents a series of blue bars that represent the bit rate for the multiplexed data stream. These two meters conspire to grab your attention, but the Progress window has several other features that are just as useful.

At the very top of the Progress window, DVD Studio Pro lists the project item that's currently being multiplexed and shows how many items are left to be processed. Directly below that, a throughput meter shows how many megabytes DVD Studio Pro has already chewed through as well as how fast the program is chewing.

At the bottom of the Progress window, four numbers help you interpret the data rate graph above them:

Low. This value is the lowest data rate encountered while multiplexing the disc. Although not particularly important to the overall multiplexing process, in conjunction with the High value, the Low value lets you see just how variable your variable bit rate streams are.

Current. This value is printed in blue and reflects the values of the individual blue vertical bars on the data rate chart as they're drawn. The current value lets you keep track of the data stream's bit rate as it's multiplexed, which in turn helps you locate spikes in the bit rate that exceed the maximum allowable value of 10.08 Mbps.

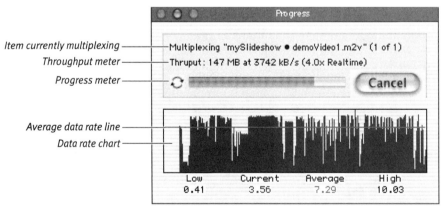

Item currently multiplexing ——— Multiplexing "mySlideshow ● demoVideo1.m2v" (1 of 1)
Throughput meter ——— Thruput : 147 MB at 3742 kB/s (4.0x Realtime)
Progress meter ———

Cancel

Average data rate line ———
Data rate chart ———

Low	Current	Average	High
0.41	3.56	7.29	10.03

Figure 13.26 The Progress window can be confusing at first, but all of the meters and graphs yield important information about how your project is multiplexing.

BUILDING THE PROJECT

Average. This number is green and reflects the value of the horizontal green line drawn across the data rate chart (if you watch the horizontal green line closely, you'll see it bob up and down in unison with the average value). If your DVD-Video is intended for playback on a slow computer, you can watch this value to make sure that your overall DVD-Video stream remains at an average bit rate that the computer can play back.

High. This value is the highest data rate encountered while recording the disc. Watch this value to make sure that your data rate stays within the acceptable limit of 10.08 Mbps. If the high value hits 10.08 Mbps, but multiplexing continues (it happens), your DVD-Video may have problems playing.

Is the QuickTime MPEG Encoder Really VBR?

The QuickTime MPEG Encoder compresses MPEG-2 streams so quickly that people often wonder if it's really a variable-bit-rate (VBR) encoder. This question becomes more perplexing as you watch tracks multiplex in the Progress window because the data rate graph usually looks pretty flat. But don't be fooled; the data rate graph uses small bars that provide an extremely low resolution, and VBR compressed video, by its nature, spends more time at the high end of its bit-rate range than at the low end. Both facts conspire to make the data rate graph look flatter than it is.

A better indication of what's going on are the Current, Low, and High values under the data rate graph. If you watch the Current value during a constant-bit-rate (CBR) build, the value hardly fluctuates because the stream's data rate remains...er, constant. During a VBR build, the current value moves around to reflect the VBR stream's ever-changing bit rate. Even more telling, the Low and High values are very close on a CBR build, but usually farther apart on a VBR build (of course, for VBR this range depends on the visual complexity of the source content).

Armed with this knowledge, multiplex a few tracks containing a single QuickTime-encoded MPEG-2 stream. You'll notice that the Current value varies (sometimes considerably), which is proof enough that the QuickTime MPEG Encoder produces VBR MPEG-2 streams.

About the Log window

While you are multiplexing a project, the Log window keeps a list of what's happening in the Progress window (**Figure 13.27**). For example, the Log window lists each multiplexed item along with the time that it was multiplexed. By checking out the time values, you can see how long multiplexing took for each item.

The Log window automatically opens when DVD Studio Pro finishes multiplexing your project. If multiplexing was successful, you'll see one of two messages printed at the bottom of the Log window:

This disc complies to version 1.0 of the DVD-Video Specification. This means that your build was successful, and the disc uses PCM and/or AC-3 audio only.

This disc complies to version 1.1 of the DVD-Video Specification. Your build was successful, and the disc uses MPEG-1 Layer 2 audio as well as PCM and/or AC-3 audio streams.

If the build is unsuccessful, the Log window opens showing you the error (**Figure 13.28**). Errors immediately stop the multiplexing process, which is handy because the item that caused the error will always be the item directly above the error, as displayed in the Log window. To fix the error, fix the item that caused it.

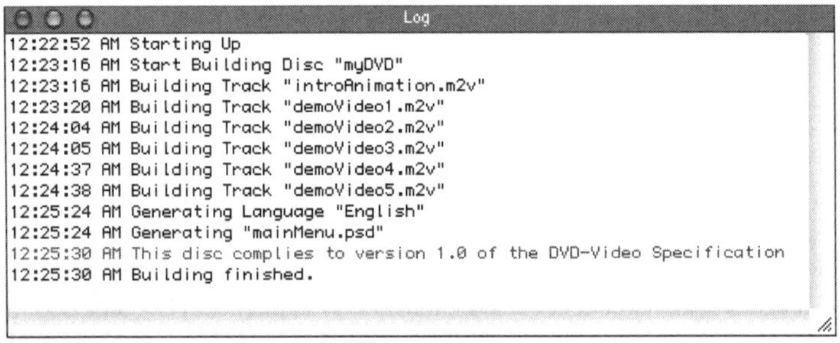

Figure 13.27 The Log window shows the order in which project items were built and finishes by showing the version of the DVD-Video specification with which the multiplexed files comply.

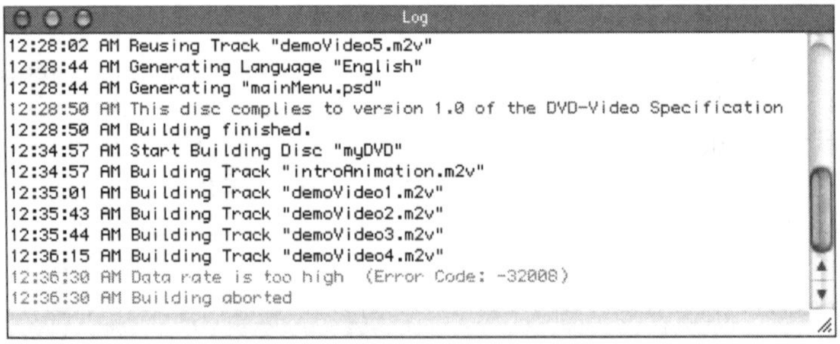

Figure 13.28 The bottom of the Log window displays the Data Rate Is Too High error message. The track listed directly above it is the offending item.

Figure 13.29 DVD Player's Controller (top) is used to control the DVD-Video displayed by the Viewer (bottom).

Figure 13.30 To open a VIDEO_TS folder stored on your computer's hard disks, choose File > Open VIDEO_TS Folder or press Command-O.

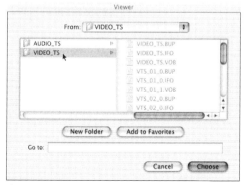

Figure 13.31 The Choose a Folder dialog box lets you select a VIDEO_TS folder for DVD Player to play.

Using Apple DVD Player

Apple DVD Player (DVD Player) plays your DVD-Video exactly as a set-top DVD-Video player would. DVD Player has two main parts: the Viewer and the Controller (**Figure 13.29**). The Viewer is the screen that displays your DVD-Video. The Controller mimics a DVD-Video player's remote control by allowing you to select menu buttons, start and stop playback, or select alternate angles.

Earlier in this chapter, you learned that multiplexing a project writes a VIDEO_TS and an AUDIO_TS folder to your computer's hard disks (see "Building the Project" earlier in this chapter). The VIDO_TS folder is an exact copy of the final DVD-Video. By opening the VIDEO_TS folder in DVD Player, you can check out your DVD-Video to see that it plays correctly before you record a DVD-R disc.

To open a VIDEO_TS folder in DVD Player:

1. Launch DVD Player.

2. Choose File > Open VIDEO_TS Folder (**Figure 13.30**) or press Command-0. The Choose a Folder dialog box opens (**Figure 13.31**).

3. In the Choose a Folder dialog box, navigate to the VIDEO_TS folder and click Choose.

   DVD Player plays the DVD-Video that's inside the VIDEO_TS folder.

   continues on next page

✔ Tips

- If the File menu doesn't show the Open VIDEO_TS Folder option, it needs to be enabled. To turn on the Open VIDEO_TS Folder option, open DVD Player's Preferences dialog box and select the Add 'Open VIDEO_TS' Menu Item to File Menu check box (**Figure 13.32**).

- In Mac OS 9, make sure that you're using DVD Player 2.7 or higher. Earlier versions of DVD Player had a few playback problems, including a gradual loss of synchronization between audio and video content.

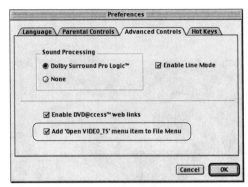

Figure 13.32 To open a VIDEO_TS folder in DVD Player for Mac OS 9, you must enable the Add 'Open VIDEO_TS' Menu Item to File Menu preference. While you're in the Preferences window, you should also make sure that the Enable DVD@ccess Web Links check box is selected.

Recording a DVD-R Disc

This shot is for all the marbles. Formatting the final DVD disc can be a nerve-wracking process; DVD-Rs are expensive, and wasting them on bad burns means you're losing money. You can minimize problems by carefully previewing every part of your project before you burn it (see "Previewing the Disc" and "Building the Project" earlier in this chapter). If everything plays correctly, you're ready to record.

Building and formatting a DVD disc is a two-part process. The first part, the build, multiplexes your project into a VIDEO_TS and an AUDIO_TS folder on your computer's hard disks. Once multiplexing is complete, DVD Studio Pro records, or formats, a DVD disc with the multiplexed files.

Rock-Solid Burns

DVD Studio Pro rarely makes mistakes as it burns DVD discs, but there are a few precautionary settings that will ensure a smooth recording process. Start by closing all other applications so that nothing unexpectedly jumps to life and interrupts DVD Studio Pro as it records the disc. Also, burning a DVD disc can take quite a while, so set your hard disk so that it doesn't go to sleep (**Figure 13.33**). For that extra level of security, you should also turn off AppleTalk, file sharing, and Web sharing. The only thing left running should be DVD Studio Pro, which can safely record the DVD disc, free from interruption.

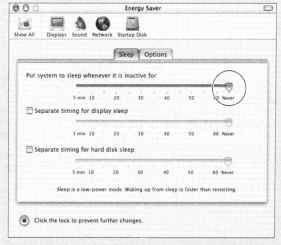

Figure 13.33 To keep your computer from going to sleep as it multiplexes and records your project, set all of the Energy Saver preferences to Never.

To build and format a DVD disc:

1. Choose File > Build and Format Disc "myDVD" (Option+Command-B), where "myDVD" is the name of your project (**Figure 13.34**).

   The Specify Build Location dialog box opens (**Figure 13.35**). Before DVD Studio Pro can record your project to a DVD disc, it needs to multiplex the items into data streams that a DVD-Video player understands. This data is recorded in the folder that you choose from the Specify Build Location dialog box.

2. Navigate to a folder and click Choose.

   The Format Disc dialog box opens (**Figure 13.36**). This dialog box allows you to select the recording device that will record your DVD.

Figure 13.34 Start the recording process by choosing File > Build and Format Disc.

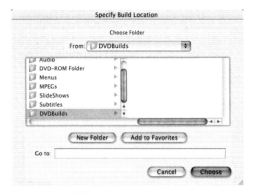

Figure 13.35 DVD Studio Pro multiplexes your project to the folder that you selected in the Select Build Location dialog box.

Figure 13.36 The Format Disc dialog box lets you select the device that you will use to record the disc.

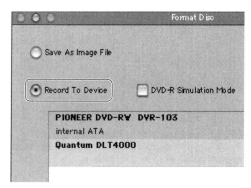

Figure 13.37 Select the Record To Device radio button (choosing Save As Image File writes an image of the final DVD disc to one of your computer's hard disks, as discussed in the section "Building Disc Images" later in this chapter).

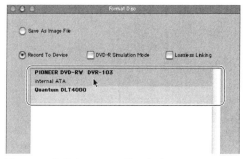

Figure 13.38 Select a recording device.

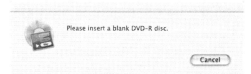

Figure 13.39 DVD Studio Pro tells you when to insert a DVD-R disc (don't insert it before DVD Studio Pro asks for it).

3. Select the Record To Device radio button (**Figure 13.37**).

DVD Studio Pro now understands that it's time to record a DVD disc. Below the Record To Device button is a central window listing all of the DVD recorders (and DLT drives) attached to your computer.

4. In the central window, select the DVD recorder that you want to use (**Figure 13.38**) and click OK.

DVD Studio Pro asks you to insert a blank DVD-R Disc (**Figure 13.39**).

5. Insert a blank DVD-R disc.

The Progress window opens (see "About the Progress window" earlier in this chapter). DVD Studio Pro multiplexes your project and then records it to the DVD-R disc.

continues on next page

RECORDING A DVD-R DISC

✔ Tips

- Do not insert a blank DVD disc until DVD Studio Pro asks for it. If you place a blank DVD disc into your computer before DVD Studio Pro needs it, a dialog box opens telling you that the disc needs to be prepared for burning (**Figure 13.40**). Click the dialog box's Eject button and wait until DVD Studio Pro asks before reinserting the disc.

- Lossless linking allows discs to successfully record even if the flow of data to the recorder is interrupted (**Figure 13.41**). A few DVD-Video players, however, may not play discs recorded using lossless linking, so you should enable this option only if you are experiencing problems burning your discs.

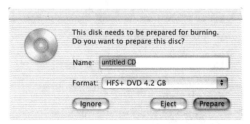

Figure 13.40 If you insert a DVD-R disc before DVD Studio Pro asks for it, this dialog box opens. Eject the disc and reinsert it when DVD Studio Pro tells you to.

Figure 13.41 Lossless linking helps slow computers safely record DVD-R discs.

DVD Studio Pro and DVD-RW

DVD Studio Pro does not officially support DVD-RW (**Figure 13.42**), which is why most people use Toast Titanium 5 to record DVD-RW discs. But if you're using Mac OS X (and feeling courageous), you can trick DVD Studio Pro into accepting DVD-RW discs. To complete this deception, you need both a DVD-R and a DVD-RW disc, although in the end only the DVD-RW disc will be recorded. (Note that this is a nonsupported hack that could potentially result in the DVD-RW disc being corrupted beyond use.)

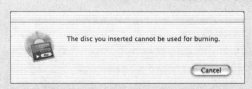

Figure 13.42 DVD Studio Pro does not officially support DVD-RW discs. If you try to use a DVD-RW disc, DVD Studio Pro displays this alert dialog box.

Follow the steps in the task "To build and format a DVD disc" and insert the DVD-R disc when DVD Studio Pro asks for it. As soon as the Progress window opens and DVD Studio Pro begins multiplexing, select your computer's desktop, eject the DVD-R disc, and replace it with an erased DVD-RW disc. Immediately click DVD Studio Pro's Progress window to bring it back to the surface; then hold your breath. If all is well, DVD Studio Pro continues to multiplex the project and then records it to the cleverly inserted DVD-RW disc.

To erase a DVD-RW disc, use Apple's Disk Utility. In Mac OS X, Disk Utility is in the Applications > Utilities folder.

Simulating a Burn

If you select the Format Disc dialog box's DVD-R Simulation Mode option (**Figure 13.43**), DVD Studio Pro reads the DVD-R disc that you placed in the recording device and simulates writing the project to it (**Figure 13.44**). Simulating a burn does exactly the same thing as a real build and format operation, but it doesn't turn on the laser in the DVD recorder. This lets you check the disc in advance for any errors that might halt the recording process (**Figure 13.45**), resulting in fewer wasted discs (but more wasted time, as it takes just as long to simulate recording as it does to record the actual disc).

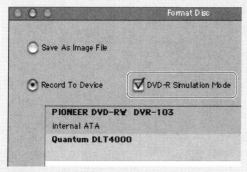

Figure 13.43 Check that the DVD-Video project will successfully record to a DVD-R disc by enabling simulation mode.

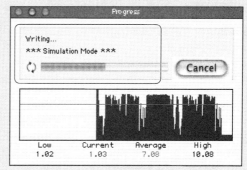

Figure 13.44 The Progress window tells you that it's writing only a simulation.

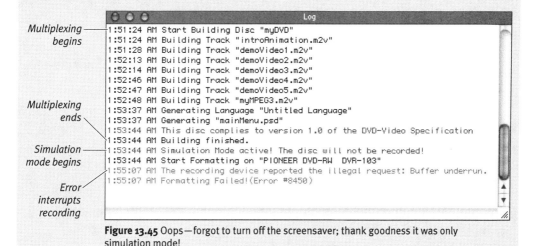

Multiplexing begins

Multiplexing ends

Simulation mode begins

Error interrupts recording

```
1:51:24 AM Start Building Disc "myDVD"
1:51:24 AM Building Track "introAnimation.m2v"
1:51:28 AM Building Track "demoVideo1.m2v"
1:52:13 AM Building Track "demoVideo2.m2v"
1:52:14 AM Building Track "demoVideo3.m2v"
1:52:46 AM Building Track "demoVideo4.m2v"
1:52:47 AM Building Track "demoVideo5.m2v"
1:52:48 AM Building Track "myMPEG3.m2v"
1:53:37 AM Generating Language "Untitled Language"
1:53:37 AM Generating "mainMenu.psd"
1:53:44 AM This disc complies to version 1.0 of the DVD-Video Specification
1:53:44 AM Building finished.
1:53:44 AM Simulation Mode active! The disc will not be recorded!
1:53:44 AM Start Formatting on "PIONEER DVD-RW   DVR-103"
1:55:07 AM The recording device reported the illegal request: Buffer underrun.
1:55:07 AM Formatting Failed!(Error #8450)
```

Figure 13.45 Oops—forgot to turn off the screensaver; thank goodness it was only simulation mode!

Building disc images

Building a disc image multiplexes the DVD-Video and then creates a complete image of the final DVD disc on your computer. Building a disc image does not record a DVD-R disc, but rather creates an exact copy of your project, including all ROM information and DVD@ccess installers for projects that include DVD@ccess links (see "Creating a Hybrid DVD" earlier in this chapter).

Building a disc image is useful for archiving projects that you are not quite ready to record to disc or for creating a disc image that you'll later open and record using Toast Titanium 5 (see "Using Toast Titanium 5" later in this chapter).

To build a disc image of your project:

1. Choose File > Build and Format Disc "myDVD" (Option+Command-B), where "myDVD" is the name of your project (**Figure 13.46**).

   The Specify Build Location dialog box opens.

2. Navigate to a folder and click Choose.

   The Specify Build Location dialog box closes, and the Format Disc dialog box opens.

3. Select the Save As Image File radio button (**Figure 13.47**) and click OK.

   The Format Disc dialog box closes, and the Save File dialog box opens (**Figure 13.48**). The Save File dialog box lets you choose where the project image will be written on your hard disks.

Figure 13.46 To build a disc image of your DVD-Video, choose File > Build and Format Disc.

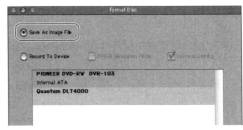

Figure 13.47 The Save As Image File button tells DVD Studio Pro to write a disc image instead of a DVD-R disc.

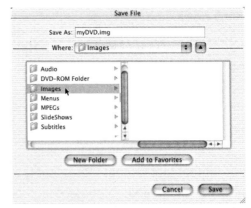

Figure 13.48 Use the Save File dialog box to name the disc image; then navigate to the folder where you want to save it.

RECORDING A DVD-R DISC

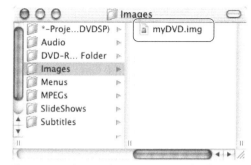

Figure 13.49 The DVD disc image on your hard disk.

Figure 13.50 Double-click a disc image file, and Apple's Disk Copy utility mounts it on your desktop.

4. In the Save File dialog box, name your file and then navigate to the folder where you want to record the project image. Click Save.

You can choose any directory that you want, but to speed writing (and save wear and tear on your hard disks), you should choose a disk other than the one containing the data streams multiplexed in step 2.

After you click Save, the Progress window opens, and DVD Studio Pro begins multiplexing your project to the folder you selected in step 2. When DVD Studio Pro is finished multiplexing, it writes the final disc image to the folder that you selected in step 4 (**Figure 13.49**). The result is a set of multiplexed files and a disc image of your final DVD-Video.

To open a disc image:

◆ Find the project image on your hard disk and double-click it (refer to Figure 13.49).

The Disk Copy utility opens (**Figure 13.50**) and mounts the disc image on your computer's desktop. Once the project has successfully mounted, DVD Player automatically launches and plays the video.

Outputting to DLT

Digital linear tape (DLT) is an older tape format that, in today's high-tech world, seems ancient, slow, and expensive. The drives that support it are clunky, and DLT tapes are both costly and hard to find. However, DLT tapes are reliable, offer massive storage capacity, and act as the standard delivery format for DVD mastering (all replicators accept DLT tapes). And if you're going to use any form of copy protection, whether it's region coding, CSS, or Macrovision, DLT is your only option (see "Protecting Your Content" earlier in this chapter).

To record a DLT tape:

1. Choose File > Build and Format Disc "myDVD" (Option+Command-B), where "myDVD" is the name of your project (**Figure 13.51**).

   The Specify Build Location dialog box opens.

2. Navigate to a folder and click Choose.

   The Format Disc dialog box opens.

3. Select the Record To Device radio button as well as the DLT drive that you want to use (**Figure 13.52**).

   At the bottom of the Format Disc dialog box, the DLT Format radio buttons become active (**Figure 13.53**). By default, the DDP button is selected. For most situations, DDP works fine, but if you need to, you can also select CMF (to learn more about these options, see "About DLT Formats" later in this chapter).

Figure 13.51 To record a DLT tape, start by choosing File > Build and Format Disc.

Figure 13.52 In the Format Disc dialog box, select Record To Device and then select your DLT drive.

Figure 13.53 Most replicators accept DDP-formatted DLT tapes, so when in doubt, select that button.

Figure 13.54 When DVD Studio Pro asks, insert a DLT tape into the DLT drive.

4. Click OK.

   DVD Studio Pro asks you to insert a DLT tape (**Figure 13.54**).

5. Insert a DLT tape.

   The DLT drive rewinds the DLT tape. When the tape is ready, DVD Studio Pro multiplexes your project and records it on the DLT tape. If you are multiplexing a DVD-9 project, you'll need to switch tapes midway through the writing process. To learn more, see the sidebar "DVD-9 Projects" on the next page.

✔ Tips

- DLT drives are plug and play. Don't be surprised if that DLT drive that you bought from eBay arrives without any software, because it doesn't need it. If the DLT drive doesn't show up in the Disc Format window, shut down your computer, power up the DLT drive, and restart the computer. If you're still experiencing problems, reinstall your SCSI card's drivers.

- Both DLT Type III and Type IV tapes are generally used for delivering DVD disc images to the replicator. At about $30 per unit, Type III tapes are half the price of Type IV tapes and provide more than enough storage space to hold a DVD-Video project (see Chapter 1, "Before You Begin"). Stick with DLT Type III tapes and save your money.

OUTPUTTING TO DLT

DVD-9 Projects

DVD-9 projects use a dual-layer DVD disc. At some point in the disc's playback, the reading laser must switch from the first layer to the second. This point is called the *layer break*.

To record a DVD-9 project, you need two DLT tapes: one for each layer of the DVD disc. DVD Studio Pro automatically decides where the project's layer break should be and tells you when it's time to insert the second DLT tape (**Figure 13.55**). DVD Studio Pro usually places the layer break between tracks. Failing that, it places the layer break on a marker.

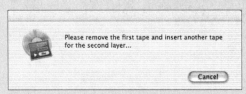

Figure 13.55 Recording a DVD-9 project takes two tapes: one for each layer. DVD Studio Pro prompts you when it's time to insert the second tape.

If you have one large track, such as in a feature movie, you'll see a slight glitch, or pause in playback, when the DVD-Video player switches layers. This glitch occurs on every DVD-9, so don't worry if you notice it when you play back your replicated project (rent a Hollywood title, and you'll see this same glitch, usually somewhere around 45 minutes into the film).

Finally, the DVD specification allows dual-layer DVD-Videos to play back using one of two methods: opposite-track path (OTP) or parallel-track path (PTP). Regardless of the method, the laser starts reading from the inside of the disc and moves toward the outer edge. When it's time to switch layers, the laser refocuses and either begins reading the second layer from the outside of the disc back toward the middle (OTP) or skips back to the middle of the disc and once again reads out toward the edge (PTP). DVDSP is OTP only, which stops the laser from having to move all the way back to the center of the disc and creates a shorter glitch as the laser switches layers.

About DLT formats

DVD Studio Pro can write DLT tapes in two formats: Disc Description Protocol (DDP) and Cutting Master Format (CMF). Both formats tell the replicator how to create a master disc that's used as the basis for each replicated copy. If you're in North America, it's pretty safe to assume that your plant will accept a DDP-formatted DLT tape, though CMF-formatted tapes are also widely accepted. DVD Studio Pro doesn't care which format you use, so phone the replicator and see which one the shop requires or prefers before you record the DLT tape(s).

✔ Tip

■ CMF's main advantage is that it's designed to work with DVD-R (Authoring) discs to create a master disc for replication. Consequently, if you have a Pioneer DVR-201 DVD recorder, you will soon be able to send a DVD-R (Authoring) disc to the replicator instead of a DLT tape—or at least that's the theory; as of this writing, CMF for DVD-R (Authoring) is still under development.

OUTPUTTING TO DLT

Testing DVD-9 Projects

Before replicating a project, you always should test it in a DVD-Video player to make sure that buttons link to the right tracks, alternate angles are in the right order, and the project generally works as expected when seen on a television. Unfortunately, testing DVD-9 projects is a bit of a hassle, as the media won't fit onto a DVD-5 DVD-R disc.

To get around this problem, encode a second set of MPEG streams using extremely low bit rates (a bit less than half the normal bit rate should work fine). Save a copy of your DVD Studio Pro project. In the project copy, use the Asset Files window to replace the high-data-rate MPEG streams with the low-data-rate imposters (see Chapter 6, "Setting Up Your Project"). You can now record the project to a DVD-R disc and test it on a television. It will look terrible, but if navigation works correctly, you can confidently open the original DVD Studio Pro project and record your DLT tapes.

About Selective Multiplexing

You've multiplexed your project and are pre-viewing it in DVD Player when you notice that a menu button links to the wrong track. But there's an even bigger problem. You must have the project done in a few hours, and there's no time to multiplex the entire project again. What do you do?

Fortunately for you, DVD Studio Pro will reuse previously multiplexed tracks! If you go back into your project and change the offending button's jump value, DVD Studio Pro will let you skip multiplexing of the unchanged tracks, saving you precious time.

To reuse project items:

1. Choose File > Build Disc or File > Build and Format Disc.

   The Specify Build Location dialog box opens.

2. Select the folder that you previously built the project to and click Choose (**Figure 13.56**).

   The folder that you've selected holds a VIDEO_TS folder. DVD Studio Pro looks inside that folder and checks to see if any of the files remain unchanged. If it finds unchanged files, a dialog box opens asking if you'd like to reuse or delete unchanged data (**Figure 13.57**).

3. Click Reuse.

   DVD Studio Pro multiplexes only menus and slideshows plus any tracks that have changed since the last time you multiplexed the project. When DVD Studio Pro finishes multiplexing, the Log window opens to show you which tracks have been rebuilt and which have been reused (**Figure 13.58**).

✔ Tip

- Only tracks escape remultiplexing. Menus and slideshows are multiplexed anew each time you build the project.

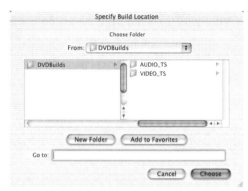

Figure 13.56 To reuse previously multiplexed data, you must choose the folder where you've previously multiplexed the project.

Figure 13.57 To avoid multiplexing items that remain unchanged from the last time that you built the project, click Reuse.

Reused project items

Figure 13.58 The Log window shows which items were reused and which items DVD Studio Pro remultiplexed.

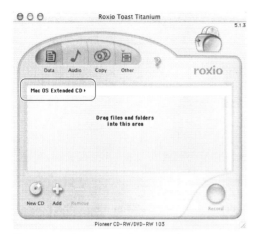

Figure 13.59 The Toast window. Here, the Toast window is set to record a CD-ROM disc.

Figure 13.60 To record a DVD-Video disc, click the Other button.

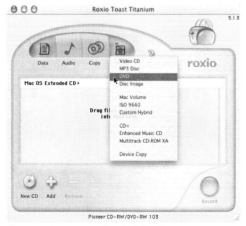

Figure 13.61 A menu of optical disc formats opens. Choose DVD.

Using Toast Titanium 5

Toast Titanium 5 (Toast) burns optical discs, allowing you to record data DVD-ROMs, DVD-Video discs, or hybrid DVDs simply by dragging files into the Toast window and clicking the Record button. Toast's advantages over DVD Studio Pro include the following:

◆ Toast officially records and erases DVD-RW discs, which can save you a bundle on wasted DVD-Rs as you test your projects.

◆ If you need to make several copies of the same disc, Toast turns your computer into a virtual assembly line; when one disc finishes burning, remove it, put in a new disc, and click Record again.

To create a DVD disc using Toast:

1. Open Toast.

   The Toast window opens (**Figure 13.59**).

2. Click the Other button (**Figure 13.60**).

   A menu opens showing several optical disc formats (**Figure 13.61**).

continues on next page

USING TOAST TITANIUM 5

3. Choose DVD.

The Toast window updates to show DVD as the format (**Figure 13.62**).

4. In the lower left corner of the Toast window, click the New DVD button (**Figure 13.63**).

A new, untitled disc is created in the Toast window.

5. Name the disc by clicking Untitled DVD (**Figure 13.64**) and then typing a new name.

This name identifies the DVD and appears every time that the disc is placed in a computer DVD-ROM drive, so make sure that you change it to something more informative than "Untitled DVD."

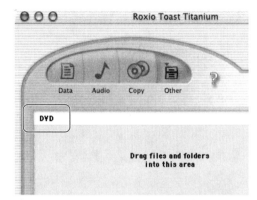

Figure 13.62 The Toast window tells you that it's ready to record a DVD.

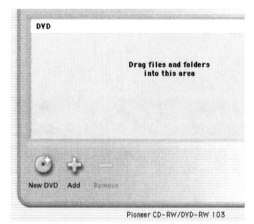

Figure 13.63 Click the New DVD button to start a new DVD disc.

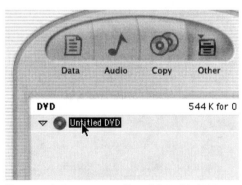

Figure 13.64 To name your disc, click Untitled DVD once and then type a new name.

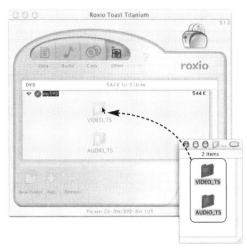

Figure 13.65 Drag a VIDEO_TS and an AUDIO_TS folder into the Toast window.

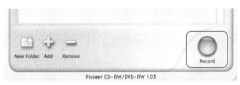

Figure 13.66 When you're ready to record the DVD disc, click the big red Record button.

Figure 13.67 When Toast asks, insert a DVD-R disc.

Figure 13.68 In the Record dialog box, click Write Disc to record your DVD-Video disc.

6. From the Finder, drag a VIDEO_TS and an AUDIO_TS folder into the Toast window (**Figure 13.65**).

   To record a hybrid DVD, drag other data files into the Toast window.

7. Click Record (**Figure 13.66**).

8. When Toast asks, insert a DVD disc (**Figure 13.67**).

   The Record dialog box opens (**Figure 13.68**). The Speed menu always defaults to the proper speed for the inserted DVD disc, so you shouldn't need to make adjustments to this dialog box's settings.

9. Click Write Disc.

   Toast records the DVD disc. When Toast is finished recording, it asks if you want to verify or eject the disc. Verifying the disc takes a while, but it ensures that all of the data has been properly recorded to the disc; if you have time, verify the disc.

✔ Tips

- Finishing the disc takes a long, long time. Don't jump the gun and abort the finishing process, or you'll just have to re-record the disc and sit through the process a second time. For even short projects, Toast needs to write the lead-out, which can take 10 minutes or more! But don't worry; Toast is not hung, and everything is working fine. Patience is not only a virtue, but in this case it will save you time and money.

- When recording DVD-RW discs, do not abort the process as Toast is recording the disc's lead-in. Doing so permanently destroys the DVD-RW disc.

USING TOAST TITANIUM 5

To erase a DVD-RW disc:

1. Open Toast.

2. Insert an already recorded DVD-RW disc.

3. Choose Recorder > Erase (Command-B) (**Figure 13.69**).

   A dialog box opens asking if you are sure that you want to erase the disc (**Figure 13.70**). At the bottom of the dialog box are three buttons labeled Cancel, Quick Erase, and Erase. Quick Erase is much faster than the Erase option, but if you choose Quick Erase, you should use only Toast to record the DVD-RW.

4. Click Quick Erase or Erase.

   The Progress window opens, alerting you that Toast is erasing the disc (**Figure 13.71**).

Figure 13.69
To erase a DVD-RW disc, open Toast, insert the DVD-RW, and choose Recorder > Erase.

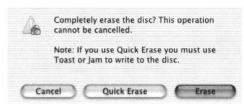

Figure 13.70 Toast gives you one last chance to make sure that you want to erase the disc. Click Erase to erase the disk (if you're in a hurry, click Quick Erase).

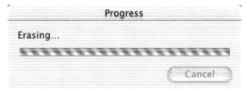

Figure 13.71 The Progress meter spins to let you know that Toast is erasing the disc.

DVD-Video on CD-ROM

If your multiplexed project is small (less then 700 MB), you don't have to record it on a DVD-R disc. Using Toast, you can instead record the DVD-Video to a CD-R disc. Apple DVD Player reads DVD-Videos recorded on a CD-R disc just as well as it reads DVD-Videos recorded on a DVD-R disc. But DVD-Video on CD compatibility *decreases* as soon as you leave the Macintosh platform. Although several Windows PC DVD-Video players also read DVD-Videos on CD, no set-top DVD-Video players support it. If your project might be played on anything other than a Macintosh, ensure its playback success by burning it to a DVD-R disc.

To record a DVD-Video on a CD, you must use Toast Titanium 5; simply record the project as if you were writing a DVD-R, but insert a CD-R disc instead.

USING TOAST TITANIUM 5

Part III:
Advanced
DVD Authoring

Part III: Advanced DVD Authoring

14

WIDESCREEN: 16:9

HDTV. Plasma displays. Widescreen television. The future of home entertainment? Definitely. In a few short years, widescreen TVs will replace their smaller counterparts to become the centerpieces of many North American living rooms. But while full-scale market penetration is still a ways down the road, you don't have to wait to jump on the widescreen bandwagon—DVD Studio Pro lets you create widescreen DVD-Video today.

Widescreen televisions are, well, wider than normal TVs. The standard television has a 4:3 aspect ratio (four units across for every three units high), whereas a widescreen TV has a 16:9 aspect ratio (in this chapter, the terms *widescreen* and *16:9* are used inter-changeably). Represented as pixels on a computer screen, the 16:9 video frame is 854 x 480 pixels for NTSC, or 1,024 x 576 pixels for PAL. The height is the same as that of a standard television, but the difference in width means that widescreen video does not fit on a standard TV without help. Fortunately, DVD-Video players can resize 16:9 video streams so that they look fine on a 4:3 television. With just a bit of extra work you can create widescreen DVDs that will play on any television, regardless of the television's aspect ratio.

As with all things DVD, the best way to understand how widescreen works is to actually create a 16:9 project. This chapter covers all of the necessary steps, including encoding 16:9 MPEG-2 streams and preparing widescreen menus.

Preparing 16:9 Video Streams

If you've read Chapter 3, "Encoding Video Streams," you've already learned how to use the QuickTime MPEG Encoder to create MPEG-2 streams suitable for standard-size televisions. The only difference in encoding widescreen streams is that instead of selecting the 4:3 radio button, you select the 16:9 radio button (**Figure 14.1**).

The 16:9 button sets a *flag* in the MPEG-2 stream. At playback, this flag tells the DVD-Video player that the stream is widescreen video. If the player is attached to a widescreen television, it displays the video at its full 16:9 resolution. If the player is attached to a normal TV, it takes certain actions to make sure that the widescreen DVD looks okay when played back on the thinner television screen (for a more technical explanation of what the player does, see "Anamorphic Video" and "16:9 Tracks" later in this chapter).

16:9 radio button

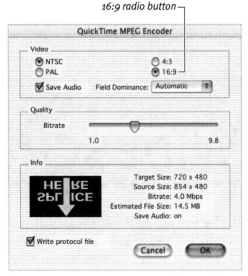

Figure 14.1 The QuickTime MPEG Encoder's 16:9 button is key to encoding widescreen MPEG-2 streams.

Figure 14.2 To encode your widescreen movie, open it in QuickTime Pro Player and choose File > Export.

Figure 14.3 The Save Exported File As window opens.

To encode a 16:9 video stream:

1. Open your widescreen video in QuickTime.

2. Choose File > Export (**Figure 14.2**) or press Command-E.

   The Save Exported File As dialog box opens (**Figure 14.3**).

3. From the Export menu, choose Movie to MPEG2 and then click the Options button.

   The QuickTime MPEG Encoder window opens.

4. Select the 16:9 radio button (refer to Figure 14.1).

5. Set the rest of the QuickTime MPEG Encoder's options as desired.

   The QuickTime MPEG Encoder is discussed in detail in Chapter 3, "Encoding Video Streams." If you have any questions about the rest of the settings in this window, refer to that chapter.

6. Click OK to close the QuickTime MPEG Encoder window.

   This leaves the Save Exported File As window open on your screen.

7. In the Save Exported File As window, click Save to begin encoding the 16:9 MPEG-2 stream.

   The MPEG Encoder progress window opens, allowing you to keep an eye on the encoder's progress.

PREPARING 16:9 VIDEO STREAMS

Anamorphic Video

When you choose 16:9 video, the QuickTime MPEG Encoder's Info area displays a curious detail (**Figure 14.4**): the source movie is sized at 854 x 480 pixels (NTSC), but the target movie is sized at only 720 x 480 pixels. What's up?

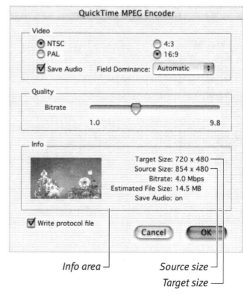

Figure 14.4 The QuickTime MPEG Encoder squeezes widescreen video into the standard 4:3 frame dimensions of 720 x 480 pixels. At playback, the DVD-Video player stretches the video back to the correct size.

Rubberized Video

Imagine that you've been asked to print a picture on a flat piece of rubber. When you compare the picture to the rubber, you notice that the picture is too wide to fit on the rubber's surface. But the rubber is pliable, so you devise a clever plan: Why not stretch the rubber before you print the picture?

Once printed, the picture looks great—as long as the rubber is stretched! As soon as you let go of the edges, the rubber snaps back to its normal shape, and the picture looks pinched. But hey, that's no problem, because to see the picture in its full glory all you need to do is stretch the rubber back out. In the anamorphic process, the video frame is the piece of rubber, and the DVD-Video player is the stretching device. Get it?

854 pixels wide

720 pixels wide

Figure 14.5 The 854-pixel-wide 16:9 video (top) is reduced to a 720-pixel-wide MPEG-2 frame (bottom) before it's stored on the DVD disc.

This seeming misfit arises from the fact that all DVD-Video must use a frame dimension of 720 x 480 pixels (NTSC). That's all the room there is on the disc; the DVD-Video specification makes no provision for larger frame sizes. Consequently, to get that extra girth into the skinny 4:3 frame, encoders strap a digital girdle around the 16:9 frame and squeeze it into the normal 4:3 MPEG-2 video frame (**Figure 14.5**). When the DVD-Video is played, the player enlarges the video back to its proper size using a process known as *anamorphic transfer* (see the sidebar "Rubberized Video").

The QuickTime MPEG Encoder creates *anamorphic* video streams. While the source video may be 854 x 480, the final stream is encoded at a dimension of 720 x 480. Were you to look at that video stream without enlarging it to its proper size, everything would appear tall and thin. The DVD-Video player stretches it back out, however, so upon playback the video looks proportionally correct to the viewer.

16:9 Tracks

When a widescreen track is played on a widescreen television, the image is stretched to appear across the widescreen TV's entire surface area. When the same track is displayed on a 4:3 television, the DVD-Video player is forced to do some work. The player must either chop off the edges of the picture, using a process called *pan and scan*, or reduce the picture so that all of it fits in the frame, which is called *letterboxing*.

Pan and scan fills the 4:3 frame by chopping the edges off of the widescreen video. At playback, the DVD-Video player stretches the 16:9 video back to its proper dimensions of 854 x 480 pixels (NTSC) and then chops 67 pixels off of each side to create an image of the correct resolution for a 4:3 TV (**Figure 14.6**).

Letterboxing displays the entire video frame on the screen by adding black mattes, or bars, to the top and bottom of the picture. The result is an onscreen image with a resolution of 720 x 404 pixels (**Figure 14.7**). In this situation, the anamorphic 16:9 video is not stretched horizontally, but rather is squeezed vertically to return the image to the proper proportions (720 x 404 is proportionally the same as 854 x 480).

As the DVD's author, the choice of whether to use letterboxing or pan and scan is yours. Each track in your project has a Display Mode property with three settings (**Figure 14.8**). Selecting one of these settings tells the DVD-Video player exactly what to do when the 16:9 video is displayed on a 4:3 television.

Figure 14.6 Pan and scan cuts off the edges of the 16:9 video.

Figure 14.7 Letterboxing 16:9 video reduces it so that its full width fits within a 4:3 television screen.

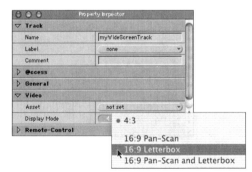

Figure 14.8 The Track Property Inspector's Display Mode menu sets a flag that tells the DVD-Video player how to display your 16:9 track on a 4:3 television.

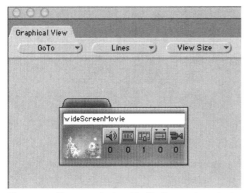

Figure 14.9 To set a 16:9 track's display mode, select the track in the Graphical View and choose a display mode, as shown in Figure 14.8.

To set a 16:9 track's display mode:

1. In the Graphical View, select a Track tile that contains a 16:9 video asset (**Figure 14.9**).

   The Property Inspector updates to display the track's properties.

2. From the Property Inspector's Display Mode menu, choose one of the following (refer to Figure 14.8):

   ▲ **16:9 Pan-Scan.** Choose this option if you want the DVD-Video player to fill a 4:3 television screen by cropping off the edges of the video.

   ▲ **16:9 Letterbox.** Choose this option if you want the DVD-Video player to letterbox your video and apply black mattes to the top and bottom of the frame.

   ▲ **16:9 Pan-Scan and Letterbox.** This option does the same thing as simple letterboxing on most players, though some players may display the video using pan and scan. To maintain full control over how your video is displayed, avoid this option and choose either Letterbox or Pan-Scan.

Vectorized Pan and Scan

Some high-end DVD-Video authoring tools let you add pan and scan *vectors* to your 16:9 MPEG-2 streams.

In video effects programs, such as Adobe After Effects or Discreet 3D Studio Max, vectors are lines, or paths, used to animate the motion of virtual cameras. Vectors in widescreen MPEG streams work similarly: the vector is used to move the pan and scan focal point back and forth across the widescreen video. This lets you define exactly which part of the widescreen video is shown on the viewer's 4:3 television screen.

DVD Studio Pro doesn't support pan and scan vectors, but rather focuses the focal point on the center of the widescreen video stream. As a result, DVD Studio Pro's pan and scan function is more like crop and chop than true pan and scan.

16:9 TRACKS

16:9 Menus

If you need a 16:9 menu that appears at full widescreen resolution, then Photoshop layer menus are your only option. Widescreen highlight menus currently don't work. If you include widescreen highlight menus in your project, your overlays won't match up with your menus' button art (**Figure 14.10**). You can, however, safely mix 4:3 highlight menus with 16:9 tracks in the same project, and indeed, that's what you'll find in most widescreen projects. But this doesn't mean that you should avoid using 16:9 Photoshop layer menus. If Photoshop layer menus are suitable for your project, there's no reason not to use them.

In Photoshop, design the source documents for your Photoshop layer menus at the following dimensions:

◆ **NTSC:** 854 x 480

◆ **PAL:** 1,024 x 576

When the document is finished, resize it to 720 x 480 (NTSC) or 720 x 576 (PAL). This creates an anamorphic menu that, upon playback, the DVD-Video player will stretch out to normal widescreen dimensions.

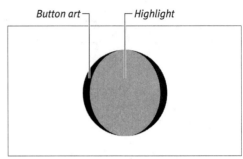

Figure 14.10 An example of what happens when a 16:9 highlight menu is played on a television.

16:9 MENUS

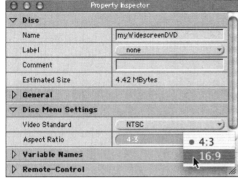

Figure 14.11 DVD Studio Pro lets you create widescreen Photoshop layer menus that are displayed across the entire surface of a widescreen television. To create a widescreen Photoshop layer menu, design the Photoshop document at 854 x 480 (NTSC) and resize it to 720 x 480 before importing it into DVD Studio Pro. Then choose 16:9 from the Disc Property Inspector's Aspect Ratio menu.

To use 16:9 Photoshop layer menus:

1. Click the Graphical View's background to select the disc.

   The Property Inspector updates to display the disc properties. In the middle of the Disc Property Inspector is a Disc Menu Settings area that has an Aspect Ratio property.

2. From the Aspect Ratio menu, choose 16:9 (**Figure 14.11**).

   DVD Studio Pro flags all of your project's menus as widescreen menus. At playback, this flag tells the DVD-Video player to stretch the menus out to the proper widescreen dimensions.

✔ Tip

- 16:9 highlight menus are displayed properly in both DVD Studio Pro's Preview mode and in Apple DVD Player, but that changes when you play the project on a set-top DVD-Video player. Don't waste valuable time messing with 16:9 highlight menus—despite appearances, they don't work.

16:9 MENUS

16:9 Slideshows

If you want to create a widescreen slideshow, you're out of luck. In Chapter 11, "Assembling Slideshows," you learned that the Slideshow editor doesn't display assets that aren't 720 x 480 pixels for NTSC or 720 x 576 pixels for PAL. As a result, your widescreen stills won't even show up in the Slideshow editor.

You can try to get around this limitation by using QuickTime to encode widescreen stills as MPEG-2 video streams. If you use these new widescreen streams in a slideshow, however, the 16:9 flag (supplied by the QuickTime MPEG Encoder) is turned off, and the resulting slideshow is displayed at 4:3. Consequently, widescreen slideshows are out of reach for the time being. Perhaps in a future version of DVD Studio Pro....

✔ Tip

■ DVD Studio Pro's Preview mode stretches widescreen MPEG stills so that they appear at the proper widescreen dimensions of 854 x 480 (NTSC). But don't be fooled; when you build the project and play it on a DVD-Video player, the slideshow will be displayed at 720 x 480, which is not 16:9.

WORKING WITH LANGUAGES | 15

As globalization brings the world's markets closer together, you increasingly may want to consider providing content in alternate languages. North America alone boasts many widely spoken languages, including Spanish, French, and Chinese, so why limit your DVD's reach by excluding viewers who don't speak English?

You can create multilingual DVDs using either of two methods. The simplest method uses subtitles to translate your video's dialog (creating subtitles is covered in Chapter 16, "Subtitles"). The second method, which you'll learn about in this chapter, uses alternate language audio streams to supply audio in virtually any language that the viewer might speak.

In addition to audio, you also need to translate any words that are printed on the screen, such as the text on your project's menus; if the viewer can't read a menu, choosing which track to play becomes an exercise in random selection. To help you, DVD Studio Pro lets you make menus in up to 16 languages. Creating all of those menus may sound like a lot of work, but as you'll discover later in this chapter, DVD Studio Pro does most of the heavy lifting for you.

All DVD-Video players have user-definable language settings, which let viewers set their players to automatically display the language that they understand. Follow the steps discussed in this chapter, and your DVD-Video will always display the correct audio streams, subtitles, and menus, no matter where in the world it is played.

Creating Multilingual Tracks

DVD Studio Pro lets you assign a different language to each audio stream in a Track tile. You might, for example, assign one audio stream to English, one to French, and one to Spanish. Although you have three different languages represented in your DVD-Video, the only audio stream that will play is the one that matches the language setting on the viewer's DVD-Video player. To viewers, the language selection process is transparent because they hear only the language that they understand.

To assign an audio stream to a track:

1. In the Graphical View, click a Track tile's Audio icon (**Figure 15.1**).

   The Audio Streams container opens (**Figure 15.2**).

2. Select an audio stream (**Figure 15.3**).

   The Property Inspector updates to display the audio stream's properties.

3. From the Property Inspector's Language menu, choose a language (**Figure 15.4**).

   If the DVD-Video player is set to the selected language, this audio stream automatically plays.

✔ Tip

■ With eight audio streams per track at your disposal, you can provide eight different audio translations for each of your project's tracks (if you need more than eight languages, use a mixture of audio and subtitle streams).

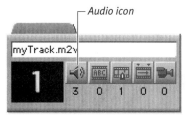

Audio icon

Figure 15.1 Each of the track's audio streams can be assigned a specific language setting.

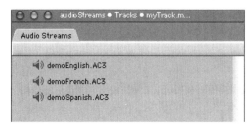

Figure 15.2 The Audio Streams container, with three alternate audio streams.

Figure 15.3 To assign each audio stream a language, first select an audio stream.

Figure 15.4 Choose a language from the Audio Stream Property Inspector's Language menu.

CREATING MULTILINGUAL TRACKS

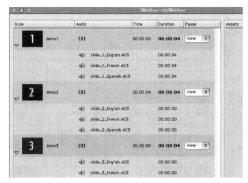

Figure 15.5 For multilingual slideshows, make sure that you add audio streams to slides in the same language order. Note how the audio streams in this slideshow are always English, then French, and then Spanish.

Figure 15.6 The Slideshow Property Inspector's Languages area contains eight Audio Language settings. The top setting applies to the first audio stream in each slide, the next setting down applies to the second audio stream in each slide, and so on.

Creating Multilingual Slideshows

Like tracks, slideshow slides can have up to eight separate audio streams that can be used to hold translations of the audio program.

When creating multilingual slideshows, however, you must add audio streams to slides in a specific progression. Although it doesn't matter which language stream you start with, you must keep the order in which they're added the same for each slide in the slideshow. Say, for example, that you're adding English, French, and Spanish streams to your slideshow. Perhaps you make English the top stream in each slide, then French, and then Spanish (**Figure 15.5**).

The reason for adding audio streams in an orderly fashion becomes apparent as soon as you open the Slideshow Property Inspector to set the audio streams' language values. Toward the bottom of the Slideshow Property Inspector is a Languages area that holds eight audio languages (**Figure 15.6**). These eight languages are listed from number 1 at the top to number 8 at the bottom. Of course, each of these languages corresponds to one audio stream in each slide. Continuing the example from the preceding paragraph, Audio Language number 1 should be English, Audio Language number 2 should be French, and Audio Language number 3 should be Spanish. If you're careful to maintain this order as you add audio streams to slides, the correct language will always play when the disc is placed in a DVD-Video player.

CREATING MULTILINGUAL SLIDESHOWS

To assign languages to slides:

1. In the Graphical View, double-click a Slideshow tile's thumbnail area.

   The Slideshow editor opens.

2. Add all alternate-language audio streams to your slides (refer to Figure 15.5).

   Add the streams in the same language order: for example, the English stream first, then French, and then Spanish.

3. In the Slideshow editor's lower right corner, click OK.

   The Slideshow editor closes. If you look at the Property Inspector, you'll see that it displays the slideshow's properties (if it doesn't, in the Graphical View click the Slideshow tile to select it). Toward the bottom of the Property Inspector is a Languages area with eight languages listed (refer to Figure 15.6).

4. In the Languages area, set each language (**Figure 15.7**).

   The top language is assigned to the first audio stream in each slide, the second language down is assigned to the second audio stream, and so on.

Figure 15.7 Select languages from the menus in the Property Inspector's Languages area.

Figure 15.8 Use the Languages tab to create alternate language menus.

Figure 15.9 The Menu Property Inspector usually has only one picture and one audio asset.

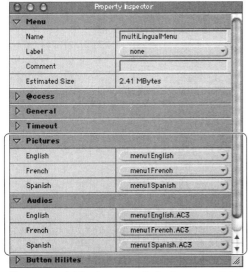

Figure 15.10 Adding languages to the Languages tab adds new asset menus to the Menu Property Inspector's Picture and Audio areas.

Creating Multilingual Menus

If you've ever poked around the DVD Studio Pro workspace, you've probably discovered the Project View's Languages tab and wondered what it does (**Figure 15.8**). Well, your curiosity is about to be satisfied: you use the Languages tab to construct multilingual menus. In most cases, Menu tiles use only a single picture asset (**Figure 15.9**), but when you add languages to the Languages tab, the Menu Property Inspector expands to include new assets for each language, as shown in **Figure 15.10**.

To create multilingual menus, you must translate the text from each of your project's menus and design a separate set of menu graphics for each language. For example, if your project contains English, French, and Spanish, you should create three separate sets of menu graphics: one in English, one in French, and one in Spanish. Back in DVD Studio Pro, you'll assign each translated menu to its corresponding picture asset property. When DVD Studio Pro multiplexes your project, it automatically constructs a different menu for each language.

Here are a few rules to keep in mind when you create alternate language menus:

◆ Hotspots are set once per Menu tile. Button hotspots must remain in the same place for each alternate language version of the menu.

◆ For highlight menus, each alternate language menu must use the same overlay image and highlight sets.

◆ Each alternate language menu must use exactly the same type of audio stream as the others. If one uses an AC-3 stream, for example, the rest must also use AC-3 streams.

CREATING MULTILINGUAL MENUS

305

To create a multilingual menu:

1. In the Project View, select the Languages tab (**Figure 15.11**).

   By default, the Languages tab lists one untitled language.

2. Select the untitled language.

   The language is highlighted, and the Property Inspector updates to display the language's properties.

3. In the Property Inspector, click the Name text box and type a name for the language (**Figure 15.12**).

   You can name the language whatever you want, but to avoid confusion, name it after the language that it represents.

4. From the Property Inspector's Language menu, select a language (**Figure 15.13**).

5. Choose Item > New Language (**Figure 15.14**), or press Command-K.

   A new, untitled language is added at the bottom of the Languages tab (**Figure 15.15**).

Figure 15.11 By default, the Languages tab contains a single, untitled, unassigned language.

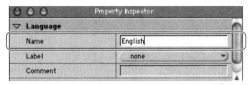

Figure 15.12 Give your language a suitable name (to help you remember which language is which).

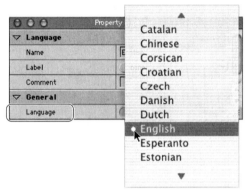

Figure 15.13 Choose a language setting from the Property Inspector's Language menu.

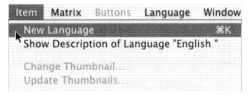

Figure 15.14 Create a new menu language by choosing Item > New Language.

Figure 15.15 A new, untitled language appears on the Languages tab.

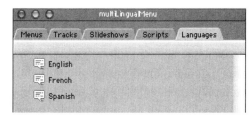

Figure 15.16 The Languages tab lists three languages, which means that the finished project will have three versions of each menu: one English, one French, and one Spanish.

Figure 15.17 Now that you've defined the languages for your menus, select a Menu tile and look at the Property Inspector.

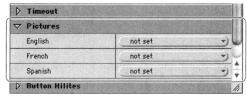

Figure 15.18 The Property Inspector now has several picture properties: one for each language on the Project View's Languages tab.

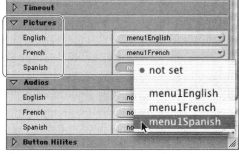

Figure 15.19 Choose a picture asset for each menu.

6. Repeat steps 2 to 5 until you've added all of the necessary languages to the Languages tab (**Figure 15.16**).

7. In the Graphical View, select a Menu tile (**Figure 15.17**).

   The Property Inspector updates to display the menu's properties (**Figure 15.18**). The Picture area now contains a separate Picture menu for each language that you've added to the Project View's Languages tab.

8. From the menus in the Property Inspector's Picture area, choose picture assets that correspond to each language (**Figure 15.19**).

   If your menu uses audio, the Property Inspector's Audio area expands to include an audio property for each alternate language menu.

continues on next page

9. From the menus in the Property Inspector's Audio area, choose an audio stream for each language (**Figure 15.20**).

When DVD Studio Pro multiplexes your project, it builds a separate menu for each alternate language. When the project is placed in a DVD-Video player, the menu that matches the player's language setting is the only menu that appears on the screen.

✔ Tips

■ The DVD specification limits every DVD-Video to 1 gigabyte of menus. If you are using MPEG-2 video to create motion menus, it is conceivable that you could surpass this 1-gigabyte limit.

■ As DVD Studio Pro multiplexes your multilingual menus, the Menu tile's thumbnail image updates to show you which menu is currently being built.

To delete a menu language:

1. On the Project View's Languages tab, select a language (**Figure 15.21**).

2. Press the Delete key.

✔ Tip

■ If any of your project's menus have picture or audio assets that use a specific language, you will not be able to delete that language from the Project View's Languages tab. Attempting to delete the language results in the dialog box shown in **Figure 15.22**. This dialog box is tenacious, and to shake it you must comb your entire project for menus that reference the language that you are trying to delete (check all of your menus' picture and audio properties).

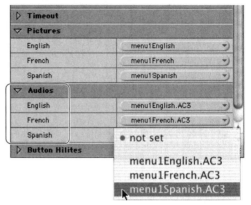

Figure 15.20 If your menu contains audio, select an audio stream for each language.

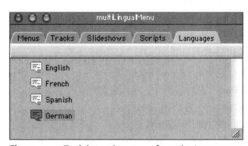

Figure 15.21 To delete a language from the Languages tab, select it and press the Delete key.

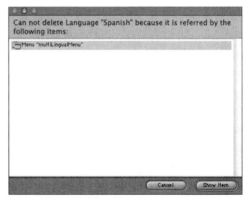

Figure 15.22 Uh-oh. DVD Studio Pro won't let you delete a language from the Project View if it is used in any of your menus.

Figure 15.23 From the Language menu, choose the language that you want to preview.

Thumbnail area

Figure 15.24 The Menu tile's thumbnail changes to show the picture asset for the language selected from the Language menu.

Previewing multilingual menus

For each language that you add to the Project View's Languages tab, a new option appears on DVD Studio Pro's Language menu (**Figure 15.23**). Choosing a language from DVD Studio Pro's Language menu causes your project's menus to display the selected language's picture and audio assets, both in the Menu editor and the Preview mode.

To preview a multilingual menu:

1. Choose Language > and select a language (refer to Figure 15.23).

   If you look closely at the Menu tile in the Graphical View, you'll notice that its thumbnail area has changed to show the alternate language menu (**Figure 15.24**).

2. In the lower left corner of the Graphical View, click the Preview button.

   The Preview mode plays the menu, using the language that you selected from the Language menu. To preview other language menus, exit the Preview mode and follow these steps again, selecting a new language each time.

CREATING MULTILINGUAL MENUS

Linking Menus to Alternate Audio Streams

Earlier in this chapter, you learned how to set audio streams so that the correct language always plays. But this doesn't help viewers if their DVD-Video player's audio language setting isn't correctly configured. To guard against this possibility, supply your project with a language (or audio) menu that viewers can use to select the audio stream that they want to hear.

A language selection menu has several buttons: one for each language in the project (**Figure 15.25**). By setting a few options in the Button Property Inspector, you can link each of the menu's buttons directly to the corresponding alternate language audio stream.

To link a menu button to an alternate language audio stream:

1. In the Graphical View, double-click the thumbnail area of the Menu tile that holds the Language menu.

   The Menu editor opens.

2. Select a button (**Figure 15.26**).

   The Property Inspector updates to display the Button's properties.

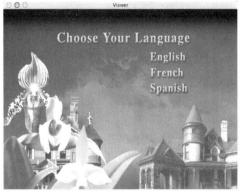

Figure 15.25 A language selection menu.

Figure 15.26 To link a button on a language selection menu to a specific audio stream on a track, first select the button.

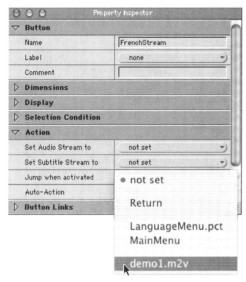

Figure 15.27 Next, choose the track that the button jumps to by setting the button's Jump When Activated property.

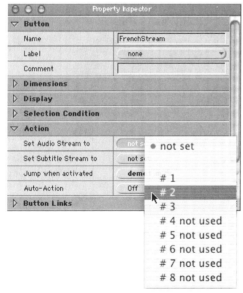

Figure 15.28 Finish the button by choosing an audio stream from the Set Audio Stream To menu.

3. From the Jump When Activated menu, choose the track with the alternate language audio streams (in **Figure 15.27**, the multilingual track is called demo1.m2v).

This is the track that will play when the button is activated. If you look above the Jump When Activated property, you'll see a Set Audio Stream To property. This property selects an audio stream from the track defined in the Jump When Finished property.

4. From the Set Audio Stream To menu, choose an audio stream (**Figure 15.28**).

Activating the button now jumps the DVD-Video to the multilingual track and automatically plays the audio stream that the viewer wants to hear.

✔ Tip

■ The Button Property Inspector's Action area also has a Set Subtitle Stream To menu that you can use to link the button to a specific subtitle stream.

Previewing Multilingual Projects

Multilingual projects use a lot of assets. With so much going on in the project, it's easy to mistakenly assign, for example, the wrong language setting to an audio stream. If a French viewer clicks a menu button and a Spanish audio track starts playing, the French viewer is going to be left wondering what's up. As a result, when creating alternate language projects, you must verify that all menus navigate as expected and that audio streams all play in the proper tongue.

To see how your multilingual project will behave in the real world, preview it in Apple DVD Player (DVD Player). DVD Player's Preferences dialog box holds three menus that let you choose a default audio, subtitle, and menu language. When you play a DVD-Video, DVD Player checks to see whether any of the project items match its language settings. If a matching project item is found, DVD Player displays it.

To preview languages in DVD Player:

1. In DVD Studio Pro, choose File > Build Disc "multiLingual" (Command-B), where "multiLingual" is the name of your project (**Figure 15.29**).

   This builds a copy of your project to your computer's hard disk. Building a project creates a VIDEO_TS and an AUDIO_TS folder on your computer's hard disks. To learn more, see Chapter 13, "Finishing the DVD."

2. Open DVD Player.

3. Choose DVD Player > Preferences (**Figure 15.30**).

   DVD Player's Preferences dialog box opens.

Figure 15.29 Multiplex your project by selecting File > Build Disc "multiLingual," where "multiLingual" is the name of your project.

Figure 15.30 To specify which language to use as you watch the DVD-Video, choose DVD Player > Preferences.

Figure 15.31 When the Preferences window opens, select the Disc tab.

Figure 15.32 Choose languages from the Default Language Settings area.

Figure 15.33 In DVD Player, choose File > Open VIDEO_TS Folder (Command-o); then navigate to the VIDEO_TS folder that contains your multilingual DVD-Video and open it.

4. In the Preferences dialog box, select the Disc tab (**Figure 15.31**).

On the center of the Disc tab is a Default Language Settings area containing menus labeled Audio, Subtitle, and DVD Menu.

5. From the Default Language Settings area's menus, choose a language (**Figure 15.32**).

6. Click OK.

The Preferences dialog box closes.

7. Choose File > Open VIDEO_TS Folder (Command-0) (**Figure 15.33**).

8. Navigate to the VIDEO_TS Folder that you built in step 1 and open it.

9. Play the DVD-Video.

Preview all tracks, slideshows, and menus to make sure that they play and display the correct languages. If everything looks good, close the DVD-Video and follow steps 3 to 9 to select another language to preview. Repeat the process until you've previewed all of the alternate languages in your project.

✔ Tip

■ DVD Player works with languages in exactly the same way as a set-top DVD-Video player. By switching DVD Player's language preferences, you can preview all of the languages used in your DVD-Video.

PREVIEWING MULTILINGUAL PROJECTS

SUBTITLES

If you've ever rented a foreign film or read the close-captioned TVs while working out at the gym, you're already familiar with subtitles. Subtitles—text captions displayed on top of the video—are most often used to supply alternate-language translations of the video's main dialog. But there's no need to stop there, as subtitles are equally effective at captioning video for the hearing impaired or providing information to supplement the main audio and video streams.

Once brought into DVD Studio Pro, subtitles are extremely easy to use. But subtitle streams are like all other assets, and before you can import them into DVD Studio Pro, you must create them. To this end, Apple has supplied you with a handy little helper application called the Subtitle Editor, which is installed at the same time as DVD Studio Pro.

The Subtitle Editor works with the fonts on your computer to create text-based subtitles. While it's possible to store pictures and even basic animations in a subtitle stream, the Subtitle Editor that comes with DVD Studio Pro is not meant for this purpose. With a bit of work, you can use a third-party application such as Macromedia Fontographer to turn pictures into custom fonts, but in general you'll use the Subtitle Editor to provide nothing more complex than alternate-language subtitle streams.

About the Subtitle Editor

The Subtitle Editor is composed of three
main windows: the Preview window, the
Subtitle window, and the Marker window
(**Figure 16.1**).

The Preview window displays a reference
movie that you watch to locate sections of
dialog that need to be subtitled. Directly
below the Preview window sits the Subtitle
window. This window contains a list of subtitle cells that hold subtitle text—but more on
that later. The Marker window in the upper
right corner of the Subtitle Editor lets you
define and jump straight to specific points in
the reference movie displayed in the Preview
window. If you are working on a long movie,
creating markers lets you quickly navigate
among the movie's various sections.

Preview window ⌐   Marker window ⌐

Subtitle cell ⌐   Subtitle text ⌐   Subtitle window ⌐

Figure 16.1 The Subtitle Editor's workspace.

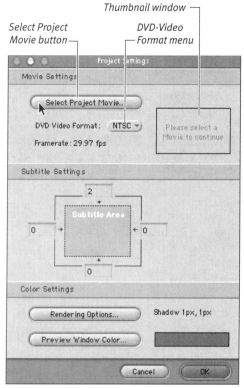

Thumbnail window

Select Project Movie button

DVD-Video Format menu

Figure 16.2 Use the Project Settings dialog box to choose the reference movie to use as the basis for your subtitles.

Setting up a subtitle project

The Project Settings dialog box is the first thing that you see when you open the Subtitle Editor (**Figure 16.2**). This dialog box lets you choose the QuickTime movie that will act as the reference movie for your subtitle stream.

The reference movie itself can be any QuickTime movie at all, compressed using any codec. For short movies, it's common to use the original source QuickTime file (the one that served as the source for your MPEG-2 stream). For longer movies, you might want to save your computer the hassle of chewing through a huge movie by compressing a low-bandwidth version of the original QuickTime file (see "Lower the Resolution" below).

Lower the Resolution

Although you *can* use your MPEG-2 stream's original QuickTime movie as your reference movie, you don't have to, and you probably shouldn't. The original QuickTime file is large and may slow down the Subtitle Editor. You're better off compressing a low-resolution version of the source movie and using that as your guide. As long as you can hear the dialog and see the lips moving on your characters, you'll be able to create subtitles. You can, for example, compress a 360 x 240 pixel version of your movie at a drastically reduced data rate (say, 400 kbps). The Subtitle Editor will expand the compressed movie to 720 x 480, so that you'll still see the full frame (though the expanded picture will look pixelated and a bit blurry).

If you decide to use a compressed reference movie, make sure that it uses exactly the same frame rate as the source movie (that's 29.97 *nondrop frame* frames per second for NTSC, and 25 frames per second for PAL). The Subtitle Editor uses this frame rate to determine the time codes for your subtitles. Whatever you do, don't compress your reference movie at a lower frame rate, or your subtitles won't appear when or where you want them to appear.

To open the Subtitle Editor:

1. Locate the Subtitle Editor application on your hard disk and double-click it (**Figure 16.3**).

   The Project Settings dialog box appears (refer to Figure 16.2). At the top of the Project Settings dialog box is a Movie Settings area used to choose the QuickTime reference movie.

2. Click the Select Project Movie button.

   An Open Movie dialog box appears (**Figure 16.4**).

Figure 16.3 The Subtitle Editor is located in the DVD Studio Pro application folder.

Figure 16.4 In the Open Movie dialog box, you can navigate to the subtitle reference movie.

ABOUT THE SUBTITLE EDITOR

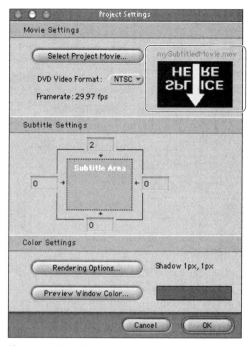

Figure 16.5 The thumbnail area in the Project Settings dialog box shows a preview of the reference movie, so you can be sure that you've selected the right one.

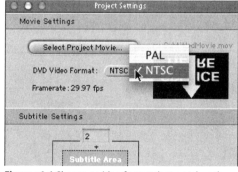

Figure 16.6 Choose a video format that matches the format of your selected QuickTime movie.

3. Use the Open Movie dialog box to find the reference movie and click Open.

In the Project Settings dialog box, the movie appears in the Movie Settings thumbnail area (**Figure 16.5**). The thumbnail area usually shows the first frame of the QuickTime movie, so if the area looks black, it's probably because your movie begins with a fade in.

4. From the DVD Video Format menu, choose either NTSC or PAL (**Figure 16.6**).

Chapter 3, "Encoding Video Streams," explains that NTSC and PAL video use different frame rates and resolutions. As a result, subtitles calibrated for NTSC video play back at a different rate and in a different place in the frame than subtitles calibrated for PAL video, so make sure you choose the correct format.

5. In the lower right corner of the Project Settings dialog box, click OK.

The Project Settings dialog box closes, and the subtitle project opens to a fresh workspace on your screen.

About the Preview Window

The Subtitle Editor's Preview window plays the reference movie (**Figure 16.7**). Below the reference movie is a *timeline slider* and a *playhead*. If you drag the playhead along the slider, or *scrub* through the movie, you can use the Preview window to locate the position where subtitles need to go.

In the upper left corner of the Preview window is a time code display. The time code returned in this box precisely matches the playhead's position in the reference movie. At the top center of the Preview window is a Zoom menu that lets you reduce or increase the Preview window's size, and in the upper right corner of the Preview window is the Subtitle and Video menu, which lets you turn the reference movie's picture on and off.

To play the reference movie:

◆ *Do one of the following:*

   ▲ To the left of the timeline slider, click the Play button (**Figure 16.8**).

   ▲ Double-click the reference movie.

   ▲ Press Command and the right arrow key.

   ▲ Press the spacebar.

   ▲ Press the Enter key on the numeric keypad.

To the left of the timeline slider, the Play button changes into the Pause button, and the reference movie begins playing.

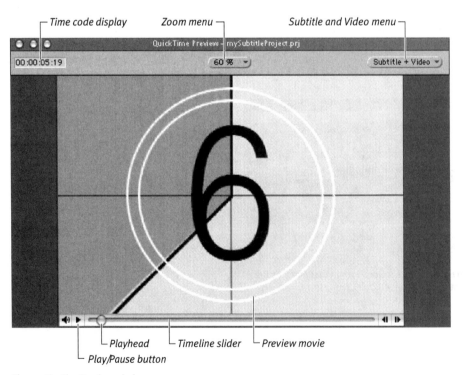

Time code display   *Zoom menu*   *Subtitle and Video menu*

Playhead   *Timeline slider*   *Preview movie*

Play/Pause button

Figure 16.7 The Preview window.

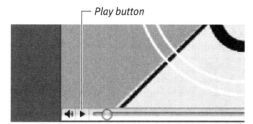

Figure 16.8 To play the reference movie, click the Play button or double-click the reference movie itself.

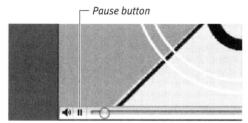

Figure 16.9 To stop the movie, click the Pause button or the reference movie itself.

To stop playback of the reference movie:

◆ With the preview movie playing, *do one of the following:*

▲ Click the Pause button (**Figure 16.9**).

▲ Click the preview movie.

▲ Press the spacebar.

▲ Press the period key on the numeric keypad.

To the left of the timeline slider, the Pause button changes into the Play button, and the preview movie stops playing.

To rewind the movie:

◆ Press and hold the left arrow key.

The movie plays in reverse.

To step forward through frames:

◆ Press and release the right arrow key.

The playhead moves forward through the movie two frames at a time.

✔ Tip

■ Press the number 3 on the keyboard's numeric keypad to advance through the movie one frame at a time.

To step backward through frames:

◆ Press and release the left arrow key.

The playhead moves in reverse through the movie two frames at a time.

✔ Tip

■ Press the number 1 on the keyboard's numeric keypad to reverse the movie one frame at a time.

ABOUT THE PREVIEW WINDOW

Creating Subtitle Cells

Subtitle cells hold the text that makes up the individual subtitles you see on the screen. The time value where a subtitle cell begins is called its *In point*, and the time value where it ends is called its *Out point*. The length of time between each specific subtitle cell's In and Out points is its *duration*. Individual subtitle cells can't overlap, but they can be as long or as short as you like (although some DVD-Video players have a hard time displaying subtitles less than 10 frames in duration).

Figure 16.10 In the Preview window, move the playhead to the place where you want the subtitle to begin.

To add a subtitle cell:

1. In the Preview window, move the playhead to the point in the movie where you want the subtitle cell to begin (**Figure 16.10**).

2. In the upper left corner of the Subtitle window, click the New button (**Figure 16.11**).

   A new subtitle cell is created in the Subtitle window (**Figure 16.12**).

3. In the Preview window, double-click anywhere on the preview movie to start playback (pressing the spacebar also starts a stopped reference movie).

   The reference movie plays.

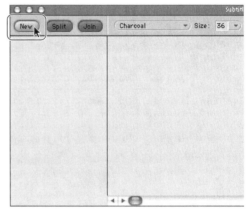

Figure 16.11 Click the Subtitle window's New button to add a subtitle cell.

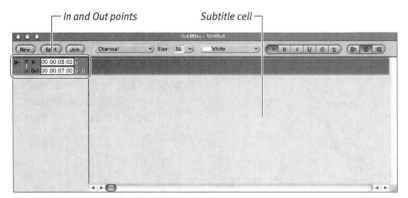

Figure 16.12 A new subtitle cell in the Subtitle window. The text boxes on the left side of the subtitle cell set the subtitle's In and Out points.

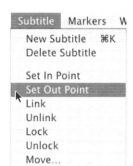

| Subtitle | Markers | W |
| New Subtitle | ⌘K |
| Delete Subtitle |
| Set In Point |
| Set Out Point |
| Link |
| Unlink |
| Lock |
| Unlock |
| Move... |

Figure 16.13 Choose Subtitle > Set Out Point to set the point where the subtitle turns off.

4. As soon as you hear the last word of dialog for the subtitle, stop playback by quickly clicking once anywhere on the reference movie (pressing the spacebar also stops playback).

Playback stops (if you need to adjust the playhead forward or backward a few frames, use the left or right arrow key).

5. Choose Subtitle > Set Out Point (**Figure 16.13**).

The subtitle cell's Out point is set to the playhead's current time code value (shown in the time code display in the upper left corner of the Preview window).

✔ Tip

■ Individual subtitles cannot cross chapter boundaries. Consequently, if you know in advance that the subtitle stream is destined for a DVD Studio Pro track that will have chapters, you must do a bit of preplanning before creating the subtitle stream.

In DVD Studio Pro, check the time code values of all of the track's chapter markers and write these values on a piece of paper. Back in the Subtitle Editor, make sure a blank space with no subtitles appears at the time code values corresponding to the track's chapter markers. For more information, see "Using Subtitles in DVD Studio Pro" later in this chapter.

To enter subtitle text:

1. In the Subtitle window, double-click the subtitle cell's text edit field (**Figure 16.14**).

   The subtitle cell's text edit field expands, and a text insertion point begins blinking.

2. Type the subtitle text (**Figure 16.15**).

   The text that you type appears over the movie in the Preview window, as shown in **Figure 16.16** (if you don't see the subtitle text, jar the Subtitle Editor to attention by clicking the Preview window and then clicking the subtitle cell again).

✔ Tip

■ You may notice that subtitles are incorrectly positioned on the screen (refer to Figure 16.16). Read the next section, "Positioning Subtitles," to learn how to place your subtitles where you want them.

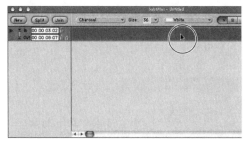

Figure 16.14 To enter subtitles, begin by double-clicking the subtitle cell's text edit field.

Figure 16.15 Type subtitle text directly in the subtitle cell's text edit field.

Figure 16.16 These subtitles are close to the top of the screen, not the bottom where subtitles usually appear. To fix subtitle placement, you'll need to set your margins.

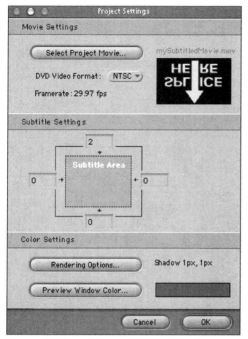

Figure 16.17 The subtitle area is defined by the margins that you set in the Subtitle Settings area of the Project Settings dialog box.

Figure 16.18 To open the Project Settings dialog box, choose File > Project Settings.

Positioning Subtitles

To position your subtitles inside the video frame, you need to set up margins in the Subtitle Editor. This task is accomplished using the Subtitle Settings area of the Project Settings window (**Figure 16.17**).

Subtitles, of course, are text, and just as with any other text in your project, you must make sure that they sit inside the video frame's title safe area (see Chapter 3, "Encoding Video Streams"). This area is represented by a border set 10 percent in from the edge of the video frame. For subtitles in NTSC video, the left and right margins should be no less than 72 pixels, and the top and bottom margins should be at least 48 pixels. For PAL video, the margins should be 72 pixels from the left and right edges and 58 pixels from the top and bottom.

Setting a top margin of 48 pixels places your subtitles at the top of the screen instead of in their customary place at the bottom. To move the subtitles closer to the bottom of the screen, choose a top margin of around 350 to 400 pixels. Whatever setting you choose, keep a careful eye on the bottom of your subtitles to make sure that they don't get cropped off (especially if the subtitles extend over more than one line).

To set subtitle margins:

1. Choose File > Project Settings (**Figure 16.18**).

   The Project Settings dialog box opens (refer to Figure 16.17).

continues on next page

2. In the Subtitle Settings area, enter values for your margins (**Figure 16.19**).

Your subtitles are squeezed into the margins that you've defined (**Figure 16.20**).

✔ Tip

■ The Subtitle window's text edit fields change size to match the subtitle project's margins. While typing subtitles, watch the subtitle cell to make sure that the text fits inside the margins that you've created (**Figure 16.21**).

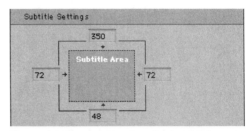

Figure 16.19 Type margin values (in pixels) in the Subtitle Settings area's text boxes.

Figure 16.20 The Preview window shows you where the subtitle will be placed within the video frame.

Figure 16.21 The subtitle cell changes in size to match the margins that you set in the Project Settings dialog box.

Formatting Subtitles

Chances are good that the Subtitle Editor's default font doesn't match the style, size, or color you want for your subtitle stream. Fortunately, changing any or all of these attributes is easy, because the menus and buttons along the top of the Subtitle window give you instant access to several text customizing features (**Figure 16.22**).

Figure 16.22 Use the buttons and menus across the top of the Subtitle window to change the font, style, and justification of your project's subtitles.

To set the font:

1. In the Subtitle window, select the text in a subtitle cell.

2. Choose a font from the Subtitle window's Font menu (**Figure 16.23**), or choose Text > Font > and pick a font.

   The subtitle text changes to the selected font.

Figure 16.23 Choose text fonts from the Subtitle window's Font menu.

To set the font size:

1. In the Subtitle window, select some text in a subtitle cell (**Figure 16.24**).

2. Choose a font size from the Size menu (**Figure 16.25**), or choose Text > Size > and pick a size.

   The subtitle text changes to the selected size (**Figure 16.26**).

✔ Tip

■ The Font Size menu lists only commonly selected font sizes. To enter your own font size, choose Text > Size > Custom and enter a value in the Text Size dialog box (**Figure 16.27**).

Figure 16.24 To change the font size, select some text in a subtitle cell.

Figure 16.25 Choose a value from the Subtitle window's Size menu.

Figure 16.26 The selected text changes size.

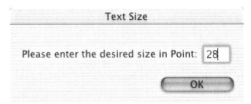

Figure 16.27 If the Size menu doesn't offer the text size you need, enter your own custom text size in this dialog box.

Figure 16.28 Select one or more style buttons to add an underline, italics, an outline, or other emphasis to your subtitle text.

Right align —
Center align —
Left align —

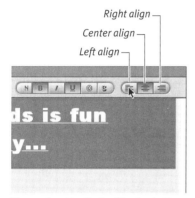

Figure 16.29 Use the justification buttons to left align, center, or right align your subtitles in relation to their margins.

To set a font style option:

1. In the Subtitle window, select some text in a subtitle cell.

2. Select a font style using the Subtitle window's style buttons (**Figure 16.28**), or choose Text > Style > and choose a style.

To justify text:

1. In the Subtitle window, click a subtitle cell to select it.

2. Click a justification option from the Subtitle window's justification buttons (**Figure 16.29**).

Using Color

The Subtitle Editor provides a preset palette of 16 subtitle colors. Subtitle color applies to all of the characters in the selected subtitle cell, which means that you can't change the color of certain text characters in a cell without changing the color of all of the others (however, text color *can* vary from subtitle cell to subtitle cell).

To set a subtitle's color:

1. Click inside a subtitle cell to select it.

2. Choose a text color from the Subtitle window's Color menu, or choose Text > Color > and pick a color (**Figure 16.30**).

Changing default colors

If the subtitle color that you want is not offered in the set of 16 preset colors, open the Subtitle Editor's Preferences dialog box and change the default colors.

To change the default subtitle colors:

1. Choose Subtitle Editor > Preferences (Mac OS X) or Edit > Preferences (Mac OS 9).

   The Preferences dialog box opens (**Figure 16.31**).

2. Click the Color Menu Settings button.

   The Color Menu Settings dialog box opens (**Figure 16.32**).

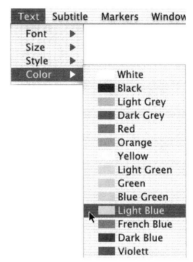

Figure 16.30 Set the text color by choosing Text > Color > and choosing a color.

Figure 16.31 The Subtitle Editor's Preferences dialog box.

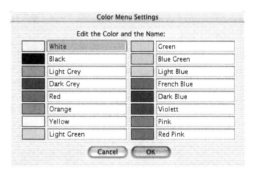

Figure 16.32 You can use the Color Menu Settings dialog box to change any of the 16 default colors used by the Subtitle Editor.

USING COLOR

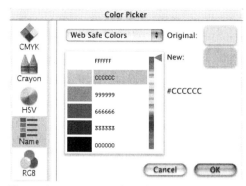

Figure 16.33 You can use the Color Picker to select custom colors.

Eyedropper

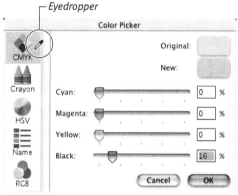

Figure 16.34 With the Color Picker open, press the Option key to enable the Eyedropper tool and sample colors from anywhere on the screen.

3. Click a color patch to open the Color Picker; then choose a color (**Figure 16.33**).

4. Click OK to close the Color Picker.

5. To change the color's name, click its text field and type a new name.

6. Click OK to close the Color Menu Settings window and then the Preferences dialog box.

The newly defined color is available in the Subtitle Editor's color menus.

✔ Tip

■ With the Color Picker open, press the Option key to enable the Eyedropper tool and sample colors from anywhere on your screen (**Figure 16.34**).

USING COLOR

Setting background colors

By default, subtitle cells are black. If you are using dark subtitles, a black background does not provide enough contrast for you to see your subtitle text. To bump up the contrast between the text and the background, change the color of the subtitle cells.

To change the color of subtitle cells:

1. Choose File > Project Settings.

   The Project Settings dialog box appears.

2. In the Color Settings section, click the Preview Window Color button (**Figure 16.35**).

   The Color Picker opens (refer to Figure 16.33).

3. Choose a color and click OK.

   The Color Picker closes, leaving the Project Settings dialog box open on the screen.

4. In the lower right corner of the Project Settings dialog box, click OK.

   The Subtitle window's subtitle cells change to the new color (**Figure 16.36**).

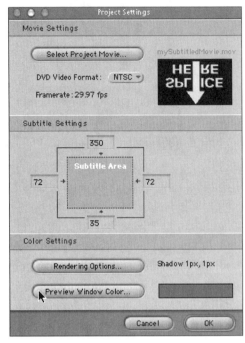

Figure 16.35 The Preview Window Color button changes the subtitle cells' background colors. Don't be fooled; despite its name, this button has nothing to do with the Preview window. (The Preview window displays the reference movie that you are subtitling.)

Subtitle cell ⌐   Background color ⌐

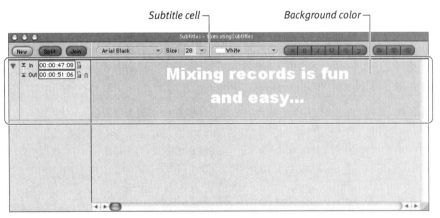

Figure 16.36 The subtitle cells in this figure have a very light background color, which makes the subtitle text hard to read—better change that background color to provide more contrast!

USING COLOR

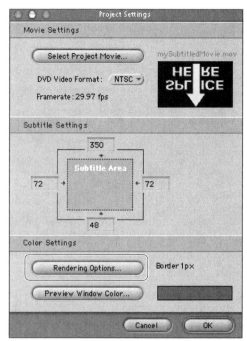

Figure 16.37 To create a stroke or drop shadow, click the Project Setting dialog box's Rendering Options button.

Setting Strokes and Drop Shadows

Adding a stroke or a drop shadow enhances the readability of subtitles and gives them a greater presence on the screen. Small fonts (particularly serif fonts) benefit from drop shadows (to learn more, see the section "Preventing Menu Flicker" in Chapter 8, "Photoshop Layer Menus").

Strokes and drop shadows are applied globally to the entire project, so you can't enable drop shadows for certain subtitle cells and not others.

To add a stroke or drop shadow:

1. Choose File > Project Settings.

   The Project Settings dialog box opens.

2. In the Color Settings section, click the Rendering Options button (**Figure 16.37**).

   The Rendering Options dialog box opens (**Figure 16.38**).

continues on next page

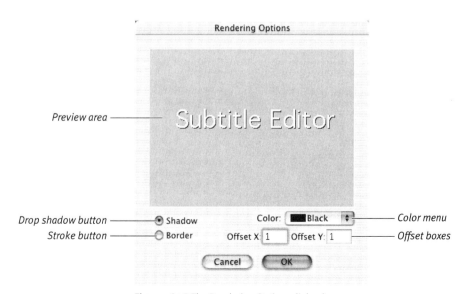

Figure 16.38 The Rendering Options dialog box.

3. Click either the Shadow or Border radio button.

The Border button creates a stroke around the text while the Shadow button creates a drop shadow.

4. From the Color menu, select a color (**Figure 16.39**).

5. Enter a stroke width (if you select Border) or drop shadow offset (if you select Shadow) (**Figure 16.40**).

6. To close the Rendering Options dialog box, click OK.

When the Subtitle Editor compiles your final subtitle stream, the stroke or drop shadow will be applied to your subtitles.

✔ Tips

■ Strokes and drop shadows are applied to subtitles when the subtitle stream is *rendered*, or compiled. The Subtitle Editor does not display strokes or drop shadows, so don't worry if you don't see them in the Preview window. When you compile the subtitle stream and bring it into DVD Studio Pro, the drop shadow or stroke will be present.

■ Positive offset values move the drop shadow down and to the right by the specified number of pixels. To move the drop shadow up or to the left, enter negative values.

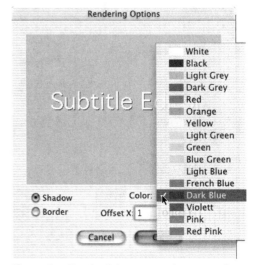

Figure 16.39 Use the Color menu to choose a stroke or drop shadow color.

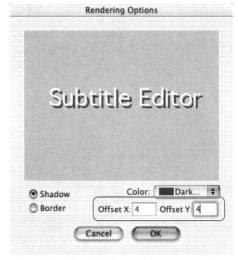

Figure 16.40 Use the Offset text boxes to specify how far from the text the drop shadow should be.

00:00:09:08	00:00:12:17	Mixing records is fun<P>and easy
00:00:13:02	00:00:18:21	You can learn it<P>in just two minutes!
00:00:20:07	00:00:25:07	Listen to the beat...
00:00:27:09	00:00:31:19	Mixing record is all in the feet.
00:00:32:02	00:00:37:29	Start tapping your left foot<P>to the beat o
00:00:42:05	00:00:45:19	Select another record
00:00:45:20	00:00:49:00	and place it on turntable B.
00:00:53:04	00:00:57:21	Back cue to find your cue beat
00:00:57:22	00:00:61:00	and let it play
00:00:63:00	00:00:66:26	Start tapping<P>your second foot
00:00:66:27	00:00:70:14	to the beat of record B.

└─ *Tabs* ─┘

Figure 16.41 The Subtitle Editor imports properly formatted plain text files.

Keep Tabs on the Tabs

If the Subtitle Editor won't import your plain text file, check or do the following:

◆ Make sure that the subtitle list begins on the first line of the text document. The Subtitle Editor stops importing a text file as soon as it encounters something it doesn't understand. If you leave the first line blank, the Subtitle Editor gets confused and will stop importing before it begins.

◆ Check that the spaces between the time code values and the subtitle text are all tabs and not spacebar spaces. If the Subtitle Editor imports your text file only up to a certain point, chances are good that a space has crept in where it's not wanted. Open the file in a text editor and check that the tabs are really tabs.

◆ Save the text file as an Apple Simple Text document. (Bare Bones Software's BBEdit is a good choice for producing these files.)

Importing Subtitles

Entering subtitles can be a time-consuming task. Moving the playhead along the reference movie and typing subtitle text is tedious at best. But there is an easier way: you can also create subtitles by listing them in a plain text document along with their corresponding In and Out time code values and then importing that text file straight into the Subtitle Editor.

Defining subtitles in a text file has several advantages. Not only is the process quick, but you can also use your word processing program's spell checker to make sure that no typos creep into your text. The greatest benefit, however, comes when you need to translate the subtitles into other languages. Rather than struggle through the translation yourself, you can simply send the text file to a translator. When the translated text file is returned, you just import the file into the Subtitle Editor, and you're instantly ready to compile the subtitle stream.

Formatting the text file

The text file is a list of subtitles with their corresponding time codes (**Figure 16.41**). Each subtitle in the list must have three values, all separated by a single Tab stroke:

◆ In time code value

◆ Out time code value

◆ Subtitle text

If a subtitle needs to be spread over two or more lines, you can add a line break using a capital *P* surrounded by angle brackets (make sure it's an uppercase *P*, as a lowercase *p* won't work): <P>.

To import subtitles from a text file:

1. Start your subtitle project as described earlier in this chapter in the section "About the Subtitle Editor."

2. Choose File > Import > Subtitles (**Figure 16.42**).

   An Open dialog box appears.

3. Navigate to the simple text file that holds your subtitles and click Open.

   The Import Subtitles dialog box opens.

4. Choose Skip Read Subtitle and click OK (**Figure 16.43**).

   The text file is imported into the Subtitle Editor and appears in the Subtitle window.

✔ Tip

■ If you find the Subtitle Editor finicky or prone to crashing, you can create subtitles just as effectively using QuickTime and a text editor such as Bare Bones Software's BBEdit. Use QuickTime to play your reference movie and locate the time code values for subtitle In and Out points; then type those values straight into BBEdit. When your list of time codes and subtitles is complete, import it into the Subtitle Editor and compile the subtitle stream.

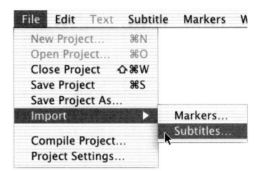

Figure 16.42 To import a text file into the Subtitle Editor, choose File > Import > Subtitles.

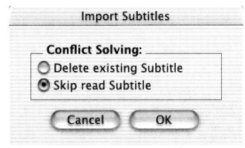

Figure 16.43 When the Import Subtitles dialog box appears, choose Skip Read Subtitle.

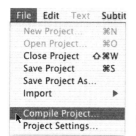

Figure 16.44 To compile a subtitle stream, choose File > Compile Project.

Figure 16.45 Use the Save dialog box to name your subtitle stream; then find the folder on your hard disks where you will save it and click Save.

Figure 16.46 The Subtitle Editor's progress window.

Compiling Subtitle Streams

Compiling takes the subtitle project and turns it into a subtitle stream that you can import into DVD Studio Pro.

To compile a subtitle stream:

1. Choose File > Compile Project (**Figure 16.44**).

   A Save dialog box appears (**Figure 16.45**).

2. Name your subtitle stream, navigate to the folder where you want to save it, and click Save.

   A progress window opens to keep track of the action as the Subtitle Editor compiles the subtitle stream (**Figure 16.46**). When the compiling process is complete, a file with the .spu extension is created on your hard disk. You can now import this subtitle stream directly into DVD Studio Pro.

Using Subtitles in DVD Studio Pro

Once they are imported into DVD Studio Pro, subtitles behave a lot like alternate audio streams. Each Track tile has a Subtitle icon that opens a Subtitle container used to hold and organize subtitle streams. Like alternate audio streams, each of these subtitle streams can be assigned a separate language, and it's this language value that the DVD-Video player reads to determine which subtitle stream to play. There's no real magic to using subtitles; as long as you appropriately set each subtitle stream's language (and have faith that the viewer has correctly specified the DVD-Video player's language settings), you can be sure that the proper subtitle will always appear on the screen.

However, there are a few things to keep in mind as you add subtitles to Track tiles:

◆ The DVD-Video specification allows only up to 32 separate subtitle streams per track. (Only? For most purposes that's way more than enough!)

◆ Individual subtitles must not cross chapter boundaries. To avoid problems, make sure that chapter markers are inserted at the In or Out point of specific subtitles and not in the middle of a subtitle. If a subtitle spans a chapter marker, attempting to build your project results in the error display shown in **Figure 16.47**.

◆ Subtitles and interactive markers both use the subpicture stream to store their graphics. Consequently, you can't have buttons and subtitles on the same track. It's one or the other, so if you use interactive markers on a track, you will not be able to add subtitles, and vice versa.

```
●●●                          Log
10:28:32 PM Starting Up
10:28:52 PM 'demoVideo5.m2v::Chapter 1' at 00:00:02:00 intersects part of 'english.spu'
10:28:52 PM 'demoVideo5.m2v::Chapter 1' at 00:00:02:00 intersects part of 'french.spu'
10:28:52 PM 'demoVideo5.m2v::Chapter 1' at 00:00:02:00 intersects part of 'spanish.spu'
```

Figure 16.47 If a single subtitle (the text on the screen, not the subtitle stream itself) spans a chapter marker, this error occurs when you attempt to build your project. To fix the error, make sure that chapter markers are at subtitle boundaries.

Figure 16.48 To import a subtitle stream, choose File > Import.

To import subtitle streams:

1. Choose File > Import or press Command-I (**Figure 16.48**).

   The Import Files dialog box opens.

2. Use the Import Files dialog box to navigate to and select a subtitle stream; then click the Import button (**Figure 16.49**).

   The Subtitle stream is added to the bottom of DVD Studio Pro's Assets container.

Figure 16.49 Choose your subtitle streams from the Import Files dialog box.

About the Subpicture Stream

Subtitles are stored in a special graphics layer called the *subpicture stream*, which uses a maximum of four colors to display the text. Subpicture streams take up little bandwidth when compared to MPEG-2 video, but you still need to account for them when determining your project's data rate. All subpictures are multiplexed right along with the video and audio streams to create the finished DVD-Video, so if your project uses several subtitle streams, you should prepare for an increase in your DVD-video's overall data rate (for more information, see Appendix B, "Making a Bit Budget").

To add subtitles to a Track tile:

1. In the Graphical View, click the subtitle icon on a Track tile (**Figure 16.50**).

   The Subtitle container opens (**Figure 16.51**).

2. From the Assets container, drag one or more subtitle streams into the Subtitle container (**Figure 16.52**).

3. Select a subtitle stream in the Subtitle container.

   The subtitle stream is highlighted, and the Property Inspector updates to display its properties.

4. From the Property Inspector's Language menu, choose a language for your subtitle stream (**Figure 16.53**).

   Repeat steps 2 through 4 until you've added all necessary subtitle streams to the track.

Subtitle icon

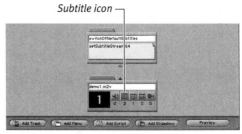

Figure 16.50 Click a Track tile's subtitle icon to open its Subtitle container.

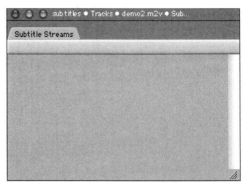

Figure 16.51 The Subtitle container holds subtitle streams. This one is empty, but it won't be for long.

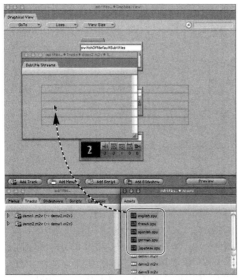

Figure 16.52 Drag subtitle streams from the Assets container directly into the Subtitles container.

Figure 16.53 To set a subtitle stream's language, select the stream in the Subtitles container and choose a language from the Property Inspector's Language menu.

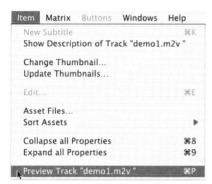

Figure 16.54 To preview your subtitles, select a Track tile and choose Item > Preview Track.

Figure 16.55 Clicking the Preview mode's Subtitle button cycles through the track's subtitle streams.

Figure 16.56 The Subpicture counter tells you which subtitle stream you are currently watching.

To preview subtitles:

1. In the Graphical View, select a Track tile that holds one or more subtitle streams.

2. Choose Item > Preview Track or press Command-P (**Figure 16.54**).

The Preview mode opens and plays the track. The first subtitle in the track is displayed automatically.

3. To view the track's other subtitle streams, click the Subtitle button (**Figure 16.55**).

Each time you click the Subtitle button, the Preview mode window switches to the next subtitle stream, and the Subpicture counter at the top of the Preview mode changes to show you which stream you're watching (**Figure 16.56**).

The Default Subtitle Stream

When you play a subtitled DVD-Video, the subtitle that matches the player's subtitle language setting is displayed automatically. If none of the subtitle language settings are a match, the player defaults to the first subtitle stream in the track.

In most situations, you'll want your project to start playing with the subtitles off, leaving the viewer to decide whether or not to turn on the subtitles (either by pressing the Subtitle button on the remote control or by choosing a subtitle stream from a subtitle menu). To set your DVD-Video so that it doesn't automatically display subtitles, either create a blank subtitle stream with no text in it or write a script. (If you just can't wait, the script that you'll need to use is pictured in Figure 16.50). For more information on creating this script, see Chapter 17, "Scripting!"

SCRIPTING!

If the thought of scripting fills you with dread, you're not alone; after all, most of us are video professionals and not computer programmers. But you really have nothing to worry about. Scripting in DVD Studio Pro is not as hard as it sounds. Apple uses a very simple and intuitive scripting language that more or less resembles plain English. In fact, most of the scripts that you'll write use *keywords* (script commands), which sound just like English words. What's more, these keywords combine into lines of script (statements), which are similar to sentences that you might speak. After a little practice, you'll start looking for excuses to use scripts, because scripting is not only powerful and easy— it's also fun!

Learning scripting is similar to learning any language: you can read about speaking Spanish all you want, but you won't become multilingual until you start talking. If you want to master scripting, you have to be hands-on. To help you hit the ground running, this chapter begins by introducing you to DVD Studio Pro's scripting language; then it moves on to explore several real-world examples, including a script that loops a menu a specific number of times and one that creates a Play All Tracks button.

This book has a companion Web site where you can find all of the scripting examples discussed in this section, plus many more. The examples at this Web site are all complete projects. In most cases, you can download these sample projects, substitute your own assets, and have a complete project ready to go in less than five minutes. When you're ready to start scripting, check out the following site: www.peachpit.com/vqp/dvdsp.

The Script Editor

The Script editor is the giant text edit field that you'll use as the writing pad for your scripts. A quick glance at the top of the Script editor reveals six drop-down menus. From the left, the first four menus list project items, such as tracks, menus, and slideshows (**Figure 17.1**). The fifth menu displays the eight variables that are available to your project, as shown in **Figure 17.2** (see "About variables" later in this chapter). The last menu, called the Helpers menu, acts like a keyword dictionary (**Figure 17.3**); if you click the menu, you'll see several keyword categories, which in turn hold all of the commonly used keywords available to DVD Studio Pro.

When you select a keyword or project item from one of the Script editor's menus, the selected keyword or item is automatically written in the text edit field. This turns writing scripts into a simple process of snapping together keywords and project items selected from the Script editor's menus. Of course, you can also type your scripts by hand, but doing so takes more time, and the potential for typos leads to the possibility of scripting errors.

Figure 17.1 The first four menus across the top of the Script editor display all of your project's items, including Script, Menu, Track, and Slideshow tiles, as well as all menu buttons, track chapters, and slides.

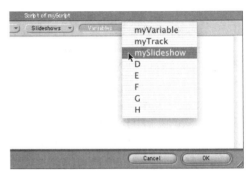

Figure 17.2 The Variables menu lists all eight of your project's variables.

Figure 17.3 The Helpers menu reveals a library of all of the scripts available to DVD Studio Pro.

Figure 17.4 At the bottom of the Graphical View, click the Add Script button to add a new Script tile to your project.

Thumbnail area —

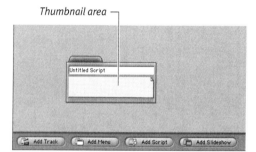

Figure 17.5 A new Script tile in the Graphical View.

To add a Script tile to the Graphical View:

◆ At the bottom of the Graphical View, click the Add Script button (**Figure 17.4**).

In the Graphical View, a new Script tile is created (**Figure 17.5**).

To write a script:

1. In the Graphical View, double-click a Script tile's thumbnail area (refer to Figure 17.5).

The Script editor opens.

2. From the menus across the top of the Script editor, select keywords and project items, or type keywords directly in the Script editor's text edit field.

continues on next page

THE SCRIPT EDITOR

3. When your script is finished, click OK (**Figure 17.6**).

After you click OK, DVD Studio Pro checks your scripts to make sure that they are written correctly. If there are no errors (called syntax errors), the Script editor closes and you can continue authoring your project. If the Script editor contains errors, a Script Error alert box opens telling you that there's a problem (**Figure 17.7**). You'll need to fix this error before you can continue using DVD Studio Pro (while this may initially seem like a frustrating feature, it actually keeps you from writing bad scripts that will come back to bite you later).

Figure 17.6 Click OK to close the Script editor.

✔ Tips

- With the Script editor open, you can check your scripts' syntax at any time by pressing the Tab key. If all scripts are syntactically correct, nothing happens and you can continue scripting. If there's a problem in your syntax, the Script Error dialog box shows you the offending line of script (refer to Figure 17.7).

- If your script contains a syntax error but you aren't quite ready to fix it, you can *comment out* the offending line of script by placing the number sign (#) in front of it and then continue authoring your project. For more information on comments, see "Using Comments" later in this chapter.

Figure 17.7 If your scripts contain errors, this alert box appears when you click the Script editor's OK button. You must fix the errors before you can continue.

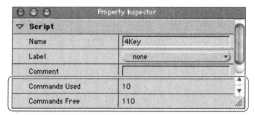

Figure 17.8 At the bottom of the Script Property Inspector, the Commands Used and Commands Free properties keep track of the number of commands that you've used in the Script tile.

Script Syntax

You can't speak a language if you don't know the words or understand how the words are put together. This section does not cover all of the keywords available in DVD Studio Pro—the manual does that just fine (flip to Chapter 5 of the DVD Studio Pro manual for a list of all DVD Studio Pro keywords). Instead, this section concentrates on the most common keywords and shows you how to link them together to form *statements* (lines of script) that DVD Studio Pro understands. In the upcoming sections of this chapter, the commands covered in this section are used to write scripts that you can also use in your own projects.

About commands

A command is part of a line of script and roughly equates to either a project item or a single script keyword. For example, in the script

`Play Track "myTrack"`

`Play` is a command, and `Track "myTrack"` is a command. Together, this statement has two commands. Why is that important, you might ask? Well, DVD Studio Pro lets you use only *128 commands per Script tile*, which is equivalent to 64 of the lines of the script just shown. Some lines of script use more commands than others, so keep this in mind as you script.

Fortunately, you don't need to count commands because DVD Studio Pro keeps track for you. If you select a Script tile and look at the Property Inspector, you'll see two properties, labeled Commands Used and Commands Free (**Figure 17.8**). As your scripts get larger, keep an eye on these two properties to see how much room remains available in the Script editor.

About variables

DVD Studio Pro lets you use up to eight variables in your project (**Figure 17.9**). Variables are containers that store the changable data used in scripts.

Variables are stored as disc properties, and their values can be used in any of your project's scripts. In fact, if you click the Graphical View's background to select the disc and then look at the Property Inspector, you'll see all of the disc's variables grouped together in the Variable Names area (**Figure 17.10**).

Variables in DVD Studio Pro must follow these guidelines:

◆ All variables in DVD Studio Pro are global, which means that any script in the project can use any variable, at any time. If you change the value of a variable in one script, that new value is used in all of the other scripts that contain that variable (that is, until the value is changed again).

◆ Variables can hold numbers or project items. If the variable holds a number, the number must be between 0 and 65535. Numbers outside of this range *wrap around*, and negative numbers are not allowed. For example, if a variable has the value of 14 and you subtract 19, you would normally get –5. But in DVD Studio Pro, 14 minus 19 equals 65530. Similarly, if you add 19 to 65530, DVD Studio Pro returns 14.

◆ Variables must have a value; they can't be empty. Consequently, when the disc starts playing, all variables are set to 0.

✔ Tip

■ In the DVD-Video specification, variables are called general parameter registers (GPRMs). The DVD-Video specification contains 16 separate GPRMs, but DVD Studio Pro gives you access to only eight of them. The other eight are reserved for automatic actions that DVD Studio Pro performs "under the hood."

Figure 17.9 The Script editor's Variables menu lists the eight variables that are available for use in your project.

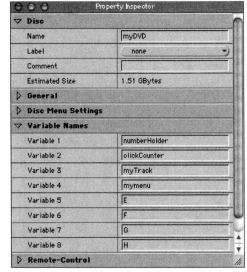

Figure 17.10 The Disc Property Inspector also lists your project's variables in its Variable Names section.

Figure 17.11 To customize your variable names, type new names in the Disc Property Inspector's Variable Names area.

To change a variable's name:

1. Click an area of the Graphical View that does not contain a tile.

   The disc is selected, and the Property Inspector updates to display the disc's properties.

2. In the Variable Names area, rename one or more variables by typing new names in the text edit fields (**Figure 17.11**).

   If you check the Script editor's Variables menu, you'll see the new variable names (**Figure 17.12**).

New variable name —

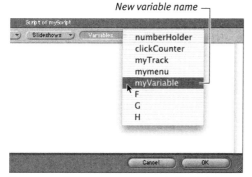

Figure 17.12 The new names appear in the Script editor's Variables menu.

Time Search/Time Play

If viewers use their remote control's Time Search/Time Play function, the DVD-Video player will reset all variables to 0. To keep this from happening, leave your project's Time Search/Time Play property set to Prohibited (**Figure 17.13**). Variables are also reset to 0 whenever the viewer presses the Stop key.

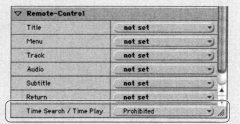

Figure 17.13 If your project depends on variables keeping their values, leave the Time Search/Time Play property set to Prohibited.

Assigning variable values

To set a variable's value, you use an assignment statement. An assignment statement is composed of three parts: the variable, a single equal sign, and the value: for example, myVariable = 3.

To assign a value to a variable:

1. In the Graphical View, double-click a Script tile's thumbnail area.

   The Script editor opens.

2. From the Variables menu at the top of the Script editor, choose the variable (refer to Figure 17.12).

   The variable is printed in the Script editor's text edit field (**Figure 17.14**).

3. Type an equal sign (=) after the variable in the Script editor.

   You can leave a space between the variable and the equal sign, or not. DVD Studio Pro doesn't care, so the choice is yours.

4. Type a value for the variable or select a project item from one of the Script editor's menus (**Figure 17.15**).

   When this script is executed, the variable will be assigned the value that you've entered to the right of the equal sign.

✔ Tip

- Assignment statements use only a single equal sign (=).

Figure 17.14 The variable that you selected from the Script editor's Variables menu is printed in the Script editor's text edit field.

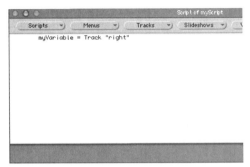

Figure 17.15 This variable has been assigned the value Track "right".

Figure 17.16 The Helpers menu lists all of DVD Studio Pro's functions.

Using functions

Functions return (or *get*) the name of a project item. Functions are always used on the right side of an assignment statement to store the name of an item in a variable: for example,

A = getLastItem()

playingVideoStream = getAngle()

In DVD Studio Pro, it's easy to figure out which commands are functions, as all functions begin with get. To see a list of functions, check out the Script editor's Helpers menu (**Figure 17.16**).

Using control statements

Control statements let your DVD-Video make its own decisions. Unlike other scripts, which simply tell the video what to do, control statements let the video check to see whether a certain *condition* has been met. If the condition has been met, then the project does something. A control statement looks like this:

if A == B then C

or more commonly in DVD Studio Pro:

if A == Track "myTrack" then Play Button
→ "Button1" of Menu "myMenu"

continues on next page

SCRIPT SYNTAX

Control statements are usually used in conjunction with an *operator*, which serves to compare two different values. In the preceding statements, the operator is the == sign. DVD Studio Pro provides four operators that you can use in your control statements.

◆ ==. Compares the values on both sides of the operator. If they are *equal*, the then statement is executed.

◆ !=. Compares the values on both sides of the operator. If they are *not equal*, the then statement is executed.

◆ >. Compares the values on both sides of the operator. If the value on the left is greater than the value on the right, the then statement is executed.

◆ <. Compares the values on both sides of the operator. If the value on the right is greater than the value on the left, the then statement is executed.

✔ Tip

■ Operators are different from assignment statements (see "Assigning variable values" earlier in this chapter). Operators use two equal symbols (==), whereas assignment statements use only one (=). To keep from getting confused, make sure that *all equal symbols in control statements are doubled-up in pairs.*

Compound Statements

A compound statement is a single line of script that does more than one thing. For example, you might want to check whether the last item played was a certain menu and then play a specific track. Such a compound statement looks like this:

```
if getLastItem() == Menu "myMenu" then Play Track "myTrack"
```

DVD Studio Pro, however, *does not allow* compound statements, so the preceding script would not work. Instead, you must divide the script into two smaller parts:

```
A = getLastItem()
if A == Menu "myMenu" then Play Track "myTrack"
```

Figure 17.17 Placing a number sign (#) at the beginning of a line of script creates a comment.

Using comments

Comments are lines of text within a script that are not executed. In complex scripts, it's easy to forget why you've written a script a particular way. Comments document the script's various parts, letting you quickly see what does what. If you are working as a member of a production team, comments also help other team members understand how the scripts work and are an invaluable aid if someone other than you needs to alter the script at a later time.

Comments can also be used to disable lines of script that you are not finished writing, and in DVD Studio Pro, this is perhaps their most useful purpose. There will be times, for example, when you need to return to the main workspace without finishing the script you're working on. Normally, attempting such antics causes a syntax error because DVD Studio Pro demands that all scripts be complete and accurate before it allows you to close the Script editor. By *commenting out* the incomplete or incorrect statement, you can close the Script editor and return sometime later when you're ready to finish the script.

To create a comment:

◆ In the Script editor, place a number sign (#) in front of a line of script or text (**Figure 17.17**).

Using the nop command

The nop command serves as a placeholder in scripts that you're not quite ready to complete (particularly control structures). If you're scripting an if then statement, for example, but you haven't decided what the statement should do (the then part), use the nop command as a placeholder until you're ready to finish the script. Here's an example of a block of script that uses the nop command:

```
A = getLastItem()
B = getCurrentTrack()
if A == B then nop
```

If you don't use nop, DVD Studio Pro will hit you with a syntax error as soon as you attempt to close the Script editor (you can also comment out the incomplete line of script).

The Script editor's Helpers menu lists the nop command as Do Nothing (**Figure 17.18**). Choosing Do Nothing prints the nop command in the Script editor. The keyword nop actually stands for "no operation." This fact, in conjunction with the nop keyword's Do Nothing label, should alert you to an important point: when the nop command executes, your project literally does nothing; no operation is performed, and your project stops playing.

Figure 17.18 The nop command is labeled Do Nothing in the Script editor's Helpers menu.

SCRIPT SYNTAX

Using labels

A label works like a reference marker inside the Script editor. Labels group blocks of scripts into sections, which you can jump to using the gotoLabel command (the Helpers menu lists this command as Goto a Label, as shown in **Figure 17.19**, but selecting this command prints gotoLabel in the Script editor).

Labels can be composed of any word or sequence of characters that you want, but they must always begin with a letter and end with a colon (:). Labels are also always placed at the start of a line of script: for example,

MyLabel: Play Track "myTrack"

button3: Play button "B3" Of menu
→ "numberPad"

You should avoid using labels that are already in use as DVD Studio Pro keywords, such as Play or nop (the Script editor will let you use a keyword as a label, but it presents you with a syntax error if you attempt to jump to the keyword label using gotoLabel). For an example of how to use labels, see "Looping a Menu X Times" or "Creating a Play All Button" later in this chapter.

Figure 17.19 The goToLabel command (listed as Goto a Label in the Helpers menu) jumps the script to a specific label. Lines of script between the goToLabel command and the labeled statement are not executed.

Assigning Scripts

After you've created a script, you can assign the script as the jump action for any button, track, marker, story, slideshow, or remote control key.

To assign a script to a project item:

◆ Select a tile in the Graphical view or a button in the Menu editor; *then do one of the following:*

▲ For a Track or Slideshow tile, select a Script tile from the Property Inspector's Jump When Finished menu (**Figure 17.20**).

▲ For a Menu tile, select the Script tile from the Property Inspector's Timeout Action menu (**Figure 17.21**).

▲ For a menu button, select the Script tile from the Property Inspector's Jump When Activated menu (**Figure 17.22**).

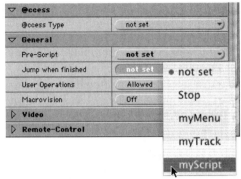

Figure 17.20 To assign a script to a track or slideshow, select it from the Property Inspector's Jump When Finished property.

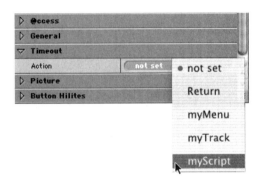

Figure 17.21 To assign a script to a menu, select it from the Menu Property Inspector's Timeout Action property.

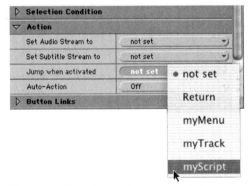

Figure 17.22 To assign a script to a menu button, select it from the Button Property Inspector's Jump When Activated property.

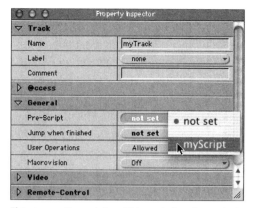

Figure 17.23 Pre-scripts, which run before the project item is displayed on the screen, can be assigned to tracks, menus, and slideshows.

Using pre-scripts

There will be times when you'll want a script to run *before* a project item plays, regardless of the track that jumped to the item. You might need a script, for example, that checks which project item played last and then selects the appropriate menu button (see "Scripting Button Selection" or "Creating a Play All Button" later in this chapter). In this situation, the script always needs to run before the menu comes on the screen. To accomplish this, you use *pre-scripts*, which are scripts that run before the items to which they are attached appear on the screen, instead of after them.

To assign a pre-script:

1. In the Graphical View, select a Track, Menu, or Slideshow tile.

   The Property Inspector updates to display the tile's properties.

2. From the Property Inspector's Pre-Script menu, select a Script tile (**Figure 17.23**).

Looping a Menu X Times

Motion menus and still menus with background audio can loop (**Figure 17.24**), causing the menu to play continually until the viewer clicks a button and jumps out of the menu. But what if you don't want the menu to loop indefinitely? With a simple script, you can set a menu to loop a specific number of times before automatically jumping to another project item.

The following task shows you how to create a counter that tracks the number of times that a menu loops (to learn more about counters, see the sidebar "Creating a Counter" later in this chapter). When a menu has looped a certain number of times (in this case, four), the script jumps to a track and plays it.

To loop a menu X times:

1. Click the Graphical View's background to select the disc.

   The Property Inspector updates to display the disc properties.

2. In the Variable Names area, name one of the variables myCounter as shown in **Figure 17.25** (to learn more about variables, see "About variables" earlier in this chapter).

3. In the Graphical View, double-click a Script tile's thumbnail area.

   The Script editor opens.

4. In the Script editor, type the following (refer to line 1 of **Figure 17.26**):

   myCounter += 1

   This line of script causes the counter to increase by one each time the script is executed.

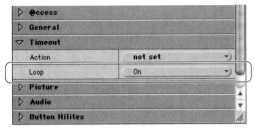

Figure 17.24 Setting a menu's Loop property to On causes the menu to loop until the viewer activates a button.

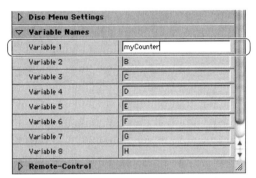

Figure 17.25 Named variables are easier to track. In the Disc Property Inspector's Variable Names area, name a variable myCounter.

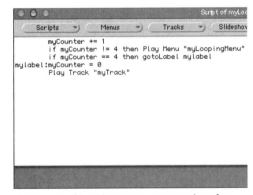

Figure 17.26 This script causes a menu to loop four times before jumping the DVD-Video to the track named myTrack.

5. Press the Return key to start a new line of script and then type the following (refer to line 2 of Figure 17.26):

```
if myCounter != 4 then Play Menu
→ "myLoopingMenu"
```

This line of script checks the value of the variable myCounter. If the counter is not yet equal to 4, this line causes the script to stop executing and jump back to the menu.

6. Press the Return key and type the following (refer to line 3 of Figure 17.26):

```
if myCounter == 4 then gotoLabel mylabel
```

If the variable myCounter equals 4, this line causes the script to jump to a label that you will write in the next step (labels are discussed in the section "Using labels" earlier in this chapter).

7. Press the Return key and type the following (refer to line 4 of Figure 17.26):

```
mylabel:myCounter = 0
```

This line resets the value of myCounter to 0. If you don't reset the value of myCounter, the next time the menu comes on the screen, it will not loop the proper number of times. Do not forget this very important step.

8. Press the Return key and type the following (refer to line 5 of Figure 17.26):

```
Play Track "myTrack"
```

This line jumps the DVD-Video to the track named myTrack. Of course, you don't need to jump to a track. You could also jump to a different menu, a slideshow, a different script, or even an individual button, chapter, or slide.

continues on next page

LOOPING A MENU X TIMES

9. In the lower right corner of the Script editor, click OK.

The Script editor closes. But you're not done—you still need to link the menu to the script so that the script plays as soon as the menu finishes. To link the menu to the script, you must assign the script as the Menu tile's timeout action.

10. In the Graphical View, select the Menu tile (**Figure 17.27**).

The Property Inspector updates to display the menu's properties.

11. From the Property Inspector's Timeout Action menu, choose the Script tile (**Figure 17.28**).

That's all there is to it! At this point, you should preview your menu to make sure that it loops properly. If there is a problem, check your script against Figure 17.26 to verify that your script is written correctly.

✔ Tip

■ In this task, clicking a menu button does not reset the myCounter variable to 0. To fix this, create Script tiles that contain the following statements and assign the scripts as the actions for each button:

myCounter = 0

Play Track "myTrack"

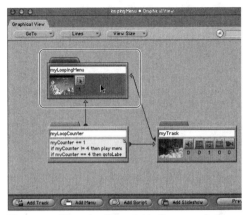

Figure 17.27 To assign the script to the menu, in the Graphical View, select the Menu tile.

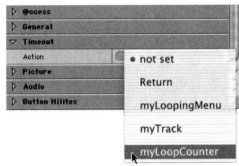

Figure 17.28 Set the menu's Timeout Action to the Script tile containing the loop counter.

Creating a Counter

A counter is a variable that increases by a certain amount each time an event occurs. You can use a counter, for example, to keep tabs on the number of times that a track has played or to monitor the number of times that a specific button has been clicked.

Counters use a special assignment operator called the addition operator (+=). The addition operator works only on numbers. If you've assigned the variable a value that isn't a number, it will do nothing. If the variable does contain a number, however, the addition operator increases the variable's value by whatever number you enter to its right: for example,

MyVariable += 1

MyVariable += 16

LOOPING A MENU X TIMES

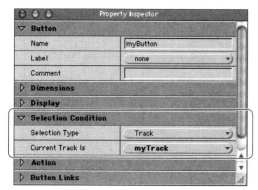

Figure 17.29 The script that you are about to learn does the same thing as the Button Property Inspector's Selection Condition area, but also works with menus and slideshows.

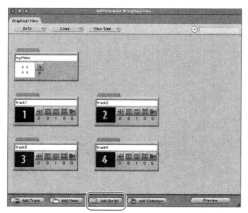

Figure 17.30 The base project, with a menu and all tracks added. This project is ready for the buttonSelector script. To start writing that script, press the Add Script button.

Scripting Button Selection

When the viewer returns to a menu, a well-designed DVD-Video will automatically select the button that corresponds to the track, slideshow, or even the menu that the viewer was just watching. In Chapter 8, "Photoshop Layer Menus," you learned how to create a button selection condition that checks which track just played and then selects the appropriate button (**Figure 17.29**). But selection conditions do not work if the last item that played was either a menu or a slideshow. Fortunately, it's easy to script button selections in DVD Studio Pro using the getLastItem() function.

The getLastItem() function returns the name of the last project item played, whether it was a track, slideshow, or menu. Chapters and slides, however, are not included in this small list of items. In fact, the getLastItem() function returns only the name of the last *tile* played. If you are jumping into a chapter or scene menu, this function will not let you program a script that selects the proper chapter button (to do that, you need to use special *system parameter registers*, which are discussed at the end of this chapter).

To script button selection:

1. Create all of the tracks, slideshows, and menus that your project needs.

   Scripting button selection is one of the last steps in the authoring process. Before you can write this script, you must have all of your project's tracks, slideshows, and menus in working order.

2. At the bottom of the Graphical View, click the Add Script button (**Figure 17.30**).

   A new Script tile appears in the Graphical View.

   continues on next page

SCRIPTING BUTTON SELECTION

361

3. Double-click the Script tile's thumbnail area.

The Script editor opens.

4. Enter the following line of script (refer to line 1 of **Figure 17.31**):

`A = getLastItem()`

When the script is executed, the last item played is stored in the variable named **A** (if you've named your variables something different, then make sure that you use the correct variable name instead of **A**).

5. Press Return to start a new line of script and then type the following text (refer to line 2 of Figure 17.31):

`if A == track "track1" then play button "1" Of menu "myMenu"`

In this line of script, `"track1"` is the name of a track in your project, and `button "1"` `of menu "myMenu"` is the name of the menu button that jumps to that track. When the script is executed, it looks at the last item that was played. If the item equals the item on the left side of the conditional statement (in this case, `"track1"`), the menu on the right side of the conditional statement opens on the screen with the correct button selected.

6. Repeat step 5 until you've populated the Script editor with a conditional statement for every button on the menu (refer to Figure 17.31).

7. In the Graphical View, select the Menu tile.

The Property Inspector updates to display the menu's properties.

8. From the Property Inspector's Pre-Script menu, select the script that you've just written (**Figure 17.32**).

The script now runs every time that the menu opens on the screen, causing the correct button to be selected automatically.

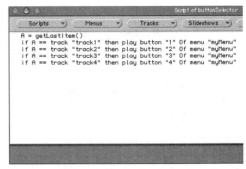

Figure 17.31 This script begins by storing the value of the last played project item in variable A. The script then uses a series of conditional statements that check the value of variable A before playing the corresponding menu button.

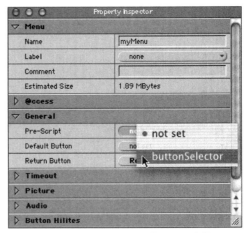

Figure 17.32 Assign the script as a pre-script for your menu so that when the menu appears on the screen, the script automatically selects the correct button.

SCRIPTING BUTTON SELECTION

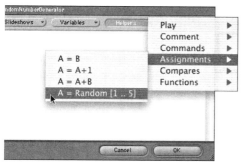

Figure 17.33 To create a random-number generator, open the Script editor and choose Helpers > Assignments > A = Random [1 .. 5].

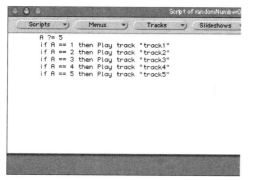

Figure 17.34 The finished random-number generator script. The first line of this script generates a random number between 1 and 5 and stores that number in variable A. The remaining lines check the value of variable A and then play the appropriate track.

Playing Tracks Randomly

DVD Studio Pro has a random-number generator that you can use to play tracks in random order. This script is particularly useful for kiosk installations where you want your project to play continuously but also want to change the order in which tracks, slideshows, and menus are displayed.

Although the random-number generator works well, the fewer project items you have, the less random the playback seems. If you randomly choose a number between 1 and 5, for example, it's common for one number to come up more than the others. If you randomly select a number between 1 and 30, the odds of choosing the same number decline.

To create a random-track script:

1. In the Graphical View, create a Script tile and double-click its thumbnail area.

   The Script editor opens.

2. Choose Helpers > Assignments > A = Random [1 .. 5] (**Figure 17.33**).

   The following script is printed in the Script editor (refer to line 1 of **Figure 17.34**):

   A ?= 5

   This is the random-number generator. With its default value of 5, the random-number generator will pick a value between 1 and 5 and store that value in the variable named **A**. To change the selection range, enter a number other than 5. (Depending on how you've named your variables, you may also need to select a different variable than **A** from the Script editor's Variables menu).

   continues on next page

3. Press Return and type the following line of script (refer to line 2 of Figure 17.34):

`if A == 1 then Play track "track1"`

In this script, `"track1"` is the name of an item in your project.

4. Repeat step 3 until you've added a conditional statement for every track in your project. Each time that you add a new conditional statement, make sure that you increase the value to the right of `A` by 1. The finished script should look similar to the script in Figure 17.34.

5. In the Property Inspector, set each track's Jump When Finished property to the randomNumberGenerator script (**Figure 17.35**).

When a track finishes playing, the random-number script is executed, and a new, randomly chosen track plays.

Figure 17.35 To execute the random-number script after each track has finished playing, set each track's Jump When Finished property to the Random Number Script tile, which in this screenshot is called randomNumberGenerator.

PLAYING TRACKS RANDOMLY

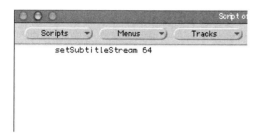

Figure 17.36 This unassuming little script will disable the subtitles for your entire project.

Disabling Default Subtitles

Under normal circumstances, subtitles always appear when the DVD-Video is played. But in most cases, you'll want your DVD-Video to start playing with subtitles disabled, allowing the viewer to turn them on and off as necessary (either by pressing the Subtitles remote-control button or by making a selection from a subtitle selection menu).

You can disable the default subtitles by creating a blank subtitle stream (one with no text) and placing it at the top of the Subtitles container. But this workaround is far from elegant. It's also a lot of work because you have to create a blank subtitle stream for each and every track in your video. A far better solution is to use this special DVD Studio Pro script:

`setSubtitleStream 64`

This script turns off every subtitle in the entire project (don't worry; viewers can still turn on the subtitles if they want to see them).

To use this script, it should be one of the first project items to play. You can attach this script as a pre-script to the project's first track or place it between an opening animation and the main menu. Where you put the script doesn't matter as long as you make sure that the script executes before the first subtitled track starts playing.

To disable default subtitles:

1. At the bottom of the Graphical View, click the Add Script button.

2. Double-click the new Script tile's thumbnail area to open the Script editor and then enter the following line of script (**Figure 17.36**):

   `setSubtitleStream 64`.

continues on next page

3. In the Graphical View, select your project's startup item.

This is the track or menu that you've defined as the startup item on the Disc Property Inspector's Startup Action menu (**Figure 17.37**).

4. From the Property Inspector's Pre-Script menu, choose the Script tile that you added in step 1 (**Figure 17.38**).

When the disc plays, subtitles are disabled until the viewer turns them on by either pressing the Subtitles remote-control button or selecting a subtitle stream from the project's subtitles selection menu (if you've provided one).

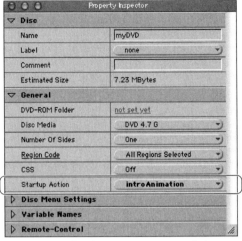

Figure 17.37 In the Disc Property Inspector, find your project's startup item by looking at the Startup Action menu.

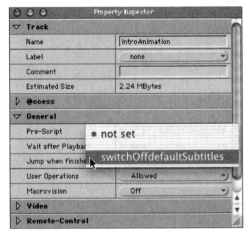

Figure 17.38 In the Track Property Inspector, assign the subtitle script as the startup item's pre-script.

DISABLING DEFAULT SUBTITLES

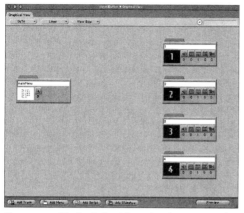

Figure 17.39 The basis for this project is a menu and four tracks. If your project has more than four tracks, don't worry; this example is easy to customize.

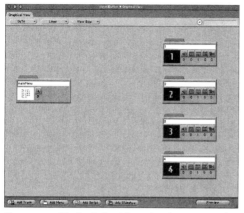

Figure 17.40 You'll need two different variables, the first named playAll and the second named lastTrack.

Creating a Play All Button

A Play All button is useful in projects with many short tracks, such as a disc filled with music videos or short tutorials. Instead of forcing viewers to watch a track, return to the main menu, and then select another track, the Play All button lets viewers make one menu selection and then watch all of the tracks in order, one after the other.

This example shows you how to script a Play All button for a project with four tracks, though you can easily modify it for a project that has more tracks. If you're careful to copy the scripts exactly as you see them in the screenshots, your Play All button is guaranteed to work.

To avoid all of the typing (and potential typos!), you can download this project from www.peachpit.com/vqp/dvdsp.

To create a Play All button:

1. Set up your project by creating the main track selection menu and adding all of the necessary tracks (**Figure 17.39**).

2. Click the Graphical View's background to enable the Disc Property Inspector.

3. In the Property Inspector's Variable Names section, name the first variable playAll and the second variable lastTrack (**Figure 17.40**).

   The playAll variable keeps track of whether or not the menu's Play All button has been selected, and the lastTrack variable holds the name of the last track that was played.

continues on next page

4. At the bottom of the Graphical View, click the Add Script button as many times as there are buttons on your menu.

In this example, there are four buttons that link to the project's four tracks, plus the Play All button, for a total of five buttons (**Figure 17.41**), so you must click the Add Script button five times.

5. Name your Script tiles and arrange them as in **Figure 17.42**.

Figure 17.41 This basic menu gives you an idea of the number of buttons used in this example.

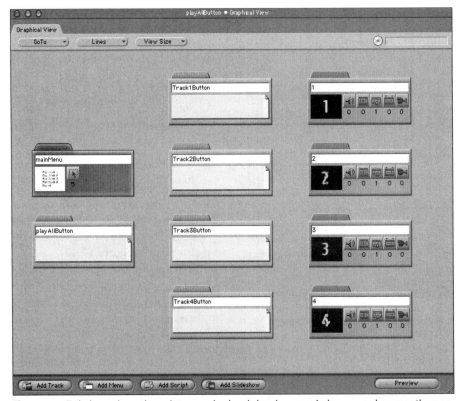

Figure 17.42 To help you keep the scripts organized and clear in your mind, name and arrange them as shown in this example.

CREATING A PLAY ALL BUTTON

6. In **Figure 17.43**, you can read the text in each Script tile's thumbnail area. Enter this text into each Script tile.

You may have noticed that the `playAll` variable is set to 0 for buttons one through four and to 1 for the Play All button. This turns on the `playAll` variable if the viewer selects the Play All button and turns off the `playAll` variable if the viewer selects any other button.

continues on next page

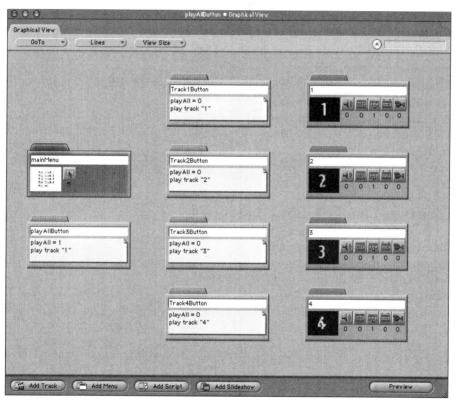

Figure 17.43 Enter the text from each Script tile's thumbnail area into the Script tiles in your project.

7. In the Graphical View, select the Menu tile and choose Matrix > Jumps of Menu "mainMenu," where "mainMenu" is the name of your Menu tile (**Figure 17.44**). The Menu Jump matrix opens.

8. Use the Menu Jump matrix to link each menu button to the corresponding Script tile (**Figure 17.45**).

9. At the bottom of the Graphical View, click the Add Script button one last time. A new Script tile is created.

10. Name the new Script tile TrackSelector and position it as in **Figure 17.46**.

11. Open the TrackSelector tile's Script editor and type the long script from **Figure 17.47** (because most of the lines are similar, copy and paste lines to save time; then change the appropriate parts).

The first line of this script sets the variable named lastTrack to equal the last project item played. Directly under that, the next line of script checks to see if the playAll variable has been turned on, which can happen only if the viewer has clicked the Play All button. If the variable has been turned on, the script instantly jumps to the playnexttrack label, and the DVD-Video begins cycling through the project's tracks. If the playAll variable has not been turned on, the script jumps back to the menu and highlights the button corresponding to the last track played.

Figure 17.44 To link the menu buttons to their corresponding scripts, open the Menu Jump matrix by choosing Matrix > Jumps of Menu "mainMenu," where "mainMenu" is the name of your Menu tile.

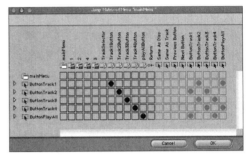

Figure 17.45 In the Jump matrix, link each menu button to the correct Script tile.

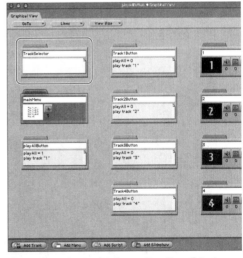

Figure 17.46 The TrackSelector tile will contain the Play All script.

CREATING A PLAY ALL BUTTON

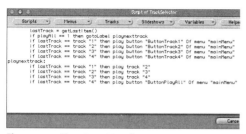

Figure 17.47 The Play All script.

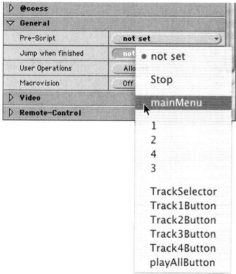

Figure 17.48 When each track finishes playing, it should return to the main menu, so select the menu from each track's Jump When Finished property.

Figure 17.49 Set the TrackSelector Script tile as the pre-script for the menu.

12. In the Property Inspector, set each track's Jump When Finished property to the Menu tile (**Figure 17.48**).

This is important because the next step assigns the TrackSelector script as a pre-script for the Menu tile. If the DVD-Video doesn't return to the menu, the TrackSelector script will not execute, so make sure that you set each track's Jump When Finished property appropriately.

13. In the Menu Property Inspector, choose the TrackSelector Script tile from the Menu tile's Pre-Script property (**Figure 17.49**).

When each track jumps back to the menu, the TrackSelector script is executed.

14. In the lower right corner of the Graphical View, click the Preview button.

The Preview mode opens. Check each button to make sure that it works.

✔ Tip

■ Sometimes the Play All button doesn't work correctly in DVD Studio Pro's Preview mode. Don't worry; the problem is in the Preview mode and not your scripting. Once you've built the project, the button will work fine in both Apple DVD Player and a set-top DVD-Video player.

Using System Parameter Registers

The getLastItem() keyword returns the last Track or Menu tile played and is integral to many of the scripts that you've learned in this chapter. But if you have a chapter (or scene) selection menu and you want the default button to always reflect the last chapter played, the getLastItem() keyword is all but useless. Until Apple stocks DVD Studio Pro with a getLastChapter() keyword, you'll need to use *system parameter registers* (SPRMs).

DVD-Video players have 24 SPRMs that hold numbers, or in some cases letter values, that correspond to various aspects of the DVD-Video being played. For example, SPRM 7 holds information about the last chapter played, and SPRM 8 contains a number corresponding to the last menu button selected. Although you won't find this trick in the manual, you can actually access all 24 SPRMs using scripts in DVD Studio Pro.

One important point to keep in mind is that scripts using SPRMs *do not currently work in DVD Studio Pro's Preview mode*. To see the results of these scripts, you must build the project and view it in Apple DVD Player (or, of course, a set-top DVD-Video player). But don't be discouraged by this limitation; the inconvenience is far outweighed by the extreme scripting control that SPRMs give you.

Table 17.1

System Parameter Registers

SPRM NUMBER	SPRM INFORMATION
SPRM 0	Menu language
SPRM 1	Audio stream number
SPRM 2	Subtitle stream number
SPRM 3	Angle number
SPRM 4	Title number
SPRM 5	VST title number
SPRM 6	Program chain (PGC) number
SPRM 7	Chapter number
SPRM 8	Selected button number
SPRM 9	Navigation timer
SPRM 10	PGC jump for navigation timer
SPRM 11	Karaoke audio mixing mode
SPRM 12	Parental management country code
SPRM 13	Parental level
SPRM 14	Video aspect ratio
SPRM 15	Player audio capabilities
SPRM 16	Initial audio language
SPRM 17	Initial audio language code extension
SPRM 18	Initial subpicture language
SPRM 19	Initial subpicture language extension
SPRM 20	Player region code
SPRM 21	Reserved
SPRM 22	Reserved
SPRM 23	Reserved

Table 17.1 lists all 24 SPRMs, but showing you how to use each one is beyond the scope of this book. Instead, the following sections demonstrate how to use SPRM 7 (chapters) and SPRM 8 (buttons), with other SPRMs left to your own exploration. At any rate, the most useful SPRMs are already covered by DVD Studio Pro keywords, and the others have only limited value for scripting purposes, so adding SPRM 7 and SPRM 8 to your scripting arsenal should be enough to enable you to create any interactive feature that your project needs.

✔ Tips

■ Ralph Labarge's *DVD Authoring and Production* (CMP Books) contains the most detailed list of SPRMs and their uses that is currently available. If you want to learn more about SPRMs, page 186 of this book is the start of a valuable resource.

■ Don't forget: the projects outlined in this section are available for download from www.peachpit.com/vqp/dvdsp.

SPRM 7

Chapter selection menus should automatically highlight the button that corresponds to the last chapter played. But until a getLastChapter() keyword appears in DVD Studio Pro, the only way to return the value of the last chapter played is by accessing SPRM 7. Each track can have up to 99 chapters, and as may be expected, SPRM 7 can hold values ranging from 1 to 99.

SPRM 7 is actually very easy to use. If you've worked through the section "Scripting Button Selection" earlier in this chapter, you'll quickly come to terms with this script. The only thing to remember is that SPRMs do not work in Preview mode, so to see the results of this script you'll have to build the project and play it in DVD Player. Also, in the Script editor, SPRM 7 is written with an underscore (_) between SPRM and 7. Here's an example:

A = SPRM_7

if A == 1 then Play Button "chapter1"
→ Of menu "chapterMenu"

if A == 2 then Play Button "chapter2"
→ Of menu " chapterMenu "

In addition, a quick look at **Figure 17.50** should give you enough information to understand how to use this system parameter register.

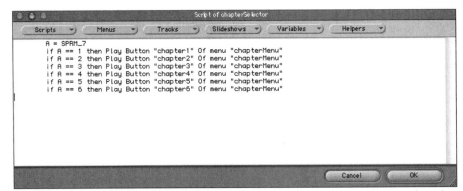

Figure 17.50 SPRM 7 stores a value corresponding to the last chapter played. You can access that value to create a script that highlights the correct button on a chapter menu.

Table 17.2

Button Selection Cross-Reference

Button Number	SPRM 8 Value
1	1,024
2	2,048
3	3,072
4	4,096
5	5,120
6	6,144
7	7,168
8	8,192
9	9,216
10	10,240
11	11,264
12	12,288
13	13,312
14	14,336
15	15,360
16	16,384
17	17,408
18	18,432
19	19,456
20	20,480
21	21,504
22	22,528
23	23,552
24	24,576
25	25,600
26	26,624
27	27,648
28	28,672
29	29,696
30	30,720
31	31,744
32	32,768
33	33,792
34	34,816
35	35,840
36	36,864

SPRM 8

Certain scripts depend on the ability to determine the last menu button selected. Without SPRM 8, these scripts are difficult to write and cumbersome to use.

SPRM 8 stores the value of the last button selected, but it works in a slightly different way than other SPRMs. Whereas SPRM 7, for example, stores the numbers 1 through 99, representing the 99 chapters available to a track, SPRM 8 uses the value 1024 for the menu's first button, and each successive button increases in value by another 1024. **Table 17.2** details the SPRM 8 value of each of the 36 possible menu buttons.

continues on next page

USING SYSTEM PARAMETER REGISTERS

Figure 17.51 demonstrates how to use SPRM 8 in a script. As with all SPRMs, keep in mind that scripts using SPRM 8 will not work in DVD Studio Pro's Preview mode, and that you must type an underscore (_) between SPRM and 8, like this:

A = SPRM_8

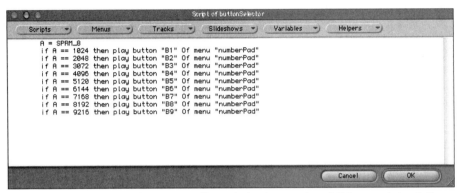

Figure 17.51 SPRM 8 stores a value corresponding to the last button selected. This comes in handy if you want to create an onscreen number pad that calculates values.

KEYBOARD
SHORTCUTS

DVD Studio Pro Menu Shortcuts

COMMAND	KEY COMBINATION	MENU SELECTION
Hide DVD Studio Pro	Command-H	DVD Studio Pro > Hide DVD Studio Pro
Quit	Command-Q	DVD Studio Pro > Quit
New project	Command-N	File > New Project
Open project	Command-O	File > Open
Import new assets	Command-I	File > Import
Close window	Command-W	File > Close
Close project	Option-Command-W	File > Close Project
Save project	Command-S	File > Save
Build disc	Command-B	File > Build Disc
Build and format disc	Option-Command-B	File > Build and Format Disc
Undo previous action	Command-Z	Edit > Undo
Cut selection to clipboard	Command-X	Edit > Cut
Copy selection to clipboard	Command-C	Edit > Copy
Paste clipboard selection	Command-V	Edit > Paste
Select all	Command-A	Edit > Select All
Duplicate selection	Command-D	Edit > Duplicate
Create new item	Command-K	Item > New
Open Tile editor	Command-E	Item > Edit
Collapse all properties	Command-8	Item > Collapse All Properties
Expand all properties	Command-9	Item > Expand All Properties
Open Preview mode	Command-P	Item > Preview
Open Asset matrix	Command-4	Matrix > Assets
Open Jump matrix	Command-5	Matrix > Jumps
Open Layers matrix	Command-6	Matrix > Layers
Show/hide Graphical View	Command-1	Windows > Graphical View
Show/hide Project View	Command-2	Windows > Project View
Show/hide Asset View	Command-3	Windows > Asset View
Show/hide Property Inspector	Command-0	Windows > Property Inspector
Show/hide Log window	Command-L	Windows > Log
Open DVD Studio Pro Help	Command-?	Help > DVD Studio Pro Help

Subtitle Editor Menu Shortcuts

COMMAND	KEY COMBINATION	MENU SELECTION
Hide Subtitle editor	Command-H	Subtitle Editor > Hide Subtitle Editor
Quit	Command-Q	Subtitle Editor > Quit
New project	Command-N	File > New Project
Open project	Command-O	File > Open
Close project	Option-Command-W	File > Close Project
Save project	Command-S	File > Save
Undo previous action	Command-Z	Edit > Undo
Cut selection to clipboard	Command-X	Edit > Cut
Copy selection to clipboard	Command-C	Edit > Copy
Paste clipboard selection	Command-V	Edit > Paste
Select all	Command-A	Edit > Select All
Create new subtitle cell	Command-K	Subtitle > New Subtitle
Show/hide Subtitles window	Command-1	Windows > Subtitles
Show/hide Preview window	Command-2	Windows > Preview
Show/hide Markers window	Command-3	Windows > Markers
Play/pause preview movie	Spacebar	
Play forward	Command-Right Arrow key	
Play reverse	Command-Left Arrow key	
Advance one frame	Keypad number 3	
Advance two frames	Right Arrow key	
Reverse one frame	Keypad number 3	
Reverse two frames	Right Arrow key	
Start of movie	Option-Left Arrow key	
End of movie	Option-Right Arrow key	

Making a Bit Budget

A bit budget helps you determine the data rate to use when encoding your MPEG-2 streams. If your project uses less than an hour of video, a bit budget isn't really important because an hour of MPEG-2 video, encoded at the maximum bit rate allowed by the DVD-Video specification (9.8 Mbps), will just fit on a DVD-5. But once you get above an hour of video, you'll need a bit budget to calculate the highest-quality MPEG-2 video that you can include on a DVD disc, given its available storage capacity.

About bit budgets

To make things easy, bit budgets are calculated in bytes, rather than kilobytes, megabytes, or gigabytes. This takes a lot of confusion out of the process, because you don't have to convert between kilobytes and megabytes or compensate for the differences between computer and DVD storage conventions. Whether on a computer or a DVD disc, a byte is always eight bits, which makes the calculations easier to handle (to learn more about how computers and DVD discs store data, see Chapter 2, "DVD Basics").

When making a bit budget, you might wonder where you can cut corners if your project is growing large. You can't control the file size of subtitle streams or menu images, and audio streams need to be encoded at very particular settings to maintain quality. Of all of your project's assets, video is the only one that can handle large shifts in encoding quality. For example, there's not a terribly noticeable difference between video encoded at 6.5 Mbps and video encoded at 7.5 Mbps. A practiced eye can see the difference, but not as easily as any old ear can hear the difference between a stereo AC-3 stream encoded at 96 kbps and one encoded at 192 kbps. You can't scrimp on the sound, but video can vary.

A bit budget subtracts the storage space needed for all of the assets with file sizes that you have little control over and fills the rest of the disc with video. The following is an overview of how to make a bit budget. Each step is explained later in this appendix.

To make a bit budget:

1. Determine the storage capacity of your target DVD.

2. Reserve 5 percent of the target DVD disc as overhead for assets that may be added later in the authoring process. Subtract this 5 percent reserve from the total capacity of the target disc.

3. Calculate the storage space needed for your project's audio streams. Subtract this figure from the value of the previous step.

4. Calculate the storage space needed for all subtitle streams. Subtract this figure from the value of the previous step.

5. Calculate the storage space needed for highlight and Photoshop layer menus. Subtract this figure from the value of the previous step.

6. Calculate the storage space needed for any DVD-ROM content (on a hybrid DVD). Subtract this figure from the value of the previous step.

7. Use all remaining storage capacity for the project's video streams (including motion menus).

Table B.1

DVD Storage Capacity	
MEDIA TYPE	DISC CAPACITY
DVD-5 (DVD-R)	4,700,000,000 bytes
DVD-9	8,540,000,000 bytes
DVD-10	9,400,000,000 bytes
DVD-18	17,080,000,000 bytes

Table B.2

Five Percent Reserve Values	
MEDIA TYPE	RESERVE
DVD-5 (DVD-R)	235,000,000 bytes
DVD-9	427,000,000 bytes
DVD-10	470,000,000 bytes
DVD-18	854,000,000 bytes

Determining disc capacity

You usually decide on a target DVD disc size before authoring a project. If you intend to use your computer's SuperDrive to record a DVD-R, you know you'll be working with a DVD-5. If you're authoring a disc that contains a feature-length movie, you'll probably need to move up to a DVD-9. This makes the first step of creating a bit budget easy: Think of the type of DVD disc on which you'll distribute your project and then look at **Table B.1** to determine its storage capacity.

Determining the reserve

Multiplexing your project creates control data (.ifo files) and backup files (.bup files) that you will not be able to account for in advance, so leaving a bit of extra room on the disc is always a good idea. There will also be times when you unexpectedly need to add assets that you didn't account for in the bit budget. Leaving a reserve gives you a margin of error that sometimes makes the difference between a project that fits on a disc and one where you must go back and re-encode video assets at a lower bit rate.

For most situations, a 5 percent reserve is more than adequate. **Table B.2** lists the reserve values to use with several types of DVD discs.

Calculating audio storage

The total storage space needed for audio streams depends on the length and bit rate of each stream. **Table B.3** lists common audio stream bit rates.

To calculate how much of the target DVD disc your audio streams will consume, use the following formula:

audio data storage (bytes) = (total audio
→ minutes x 60 x bit rate) / 8

If your project uses audio streams encoded using several different bit rates, you'll need to do some extra math. First calculate the size of each individual stream; then add the totals together to determine the storage space needed for all audio streams combined.

Calculating subtitle storage

Each individual subtitle within a subtitle stream uses around 4,000 bytes—that's 4,000 bytes for each group of letters that flicks across the screen. To calculate the storage space for subtitle streams, you must count each separate subtitle in every project subtitle stream and then multiply that number by 4,000:

subtitle storage (bytes) = # of
→ subtitles x 4,000

✔ Tip

- If you used the Subtitle editor to create the subtitle streams, open the original subtitle project and count the subtitle cells to quickly figure out the number of subtitles in the stream. It's either that or watch the video while adding ticks to a pad of paper!

Table B.3

Typical Audio Stream Bit Rates	
STREAM TYPE	BIT RATE
Stereo AC-3	192,000 bits/second
5.1 AC-3	448,000 bits/second
16-bit stereo PCM	1,500,000 bits/second

Calculating still-menu storage

Just as with a JPEG still image, the amount of space needed to store a still menu varies with the menu's visual complexity. Despite this fact, it's rare for a still menu, no matter how visually complex, to take up more than 100,000 bytes on the final DVD disc.

Highlight menus turn a subpicture stream on and off on top of a single background image, so each highlight menu uses approximately 100,000 bytes. Use the following formula to calculate the storage space needed for your highlight menus:

`highlight menus (bytes) = # of highlight`
`→ menus x 100,000`

Photoshop layer menus work differently. When DVD Studio Pro compiles your project, it creates a new I-frame for the selected and activated states of each button on the menu. When buttons are selected or activated, the DVD-Video player actually jumps between these separate I-frames to create a rollover effect. Use this formula for budgeting Photoshop layer menus:

`Photoshop layer menus = (total # of buttons`
`→ on all Photoshop layer menus x number of`
`→ button states + 1) x 100,000`

If your Photoshop layer menu uses selected *and* activated states, the `number of button states` value equals 2. If *only* selected states are used, then the `number of button states` value equals 1. All normal button states are held in the same I-frame, which is represented by the + 1 part of the equation.

✔ Tip

■ If your project uses a mix of highlight and Photoshop layer menus, calculate each group of menus separately and add the totals to find the combined storage capacity needed for all of the project's menus.

Calculating DVD-ROM storage

To calculate the size of your project's DVD-ROM content, in the Finder select the folder containing the DVD-ROM content and then press Command-I. An Info window opens telling you how big the folder is. You must convert the size of the folder into bytes using this formula:

DVD-ROM storage in bytes= size of folder
→ in megabytes x 1024 x 1024

Calculating video bit rates

In bit budget terms, calculating the video bit rate is the end game. This two-step process determines the bit rate to use when encoding MPEG-2 video streams for your project's tracks and motion menus. In the first step, you calculate the amount of space left on the disc after all of your audio, subtitle, menu, and DVD-ROM content is accounted for. This leftover space will be filled with video streams for your project's tracks and motion menus. Use the following formula to determine how much space is available for video assets:

space available for video assets = DVD
→ disc capacity – reserve – audio data –
→ subtitle data – still menu data – DVD-
→ ROM data

You want to fill the disc to the brim with video, which means that you must figure out the compression *sweet spot* for your video streams (the bit rate that creates the highest-quality video that fits in the leftover space on the target DVD disc). After figuring out how much space is left on the disc, use this formula to determine the maximum bit rate to use when encoding video:

video data rate = (space available for
→ video / video minutes / 60) x 8

✔ Tip

■ Don't forget that the total combined data rate for all assets in a single, multiplexed DVD-Video stream is 10.08 Mbps. If your bit budget says you can use a high bit rate (for example, one above 7.5 Mbps), take a moment to add up the total bandwidth needed for each individual track in your project (add the video stream's data rate to the combined sum of the track's audio and subtitle stream data rates).

Real-World Bit Budgeting

Here's a real-world example of a bit budget for a project with two menus and four tracks. Each track has three alternate audio streams.

Project Assets

Track 1: 4 minutes and 3 AC-3 stereo audio streams

Main Menu

Track 2: 30 minutes and 3 AC-3 stereo audio streams

Track 3: 45 minutes and 3 AC-3 stereo audio streams

Track 4: 60 minutes and 3 AC-3 stereo audio streams

Audio Setup Menu

Calculating DVD Capacity

1 DVD-9 = 8,540,000,000 bytes

Calculating Reserve

1 DVD-9 = 427,000,000 bytes

Calculating Audio Storage

Total length in minutes of all audio streams:

$(4 + 30 + 45 + 60) \times 3$ streams per track = 417

$$
\begin{aligned}
\textit{Audio data storage (bytes)} &= (\text{total audio minutes} \times 60 \times \text{bit rate}) / 8 \\
&= 417 \times 60 \times (192{,}000 / 8) \\
&= 600{,}480{,}000 \text{ bytes}
\end{aligned}
$$

Calculating Still-Menu Storage

$$
\begin{aligned}
\textit{Still-menu data storage} &= \# \text{ of menus} \times 100{,}000 \\
&= 2 \times 100{,}000 \\
&= 200{,}000 \text{ bytes}
\end{aligned}
$$

Calculating Video Bit Rate

$$
\begin{aligned}
\textit{Space available for video} &= \text{DVD disc capacity} - \text{reserve} - \text{audio data} - \text{subpicture data} - \\
&\quad \text{still menu data} - \text{DVD-ROM data} \\
&= 8{,}540{,}000{,}000 - 427{,}000{,}000 - 600{,}480{,}000 - 0 - 200{,}000 - 0 \\
&= 7{,}512{,}320{,}000 \text{ bytes}
\end{aligned}
$$

Total length in minutes of all video streams: $4 + 30 + 45 + 60 = 139$

$$
\begin{aligned}
\textit{Video bit rate} &= (\text{space available for video} / \text{video minutes} / 60) \times 8 \\
&= (7{,}512{,}320{,}000 / 139 / 60) \times 8 \\
&= 7{,}206{,}062 \text{ bps, or } \textbf{7.2 Mbps!}
\end{aligned}
$$

ONLINE RESOURCES

This book will have you creating professional-caliber DVD-Videos in no time. It will not, however, answer every single question you have about DVD Studio Pro, and it won't supply you with all of the cool, downloadable scripts and tools available on the Web. After you have the hang of how to create basic DVD-Videos, head to the Web for the news and tools that will help you hone your craft.

The first and best place to start? The *DVD Studio Pro 1.5 Visual QuickPro Guide*'s companion Web site, of course. As you read in Chapter 17, "Scripting!" this book describes several complicated and lengthy scripting projects that are easier to download than to explain. Point your browser to `www.peachpit.com/vqp/dvdsp` to download sample projects and get up to speed on all of the late-breaking news on DVD Studio Pro. You might also want to check out the following online resources, which will prove useful to DVD-Video authors of all levels.

DVD-Video

2-Pop www.2-pop.com/

Join the discussions at 2-Pop.com to find answers to all of your digital video questions, including those on editing video in Apple's Final Cut Pro. The DVD Authoring arena is an active bulletin board where you can post questions and get timely answers from other passionate DVD Studio Pro users. The forum's archives are extensive; a quick search offers solutions to most DVD Studio Pro problems.

The Apple DVD Studio Pro Mailing List

www.lists.apple.com/mailman/listinfo/
→ dvdlist/

The Apple DVD mailing list is devoted to all questions concerning iDVD and DVD Studio Pro. Ask questions and get answers from people who not only love the product, but know everything about it. As with all mailing lists, you should first check the archives to see if your question has been asked before. It's also polite to learn list etiquette by *lurking* before posting.

DVD Demystified

www.dvddemystified.com/dvdfaq.html

Have a general question about DVD-Video? This FAQ can help. The DVD-Video FAQ is maintained and updated by Jim Taylor, a community-recognized DVD-Video guru.

dvdsp.com www.dvdsp.com/

From this incredible treasure trove of information, glean inside tips and other DVD Studio Pro secrets.

Macrovision www.macrovision.com/

If you intend to use Macrovision AGC copy protection in your project, you need to purchase a license from Macrovision. Visit the company's Web site to learn more.

Audio

The Beta Lounge www.betalounge.com/

A symposium of modern electronic music, streamed directly to your desktop through Real Player—something to listen to during those long, long midnight hours...

Bias www.bias-inc.com/

Bias Peak DV 3.0 comes on the DVD Studio Pro application DVD-ROM. The Bias Web site contains special offers and updates for Peak DV users like yourself.

Digidesign www.digidesign.com/

Pro Tools is simply *the* industry-standard audio editing utility. You can download a free, full-featured version of Pro Tools from this site.

Dolby www.dolby.com/digital/

To really immerse yourself in the nitty-gritty of AC-3 encoding, visit Dolby's Web site. Dolby created the format, and the company's site contains PDF documents that explain everything you should ever want to know about AC-3 encoding—and more.

Hit Squad www.hitsquad.com/

If you're looking for a shareware audio editor, the Shareware Music Machine has over 4,000 applications to offer.

Propellerheads Software

www.propellerheads.se

Propellerheads Reason is a complete software-based audio recording studio. This killer sampler/synthesizer/sequencer is all you need to make copyright-free music, and it's fun to use! A demo version is available for you to download from the site.

INDEX

INDEX

bit budgets, 379–385
 formulas for calculating, 382–384
 purpose of, 379
 real-world example, 385
 steps for making, 380
bit depth, 58, 59, 62
bit rates
 audio, 70, 76, 382, 385
 CBR *vs.* VBR, 45
 multi-angle, 143
 testing, 45
 video, 44–45, 143, 384, 385
Bit Stream Mode menu, 84
bleeding, 39, 160
broadcast safe colors, 39, 160
broadcast video standards, 36
browser, setting default, 245–247
Build & Format Disc option, 266, 267, 274, 278
Build Disc options, 211, 266
building
 contrasted with formatting, 267
 disc images, 278–279
 projects, 265–270
BUP files, 265, 381
burns
 avoiding mistakes/problems with, 273
 simulated, 277
Button container, 164, 173
Button Hilites area, 181–183, 190
Button icon, 164
Button Links area, 174
Button Navigation tool, 174, 191–192
Button Selection script, 361–362
button states, 169–171
buttons, 167–177
 adding/deleting, 168
 displaying states for, 171
 editing, 116
 grouping, 163
 linking, 173–174, 191
 maximum number of, 30
 naming, 166
 numbering, 173
 opening URLs from, 240–243
 positioning, 167
 purpose of, 30
 setting actions/properties for, 164, 172, 193–194
 setting default, 175
 setting selection conditions for, 176–177
 setting states for, 169–170
 sizing, 167
 SPRM 8 values for, 375–376
bytes, 380

C

camera angles, 30
CBR encoding, 45, 269
CD discs
 contrasted with DVDs, 24–26
 labeling, 25
 reading of pits and tracks in, 24
 storage capacity of, 25–26
CD printers, 25
CD-R discs
 and desktop audio revolution, ix
 labeling, 25
 recording DVD-Video on, 288
CD-ROM discs, 25–26. *See also* CD discs
CD-ROM drives, 24
cells
 subtitle, 322–324, 332
 VOBU, 34
chains, program, 34
channels, 65–66, 73–75
chapter markers, 53–54, 338. *See also* markers
chapter menus, 374
chapters, 205
Cleaner, 21, 43, 51
CMF, 283
color depth, 39
Color Menu Settings dialog box, 330
Color Picker, 331
colors
 bleeding of, 39, 160
 broadcast safe, 39, 160
colorstripe protection, 258, 259
commands. *See also* specific commands
 DVD Studio Pro, xiii, 377–378
 script, 343, 347
Commands Free property, 347
Commands Used property, 347
comments, script, 346, 353
companion Web site, xiii, 343, 387
Compile Project command, 337
compound statements, 352
compression
 and Apple SuperDrive, 6
 artifacts, 45
 dynamic range, 80–81
 lossy, 64
 MPEG, 40–43, 46–49
 utilities, 43
compression markers, 53–54
compression profiles, 81
computer, display of video on, 36–37, 39
conditional statements, 351
Configure Lines menu, 102
Contact button, 240
container icons, 136

INDEX

INDEX

INDEX

Look to **Peachpit Press** for your digital video needs!

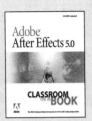